DOING REALIST RESEARCH

Sara Miller McCune founded SAGE Publishing in 1965 to support the dissemination of usable knowledge and educate a global community. SAGE publishes more than 1000 journals and over 800 new books each year, spanning a wide range of subject areas. Our growing selection of library products includes archives, data, case studies and video. SAGE remains majority owned by our founder and after her lifetime will become owned by a charitable trust that secures the company's continued independence.

Los Angeles | London | New Delhi | Singapore | Washington DC | Melbourne

DOING
REALIST
RESEARCH

Edited by

Nick Emmel, Joanne Greenhalgh, Ana Manzano,
Mark Monaghan and Sonia Dalkin

Los Angeles | London | New Delhi
Singapore | Washington DC | Melbourne

Los Angeles | London | New Delhi
Singapore | Washington DC | Melbourne

SAGE Publications Ltd
1 Oliver's Yard
55 City Road
London EC1Y 1SP

SAGE Publications Inc.
2455 Teller Road
Thousand Oaks, California 91320

SAGE Publications India Pvt Ltd
B 1/I 1 Mohan Cooperative Industrial Area
Mathura Road
New Delhi 110 044

SAGE Publications Asia-Pacific Pte Ltd
3 Church Street
#10-04 Samsung Hub
Singapore 049483

Editor: Jai Seaman
Assistant editor: Alysha Owen
Production editor: Victoria Nicholas
Proofreader: Sharon Cawood
Marketing manager: Susheel Gokarakonda
Cover design: Bhairvi Gudka
Typeset by: C&M Digitals (P) Ltd, Chennai, India
Printed in the UK

Editorial Arrangement © Nick Emmel, Joanne Greenhalgh, Ana Manzano, Mark Monaghan and Sonia Dalkin 2018

Introduction © Nick Emmel, Joanne Greenhalgh, Ana Manzano, Mark Monaghan and Sonia Dalkin 2018
Chapter 1 © Nick Tilley 2018
Chapter 2 © Malcolm Williams 2018
Chapter 3 © Gill Westhorp 2018
Chapter 4 © Brad Astbury 2018
Chapter 5 © Bruno Marchal, Guy Kegels and Sara Van Belle 2018
Chapter 6 © David Byrne 2018
Chapter 7 © Rob Anderson, Rebecca Hardwick, Mark Pearson and Richard Byng 2018
Chapter 8 © Geoff Wong 2018
Chapter 9 © Andrew Booth, Judy Wright and Simon Briscoe 2018
Chapter 10 © Mark Monaghan and Annette Boaz 2018
Chapter 11 © Mike Kelly 2018
Chapter 12 © Ray Pawson 2018

First published 2018

Library of Congress Control Number: 2017960434

British Library Cataloguing in Publication data

A catalogue record for this book is available from the British Library

ISBN 978-1-4739-7788-4
ISBN 978-1-4739-7789-1 (pbk)

At SAGE we take sustainability seriously. Most of our products are printed in the UK using responsibly sourced papers and boards. When we print overseas we ensure sustainable papers are used as measured by the PREPS grading system. We undertake an annual audit to monitor our sustainability.

DEDICATION

We dedicate this book to Professor Ray Pawson. Reflecting the practical purpose of realist methodologies, this book started out as a Festschrift dedicated to Ray but quickly turned into a much more practical and applied project. As the reader will soon recognise, the contributors to this volume find many points of agreement with Ray's work. But in the tradition of Robert Merton and Donald T. Campbell Ray championed and the realist methodology he pioneered his work provides an important stepping-off point for the disputation that informs the development of a realist methodology for evaluation, research and synthesis elaborated in this book.

CONTENTS

LIST OF FIGURES AND TABLES

FIGURES

TABLES

AUTHOR BIOGRAPHIES

Rob Anderson is Associate Professor of Health Economics and Evaluation at the University of Exeter Medical School. He has worked as an economic evaluator and applied health services researcher in the UK and Australia. He first wrote about the potential of combining realist evaluation with economic evaluation in 2003.

Brad Astbury is a Lecturer at the University of Melbourne, Centre for Program Evaluation in the Melbourne Graduate School of Education. He teaches introductory and advanced subjects within the Masters of Evaluation. His main areas of interest are evaluation theory, social research methodology and impact evaluation.

Annette Boaz is a Professor of Health Care Research in the Faculty of Health, Social Care and Education at Kingston University and St George's University of London. Her research focuses on the relationship between research evidence, policy and practice. She spent some of her formative years under the tutelage of Ray Pawson at the ESRC UK Centre for Evidence Based Policy and Practice.

Andrew Booth is a Systematic Review Methodologist, with particular interests in qualitative and realist synthesis, at the School of Health and Related Research (ScHARR) at the University of Sheffield. Andrew is a Co-Convenor of the Cochrane Qualitative and Implementation Methods Group and has published extensively on information retrieval topics.

Simon Briscoe is an information specialist at the Exeter HS&DR Evidence Synthesis Centre which is funded by the NIHR Health Services and Delivery Research Programme at the University of Exeter Medical School and NIHR CLAHRC South West Peninsula. He has contributed to several realist reviews on health care topics.

Richard Byng is a GP and Professor in Primary Care Research at Plymouth University focusing on the development and evaluation of complex interventions for mental health and marginalised groups, including the use of realist methods.

David Byrne has published widely in relation to methods and methodology and done empirical research in relation to social exclusion, health (with Blackman) and urban issues. His book, *Complexity Theory and the Social Sciences: The State of the Art*, written with Gill Callaghan, reviews how complexity theory has been used across the social sciences.

Sonia Dalkin is a Senior Lecturer in the Faculty of Health and Life Sciences at Northumbria University, UK. She is also a member of Fuse (the Centre for Translational Research in Public Health). Sonia has specific interests in palliative care, health inequalities and complex interventions. Sonia has significant experience in realist approaches, providing training in these methodologies throughout the UK and internationally.

Nick Emmel teaches interdisciplinary social research methods at the University of Leeds and researches complex social interventions, such as accessing socially excluded and vulnerable individuals and groups and explaining the results of randomised control trials. He is Director of Advanced Qualitative Methods Training for the ESRC White Rose Doctoral Training Partnership. Publications include *Sampling and Choosing Cases in Qualitative Research: A Realist Approach* (2013). He is currently writing about the case for context.

Joanne Greenhalgh is a Social Research Methodologist. Joanne's current research is focused in two main areas: (1) applying realist evaluation and realist synthesis to the evaluation of healthcare policy and practice; (2) the evaluation of the use of patient reported outcome measures (PROMs) in clinical practice and their impact on clinical decision-making and patient care. She was a member of the NIHR funded RAMESES II project to develop quality and reported standards for realist evaluation and has worked on several realist synthesis and evaluation projects.

Rebecca Hardwick is a PhD student at the University of Exeter Medical School. Her work focuses on knowledge use by third-sector healthcare organisations and she is applying a realist framework to explain these processes. Her background is health service policy and management, in the NHS and third sector.

Guy Kegels is Emeritus Professor of the Institute of Tropical Medicine (ITM). His academic career has covered research and teaching on health systems, health service organisation, research methodology and strategic management. He has guided work on realist evaluation, including PhD research projects, at ITM since 2003.

Mike Kelly is Senior Visiting Fellow in the Department of Public Health and Primary Care and is a member of St John's College, Cambridge. Between 2005 and 2014, when he retired from the NHS, he was the Director of the Centre for Public Health at the National Institute of Health and Care Excellence (NICE).

Ana Manzano is a Social Research Methodologist and Lecturer based at the University of Leeds, UK. Her specialist area is the evaluation of complex applied healthcare interventions using mainly but not exclusively the realist approach.

Bruno Marchal is Associate Professor at the Department of Public Health, Institute of Tropical Medicine (ITM) in Antwerp. His research includes local health systems and research methodology for complex issues in health. Much of his current work focuses on realist research in the field of health policy and systems research in low- and middle-income countries.

Mark Monaghan is a Lecturer in Criminology and Social Policy at Loughborough University, UK; prior to this he worked at the University of Leeds. His work focuses mainly on the scientific and political battles through which policy is made. He has applied this to the area of illicit drug and welfare policies.

Ray Pawson is Emeritus Professor of Social Research Methodology, University of Leeds, UK. Publications include *A Measure for Measures* (1989), *Realistic Evaluation* (1997 with Nick Tilley), *Evidence-Based Policy: A Realist Perspective* (2006) and *The Science of Evaluation: A Realist Manifesto* (2013). The next monograph on 'Evidence-based Medicine' is expected in 2020.

Mark Pearson is a Senior Research Fellow in Implementation Science at the University of Exeter Medical School. He critically applies theory-driven approaches such as realist evaluation and synthesis to research knowledge mobilisation and implementation processes in health, social care, and public health systems.

Nick Tilley is a Professor in the Jill Dando Institute of Crime Science, UCL and Adjunct Professor at the Griffith Criminology Institute, Brisbane. Over 40 years he has published widely on evaluation methodology, crime trends, crime prevention and policing, the consistent concern being with fostering theoretically informed applied social science.

Sara Van Belle is a Senior Researcher at ITM's Department of Public Health. As a political scientist and cultural anthropologist with a PhD in public health, she has a long experience in research, programme management and international development in Africa. Her research focus is on complexity and governance in health systems, policy analysis and realist research.

Gill Westhorp is a Professorial Research Fellow at Charles Darwin University where she leads the Realist Research Evaluation and Learning Initiative (RREALI). She is a co-author of the RAMESES standards for realist evaluation and realist review, and is interested in the use of realist approaches for hard-to-evaluate initiatives.

Malcolm Williams is Professor and Co-Director of the Cardiff University Q-Step Centre. His research is empirically promiscuous, but with an abiding interest in methodological issues such as probability, representation and objectivity. He is a realist, but not realist enough for the Critical Realists. His latest book is *Key Concepts in the Philosophy of Social Research* (Sage).

Geoff Wong is Clinical Research Fellow at the University of Oxford and an NHS General Practitioner. He has extensive expertise in both realist review and evaluation. He has collaborated with leading realist researchers to develop quality and reporting standards and training materials for realist reviews and evaluations – the RAMESES Project (www.ramesesproject.org).

Judy Wright is a Senior Information Specialist at Leeds Institute of Health Sciences, University of Leeds. Judy supports research staff undertaking systematic reviews across the university and within NHS Trusts across Yorkshire. Judy provides search methodology advice for systematic reviews and diverse evidence syntheses and also teaches research information skills.

INTRODUCTION

Doing realist evaluation, synthesis and research

Nick Emmel, Joanne Greenhalgh,
Ana Manzano, Mark Monaghan
and Sonia Dalkin

INTRODUCTION

In 'A history of evaluation in 28½ pages', a chapter in *Realistic Evaluation* (1997: 16), Ray Pawson and Nick Tilley describe the distinguished methodologist of evaluation and qualitative research M.Q. Patton as the 'Lewis Carroll of evaluators' who 'uses every analogy, tale and metaphor [...] to promote a more skilful approach to evaluation'. This was not intended as a slur but can only be interpreted as a compliment. For a little later they point out that Patton is equipping the evaluator – and we would add researcher and synthesiser – with the insights and skills they will need to deal with 'different situations, different purposes, different people, and different languages' (Patton, 1982: 49 cited in Pawson and Tilley, 1997: 16). Ray Pawson tells the story of how Patton responded to the comments in their book. At the British Evaluation Society Conference Patton announced he was establishing a prize to be awarded for 'the overuse of metaphors in methodological writing'. The first winners, deservedly, Ray Pawson and Nick Tilley, with a special citation (he might have added) for over-burdening the reader with cricketing metaphors, unintelligible to all but a select few from a handful of countries. And here is the problem every methodologist struggles with. In seeking to bridge the murky waters between a philosophy of the world and methods to investigate it, we have little choice but to fall back on an armoury of metaphor and analogy, hoping they provide a compelling and vivid account of the reasoning that guides investigation of the social world.

Inevitably these allegorical accounts encourage ambiguity, contention and uncertainty. Our job in *Doing Realist Research* is to bear down on some of the metaphors that inflect through the debates about how to understand and do realist research. The purpose of this book is to identify and explain key lessons that may be transferred across the many and varied settings in which social research, evaluation and synthesis are conducted. Drawing as much on Patton's injunction to recognise diversity of problem, purpose and audience as the body of realist evaluation scholarship that has developed since the publication of *Realistic Evaluation*, this book is about the thoughtful and critical application of realist methodologies, whether you are 'accumulating a mass of notes and a liberal coating of grime' in the library or getting 'the seats of your pants dirty in real research', as Robert E. Park (quoted in Hammersley, 1989: 76) suggested we must do. Most likely, as all the contributors to this book suggest, you will be researching back and forth between library and field-site, acknowledging the complexities of the social world and the methods to investigate it. Our purpose is to provide practical, worked-through examples of the ways in which researchers have brought theories into relation with evidence in realist evaluation, synthesis and research.

IDEAS AND EVIDENCE

For realists practical is not synonymous with empirical. Lying in a dusty box-file on an even dustier shelf in the perennially dark stack room of the Brotherton Library at the

University of Leeds is a yellowing manual-typed pamphlet, Occasional Papers in Sociology No. 14: *Monstrous Thoughts: Weaknesses in the Strong Programme of the Sociology of Science*, by Ray Pawson and Nick Tilley, published in 1982. This paper draws a distinction between a rational (read realist, although they don't use the term) scientific methodology and the two poles of the strong programme of social science. At one pole is an interpretive approach, 'all personal influence and no method', which denies the impact of ideas on the procedural rules of science. At the other is a structural version, 'all institution and no method', which casts scientists as passively responding to external resources. They chart a course between these poles to recognise that science is the synthesis of interpretation and structure. 'Social structures', they note, drawing on the work of Antony Giddens, are 'both constituted by human agency and yet, at the same time, are the very medium of this constitution. Substitute "scientific method" for "social structures" and "scientists' actions" for "human agency" in the quotation and we have the beginnings of a more complete account of science as a social activity' (Pawson and Tilley, 1982: 46–7). They develop Imre Lakatos' account of a zigzag route between proof and refutation in mathematical discovery (Lakatos, 1976) to inform an account of the way science progresses; ideas (or lemmas) are brought into relation with empirical accounts to refine these ideas in the practical progress of science.

But science is a messy business, as the contributors to this volume repeatedly observe in one way or another. Pawson and Tilley (1982) depart from Lakatos' account, whose methodology they consider too prescriptive and tidy, to emphasise that scientific change and development, like every other belief and activity, is generated within and can never be divorced from social processes.

DISPUTATION AND REALISM

Of course, science itself is a social process. Adopting Karl Popper's stance that knowledge is facilitated through criticism, Donald T. Campbell's (1988) 'disputatious community of scholars' provides a useful metaphor through which to understand the way in which realists characterise the process of science. A group whose intellectual debates help research, evaluation, synthesis and methodology to flourish through listening to each other's arguments and counter-arguments. An open system of criticism and support that brings multiple perspectives and multiple methods to bear in the crucible of substantive research, evaluation and its synthesis A continual process of development and redevelopment of interpretation, disputation of analysis and contestation of causal explanation seeking to most adequately and plausibly account for the object of our enquiry.

For physical scientists there may be an end to this disputation. Although new empirical evidence does not seem to confirm hypotheses as science is so often characterised to do, but affords new ways of thinking and opens up fresh avenues for empirical enquiry. The determination of Higgs boson[1] is neither an end to enquiry about the nature of subatomic matter nor the completion of the Standard Model of particle physics, for instance, but a step along a road that refines theory and leads to the design of previously unimagined empirical enquiry.

REALIST PRINCIPLES

The concerns for many of the readers of this edited book will not be the enduring matter of physical science's enquiry but the objects of social and human science and their application in the social or even the real world. In addition to contending with the disputations agency of scientists, the social and human scientist appreciates the emergent, transitive and only ever relatively enduring nature of the social world. A realist evaluator investigating an intervention knows it is never stationary; practitioners and participants are using resources afforded by the intervention to change (or not) their little bit of the world. Realist researchers understand that the people, groups, organisations or whosoever they are investigating may well be acting on structures that existed before them and in which they played no part in shaping, but which they are, with varying degrees of success, trying to change or keep the same.

This dynamism that results from human action is why traditional experimental methods, while not quite the anathema they have sometimes been characterised as, are certainly recognised to have significant limitations by realist evaluators and researchers. These methods ignore the emergent nature of the social world. People's agency, the factors that could make a difference, are ignored or, at best, converted from rich relational accounts into variables, things to be empirically recorded.

As all the contributors show in this volume, realists are rather less interested in methods and very much more interested in how insights, which sometimes arise from investigations, add to a pool of theory. That an RCT or a Grounded Theory study provide compelling insight into some particular process is considered important because it helps the evaluator, synthesiser or researcher to judge a theory. The same can be said for any method of insight. All the contributors in this edited collection show how wedded to multiple methods realist researchers are in their pursuit of refined theory. This once again disrupts traditional ways of thinking about research. We are often presented with a hierarchy of evidence as a given. This places experimental methods at its zenith and relegates lay-accounts to the dark reaches at its base. A realist methodology tips this hierarchy on its side, recognising that the key is not some arbitrary measure of methodological rigour but the utility of insight in crafting theory. As Pawson, Owen and Wong (2010b) show in a short paper which should be essential reading for any realist methodologist, the insights from experienced policy-makers and practitioners discussing a problem on a morning radio news programme can be as important as a study that cost many millions. Realists dig for nuggets of evidence even in 'bad' research to elaborate theories (Pawson, 2006a). This can trouble the political economy of science, of course, which is quite fun to do, but at a methodological level we are reminded that a realist methodology is, to use a phrase Ray Pawson (2003) adopted, 'theory incarnate'.

REALISM AND THEORY

What theory is and why bother with it are fundamental questions in a realist philosophy of science. Each of the contributors to this book showcase how theory is crafted in the day-to-day activities of realist studies. They demonstrate what theory is and how it is uncovered, challenged and enhanced through empirical investigation in the library and in the field and also demonstrate the utility of theory.

In this introduction we want to provide a sketch to answer what theory is and why it is ubiquitous in a realist methodology, not least because each of the contributors to this volume assumes the reader will have this understanding. Returning to the earlier observation arising from Ray Pawson and Nick Tilley's investigation of the weaknesses in the strong programme of the sociology of science, science for realists is the synthesis of interpretation and structure. The significant achievement of realist science is to marry epistemological narrative and ontological depth (Bhaskar, 2008). Explanations are a product of both the social character of scientific progress and the role played by models in scientific thought. We have already emphasised how important disputation is to the progress of science. As Karl Popper observes in richly metaphorical language, there is nothing absolute about science: 'It is like a building erected on piles. The piles are driven down from above in the swamp.' But these piles never reach a rock-steady foundation, they are driven down just far enough to hold the structure steady for the moment. And as Popper (2002: 94) goes on to observe, '[w]e simply stop when we are satisfied that they are firm enough to carry the structure, at least for the time being.'

So far, so measurable, logical and positivist. There is a further step. Realist science proposes models which are necessary because they seek to explain real social processes. For realists the real exists, but is independent of our knowing it. Realists acknowledge a stratified account of reality, which in practical terms means moving beyond describing what can be measured in the social world to explain the deeper causal powers that shape that which can be observed. Causality is accepted as configurational, contingent and generative of real social processes. Many of these underlying mechanisms, which shape the observable and recordable, are much less amenable to direct description. It is here that a realist methodology parts company with the approaches in science that provide descriptive accounts of 'what is' and 'what works'. Realist science answers explanatory questions as best as it can through constructing models that explain why the empirically recordable looks and behaves in the way it does. Explanations in realist science are the product of bringing ideas into relation with evidence. These theories are the fallible, provisional and testable models of realist science.

CONTINGENCY AND THEORY

To recognise ideas are as important to research (and explaining the social world) as measurements is an established principle in a realist methodology. Ideas – 'concepts, meaning, and intentions' as Joe Maxwell (2012: 18) reminds us – are:

... as real as rocks; they are just not as accessible to direct observation and description as rocks. In this way they are like quarks, black holes, the meteor impact that supposedly killed the dinosaurs, or William Shakespeare: we have no way of directly observing them, and our claims about them are based on a variety of sorts of indirect evidence.

These causal powers are emergent; they will only exert their generative influence in an arrangement with other parts. Causal powers work in a disposition to their context and shape particular regularities, which in turn produce outcomes. Outcomes, regularities within and across the outcomes, and aspects of context are features of the social world that are most amenable to measurement, observation and description. Positivist and constructivist social and human science dutifully record these observations, and sometimes peer as far back as they can empirically along the path from which the outcome came to make claims to what preceded an empirical observation. Such accounts of path dependency have their value of course, but realists are concerned to make claims to underlying factors that support, help, shape and make a difference (or not). These claims form the basis of explanations and they have practical utility. They provide policy-makers, practitioners and people with accounts of why something happened (or why it didn't happen), where and under what circumstances. For evaluators and researchers these theories provide guidance about where to look to next, who to purposefully sample (Emmel, 2013) and the most appropriate method to use to test and refine theory.

REALIST EXPLANATION

In a further step, realists recognise that a methodology that brings ideas into relation with evidence is ideally suited to explore complex systems. They draw on an interpretation of complexity, which is non-linear, locally adaptive, emergent and path-dependent (see Byrne and Callaghan, 2013). The possibilities to exercise human agency are contingent upon factors in particular contexts. Recognising that measurable outcomes may be arrived at by many potential means or regularities shaped through the reasoning and resources of evaluative human agents, is also part of the explanation of complexity in a realist social and human science.

Inevitably realist methodologists fall back on metaphor to describe these complex relational processes in a realist methodology. Perhaps the richest metaphorical device in Ray Pawson and Nick Tilley's seminal book *Realistic Evaluation* is the CMO configuration. All realist explanations should, in some way, include an account of context, mechanisms and outcome.

It is hard, given our training in scientific method, to break away from two particularly dominant narratives. The first is that there is a tool available to address each problem. The second is that data trumps everything else. The idea of the CMO configuration undermines both these parts of classic training.

The CMO, as all the contributors to this edited collection remind us in one way or another, is a heuristic device. Many an hour/day/month can be spent trying to organise data into these three categories. But anyone who tries soon finds these typologies are not clear cut. They are, as we have emphasised, contingent upon each other, the epitome of complexity. They only work in relationship to each other: split them apart and they no longer offer up an explanation of the social process under investigation.

Ray Pawson described the CMO configuration as an 'ugly circumlocution' (Pawson, 2013: 21), which sums up the trouble with the matter. This phrase reminds us of the Circumlocution Office Charles Dickens describes in Little Dorrit. Dickens' account of the Circumlocution Office is a theme he wrote of often, resisting rigid institutional rules, which helps us to understand the CMO metaphor. Do we follow the authority of a rigid method called CMO, or critically and creatively engage with it, recognising the value of this necessary flagrant nuisance and how difficult causal attribution is in supporting our explanation of social processes?

Such a nursery of statesmen had the Department become in virtue of a long career of this nature that several solemn lords had attained the reputation of being quite unearthly prodigies of business, solely from having practised, How not to do it, as the head of the Circumlocution Office. As to the minor priests and acolytes of that temple, the result of all this was that they stood divided into two classes, and, down to the junior messenger, either believed in the Circumlocution Office as a heaven-born institution that had an absolute right to do whatever it liked; or took refuge in total infidelity, and considered it a flagrant nuisance. (Dickens, 1996: 102)

Realists, you will have gathered by now, are of course infidels, the methodology a flagrant nuisance, the CMO pedagogy incarnate. The last thing the contributors to this volume would suggest doing is imposing context, mechanism, outcome and their infinite configurations as tools or tropes to answer all scientific questions.

Indeed, as Bruno Marchal and colleagues and David Byrne show in Chapters 5 and 6, this heuristic needs modification if the CMO configuration is to fill in the realist and complex question, 'what works for whom, in what circumstances, and why?'. It has a special place in realist explanation, as one of its originators, Ray Pawson, asserts in the concluding chapter, because it contributes to the development of another kind of theory, the theory of the middle range. The idea of middle-range theories, put forward by Robert Merton (1968), developed by Raymond Boudon (1991) and adapted by Raymond Pawson and Nick Tilley (1997), is considered central to a realist methodology. They are bundles of hypotheses that can be tested empirically. They are also abstract enough from particular instances that these theories can be transferred between cases that might have quite different empirical characteristics.

THE CHAPTERS

Cases are an important feature of a realist methodology. And for the reader eager to go straight to the chapters that will directly support their research we provide an overview of the cases in Table I.1. After Ragin and Becker (1992) the descriptions of the cases in Table I.1 work out of the relationship between ideas and evidence. The key theoretical focus of each chapter is divided from its empirical case studies by a semi-colon. In each chapter some kind of artificial closure has been achieved for practical purposes. For those with a little more time, a description of each of the chapters is elaborated below.

TABLE I.1 The cases by chapter in *Doing Realist Research*

	Chapter title	The cases (after Ragin and Becker, 1992)
1	The middle-range methodology of realist evaluation	The history and evolutionary mechanisms of realistic evaluation; the What Works Centre for Crime Prevention
2	Making up mechanisms in realist research	Theory, evidence and their relations to mechanism; social stratification in the United States and homelessness in the United Kingdom
3	Understanding mechanisms in realist evaluation and research	Applying mechanisms in evaluation and research; youth programmes and public disclosure initiatives identifying under-performance or deviant behaviour
4	Making claims using realist methods	Generalisation through explanation; early intervention and prevention programmes
5	Theory and realist methods	Theories; health systems in resource-constrained settings of low- and middle-income countries including Ghana, Uganda and South Africa
6	Researching complex large-scale nested interventions	Explaining complex social interventions; housing regeneration and renewal programmes
7	Using realist approaches to explain the costs and cost-effectiveness of programmes	Economic evaluation and realist evaluation; shared care
8	Data gathering for realist reviews	Relevant rigours data in realist reviews; looking for needles in the haystack of evidence
9	Scoping and searching to support realist approaches	Evidence of synthesis reviews; from grey literature to peer-reviewed papers
10	Evidence from realist research, its influence and impact	The processes of engaging with policy-makers during realist synthesis; youth mentoring
11	Realist research, guidelines and the politics of evidence	Policy, politics and evidence; the National Institute for Health and Care Excellence (NICE), regulating alcohol consumption and prevention of cardiovascular disease through diet
12	Realist memorabilia	The body of realist literature; youth mentoring; problem-orientated policing

The striking feature of Nick Tilley's contribution to this edited collection in the first chapter is the ways in which the features of realist explanation discussed in this introduction are put to practical purpose. In a personal account of an intellectual journey and friendship, Tilley demonstrates how disputation, intellectual engagement and practical reckoning lie at the foundation of a realist methodology. Not least, he shows how his recent work in policy and practice, as a partner in the What Works Centre for Crime Prevention, has spawned a new evaluation approach: 'EMMIE' (effect, mechanism, moderator, implementation and economy). He accepts this approach does not hold to a rigid interpretation of realist methodology, but responds pragmatically to the needs of research funders, policy-makers and practitioners. Nonetheless, the principles of realism underwrite this new method. Its purpose, to draw on different types of evidence used to support or refute theories of the middle range. Tilley shows how through bringing diverse evidence to theory, better understanding of the causal liabilities that produce real outcomes to inform policy and practice can follow.

In Chapter 2 Malcolm Williams focuses on one of the key components of the relationship between evidence and theory, the mechanism. He shows how mechanistic thinking aims to close the gap between the real intransitive objects of nature and the transitive objects of our explanation in social science. This account emphasises the importance of cumulative theorising to realist explanation and shows why we must make up mechanisms, not as works of fiction but from the phenomena we can observe and measure. Drawing on empirical evidence from investigations of social stratification in the US and homelessness in the UK and methodological writing from realism and from interpretive causal analysis, Williams demonstrates how our explanation of complex social phenomena through a mechanism will always be incomplete, how our theories and methods must be eclectic and forever testable, and, because they are testable, our models will be forever falsifiable.

In Chapter 3, Gill Westhorp extends the definitions of mechanism. Pawson and Tilley (1997) described mechanisms as reasoning and resources in social programmes. In one of the few discussions of social mechanisms in Roy Bhaskar's work, mechanisms are similarly described:

Thus a person may possess a reason for acting in a certain way and not act in that way under appropriate circumstances if, at the time, he possesses in addition a set of overriding or more compelling reasons [which reads better as 'resources'] for not acting in that way. (Bhaskar, 2008: 234)

Extending these definitions, Westhorp argues that other constructs of mechanisms might be equally useful to understand how some types and aspects of policies and programmes work in different contexts. Mechanisms, Westhorp suggests, may work at different levels of stratification – some seen and empirically measurable, some deep below the surface of that which can be measured – and at different times, for instance the effects of a mechanism that fired in the past may be felt in a present evaluation. Mechanisms are always nested in and contingent upon a set of relationships as well, a point David Byrne picks up on in Chapter 6. These methodological observations, derived from a realist philosophy, lead Westhorp to propose a new and elaborated typology of mechanisms, along with a practical account of what these might look like at different scales and in different circumstances.

Two key messages contributors to this collection keep returning to are, first, that realist methodologies must be rigorous and systematic but never mechanical and, second, that they require a flexible and creative mind-set. In Chapter 4 Brad Astbury examines the explanatory potential of mechanisms, their contribution to developing middle-range theory-building and modest forms of theoretical generalisability. Developing these methodological lessons from an evaluation of an early intervention and prevention programme, Astbury emphasises the limits of logic models in identifying causal mechanisms. In developing theories of the middle range through empirical engagements in evaluation, he emphasises the importance of learning cumulatively, drawing on existing theoretical resources, and the value of casing – bringing ideas into relation with evidence. Focusing attention on aspects of causal explanation will help to answer the 'will it work elsewhere' question.

In Chapter 5, Bruno Marchal, Guy Kegels and Sara Van Belle examine the ways in which different kinds of theory are used in realist research. They explore the differences, commonalities and the value of theory. These include folk theories and programme theories, which in some way articulate what is happening in a particular context. These allow for the elaboration of CMO configurations, to which they consider it useful to add explicit details about intervention and actors. Marchal and colleagues also consider grander social theories, which are often rather abstract from a particular setting, but which, along with the other types of theory they discuss, contribute to the development and testing of middle-range theories. These, as each of the chapters discusses, are central to realist explanation. Marchal and colleagues elaborate the ways in which these theories are developed and relate to each other, providing a wealth of practical examples for conducting research, working in multidisciplinary teams and adopting methods, including Charles Ragin's Qualitative Comparative Analysis, to equip researchers with a rich portfolio of readily useable and topical theoretical framings to capture unpredictable and emergent phenomena.

Marchal and colleagues' concern with theory development is tested in quite specific and well-defined interventions. In Chapter 6 David Byrne considers a quite different kind of evaluative environment: multi-layered and multi-faceted programmes where the boundaries of systems are highly permeable and interpretable and causal chains run in all directions. His case is the history of housing regeneration and renewal programmes conducted through an extended period of de-industrialisation. Byrne argues that the evaluation of large complex systems should not abandon the language of mechanisms operating in context, but they do need to specify outcomes in terms of a system state that is the result of the interaction of many mechanisms and contexts. The pedagogy of the CMO configuration leads to its rewriting.

The pedagogic value of the CMO leads Rob Anderson, Rebecca Hardwick, Mark Pearson and Richard Byng into a relatively new area for a realist methodology, that of realist economic cost-benefit analysis. In Chapter 7 they juxtapose the black-box approaches of traditional economic evaluation, measuring what goes into a programme and what comes out with no concern for what happens between these measures, with a realist methodology. Anderson and colleagues demonstrate how investigation of resources, a key part of a realist account of mechanisms, can aid researchers to theorise mechanisms, outcomes and contexts. They show, in particular, how evidence derived from conventional economic evaluations may generate data to refine programme theories and lead to causal explanations, which address the realist questions about what works for whom in what circumstances and why.

Refining theory is Geoff Wong's concern in Chapter 8, where he provides practical guidance for any researcher setting out to undertake a realist review and who must address the issues of both their sources of data and their quality. As Wong explains, realist reviews are much more about explaining phenomena than calculating the size of their effects. This chapter encourages researchers to be imaginative and inclusive in searching for evidence to develop plausible yet fallible programme theories. Wong uses practical examples from published work to show how evidence can be applied in real-world reviews. The chapter offers up suggested solutions in the development of a rigorous process for realist review. These, in common with all the contributions in this edited collection, emphasise the relationship between evidence, theory and useful explanation in a realist methodology.

Andrew Booth, Judy Wright and Simon Briscoe elaborate ideas about realist review further in Chapter 9. Contrasting realist synthesis reviews with systematic reviews, these authors explain the strategies realist researchers might adopt and how these are continually informed by a realist methodology. Once again the methods are located around the keystone of realism, the exposure, elaboration and exposition of theory. They highlight the challenges faced in interpreting the quality standards, protocols and search methods, embodied in the systematic review methodology, in a way that is sensitive to the requirements of the realist review. Booth and colleagues promote strategies that interweave programme theory articulated by users, practitioners and policy-makers with theory gleaned from literature. They purposefully flatten the hierarchy of evidence to show why social media may be as important as peer-reviewed papers reporting from randomised control trials and systematic reviews. They address the very practical challenges of information retrieval that arise from these methodological observations.

In Chapter 10, Mark Monaghan and Annette Boaz again return to an exploration of the difference between experimental methods that assume a succession from cause to effect, with little concern for what happens between these two observable waypoints, and realism's generative, causal and mechanistic explanations. Their focus is on the ways in which realist methods can inform policy-making processes. Elaborating on the themes Nick Tilley identifies in Chapter 1 of this collection, Monaghan and Boaz chart the kinds of engagement realist researchers seek to establish with policy-makers to broker research production that addresses priorities while also contributing to identifying and refining programme theories. They point to the ways in which a realist methodology seeks to deal with the complexity in different contexts, through the cumulation of evidence about what works for whom in what circumstances and why, rather than just what works. They also show how the findings from realist research – models, diagrams and stories that elaborate theories – percolate into policy processes, stimulating often different thinking about problems rather than offering an overarching prescription to answer those problems.

In Chapter 11 Mike Kelly contrasts evidence-based medicine, which, like the economic evaluation methods of cost-benefit analysis Anderson and colleagues discuss in Chapter 7, valorises the accuracy of the relationship between intervention and outcome of traditional methods with realism's concern to understand the nature of linkages and pathways of action between intervention and outcome. Drawing on the experiences of developing guidelines for public health interventions at the National Institute for Health and Care Excellence (NICE) in the UK, Kelly shows how the mechanistic approach to explanation inherent in realist approaches extends accounts to permit forensic detection about why things are the way they are. Investigating two politically contentious areas of public health – regulating alcohol consumption and the prevention of cardiovascular disease through diet – Kelly demonstrates how real causes and explanation are possible using the best available evidence, not speculation and supposition, and how this interpretation leads to proposals for cost-effective strategies. He also shows how these proposals bump up against political considerations that shape the prosaic problems of implementation. As Kelly observes, the great strengths of evidence-based medicine are its transparency, rigour, forensic approach to evidence and the fact it is based in peer-reviewed science. The great strengths of the realist approach are its acknowledgement of complexity, its refusal to be drawn into simple linear models and its ability to reframe questions in ways that are often much more illuminating than simple hypothesis testing. Both approaches must recognise the contingent nature of any evidence-based statement, however.

The metaphorical bookends of this edited collection are Nick Tilley and Ray Pawson. Nick Tilley's contribution in Chapter 1 focuses attention on the practical purpose of realist explanation. It is a theme Ray Pawson returns to in the final chapter. He asks three taxing questions, for which he of course provides answers. First, he wonders if realism will last. His answer: it will because it is not limited to realist evaluation and realist synthesis – these are part of a much older, wider and emergent interdisciplinary scholarly enterprise. Pawson's second question revisits the CMO, which we have noted is a concern of all the contributors to this collection. It is teased apart and joined back together one last time to show how the CMO configuration is the fundamental building block of *any* causal explanation. And finally Pawson ponders on the use of realist evaluation and synthesis. He points to the modest expectations of realist researchers, the ways in which explanation cumulates in realist science and how the theories that guide a realist methodology become real when they are creatively tested and are able to explain change in the social and human world. This is partial knowledge, certainly, but it represents real and practical progress.

There is a considerable – and we would argue an increasing – appetite for realist methodologies in the social and human sciences, internationally and across disciplines and fields (measured by citations). As all the authors in this edited collection stress, the strength of realist explanation lies in its ability to address complexity through recognising the contingent relationship between context and causal powers (mechanism) to bring about change (or for things to stay the same). They elaborate the metaphors that make these relations real. Realism stands apart from a science that in its pursuit of measurable precision neglects to illuminate the power of things and explain the how and why of real and complex social explanation.

NOTE

1 Higgs boson was predicted in a theory presented by a group of physicists in the 1960s. A scaler particle and field in the Standard Model of particle physics, it was tentatively confirmed by CERN, the European Organisation for Nuclear Research, on 14 March 2013. Writing about its discovery, the theoretical physicist Carlo Rovelli observes: 'Our fantasy is too limited to "imagine" how the world may be made, unless we search for inspiration in the traces we have at our disposal. The traces we have – our clues – are either theories which have been successful, or new experimental data, nothing else' (Rovelli, 2016: 189).

1

THE MIDDLE-RANGE METHODOLOGY OF REALIST EVALUATION

Forty years with Realist Ray and their unintended consequences, an affectionate and unfinished middle-range story

Nick Tilley

WHAT THIS CHAPTER IS ABOUT

The chapter describes the foundations of 'realistic evaluation' via a journey through history, detailing the meeting and ongoing relationship between Ray Pawson and Nick Tilley. Tilley describes the duo as 'the bad boys of evaluation methodology', writing with a frisson of excitement and challenging opposing established orthodoxies. A description of Tilley's work towards theory development and research use is then provided, which he states has always been underpinned by the seminal 'what works for whom in what circumstances and how'. He describes his recent work for the 'What Works Centre for Crime Prevention' and the formulation of EMMIE (Effect sizes, Mechanism or mediator, Moderator or context, Implementation and Economy). He concludes by looking to the future, describing four issues that have emerged repeatedly and require further work. Overall, the chapter describes an affectionate account of a long-term friendship, collaboration and continuing legacy.

How this chapter will help you to do realist research

The chapter provides the history of realist evaluation. Understanding the tensions that Ray Pawson and Nick Tilley encountered in evaluation research, and how as a result of this realistic evaluation came to fruition, will help the reader to conduct their research in a truly realist paradigm.

A practical tip: a take-home message from the chapter

Don't be afraid to be an outsider or to challenge opposing established orthodoxies. The realist community is, and continues to strive to be, a community of disputatious scholars.

This is the story of 40 years with Realist Ray and their unintended consequences. It is an affectionate and unfinished middle-range story of realist methods.

Ray Pawson has always been interested primarily in methodology. He has also, for as long as I've known him, been a realist. The social world is real and is populated with real causal liabilities which when actualised produce real outcomes. The activation of causal liabilities is never unconditional. The job of social science is to produce and test theories about the kinds of condition in which given forms of causal liability are activated to produce patterned intended and unintended outcomes. The causal liabilities or mechanisms are relatively fundamental and enduring, the conditions for their activation less so. But there are levels of abstraction at which contexts and mechanisms can be specified that enjoy sufficient generality for explanatory purposes across multiple settings. In this, social science accords with what is done unself-consciously in many of the natural and life sciences. One difference, however, is the capacity humans have for intentional behaviour in the light of their understandings of the social world.

The techniques used by social scientists need to attend to the distinctive qualities of the social world (including the human capacity for sense-making and intentional behaviour), but the techniques are otherwise diverse, as in the physical sciences, and to be chosen in light of the nature of the theory being tested, data availability and scope for collecting further evidence. Fetishes for one technique or another are anathema. And Ray has been merciless in poking fun at serial methodological madnesses, as tribes of fanatics (including various anti-data brigades) have fought battles and as fashions in favour of one or the other have changed (Pawson, 1979, 1980, 1982, 1989).

So, Ray has combined an incisive ability to cut through pretentious nonsense to reveal that one emperor after another lacks clothing, with an appreciation of great sociology where imaginative theory has been tested using diverse methods. His heroes include Raymond Boudon and Robert Merton (Pawson, 2009b), both of whom conceive of, advocate for and practise the kind of sociology Ray embraces (see, for example, Boudon, 1981; Merton, 1968). Boudon's and Merton's sociology is middle-range, counterintuitive, theoretically refined and empirical. They articulate their theory and adduce relevant evidence that directly speaks to it. Under Ray's guidance I came to appreciate Boudon's *Education, Opportunity and Social Change* as an exemplar of the best that sociology should aspire to (Boudon, 1974). Ray has emulated Boudon's and Merton's work in the empirical studies he has undertaken to exemplify the methodological approach he has now been advocating for some 40 years. His early contributions to the analysis of social class as well as more recent work on health should both be recognised as substantively important in addition to the methodological contributions for which he is better known (see, for example, Pawson, 1989[1]).

At least this is the Ray I know, love and admire deeply. I have learned a great deal from talking to him, reading him and collaborating with him since the early 1970s.

Ray's and my meeting was fortuitous, as was our subsequent work together. Nothing much has been planned. We met at the then Lanchester Polytechnic (now Coventry University), when we were both young lecturers in a department where I think there was only one person over 30. I'd been appointed as a lecturer in 1971 aged 24, directly from a Master's degree a couple of years before Ray arrived. Ray was finishing off his PhD and is a year younger than I am. We lived close to one another, in Earlsdon, and walked together to and from work. As a young department we were also a pretty sociable bunch. So, there was lots of opportunity to talk ideas. I was (and remain) an unapologetic enthusiast for Popperian pragmatic piecemeal social engineering and thereby wanted to do theoretically informed non-doctrinaire empirical sociology in the service of harm reduction (Popper, 1945, 1957; Tilley and Selby, 1976; Tilley, 1982). I'd also developed an interest in the then burgeoning strong programme in the sociology of scientific knowledge (SSK) that had been highly critical of Popper, but I believed to have misread both him and studies undertaken in the name of SSK[2] (Tilley, 1981). Ray and I were on rather different tracks, albeit that our respective interests and predilections for theory and method were fairly congruent.

I moved to Nottingham Trent in May 1979 and Ray went to Leeds in the September of the same year. We kept in touch, partly for social reasons and partly because we'd enjoyed talking sociology together. Our first joint venture (and I think Ray's first research collaboration) came out in 1982 as *Monstrous Thoughts: Weaknesses in the Strong Programme of the Sociology of Science* (Pawson and Tilley, 1982). It married Ray's interests in methodology with mine in the sociology of science. It was about Euler's theorem that for all polyhedral $V - E + F = 2$, where V refers to the number of vertices or corners, E to the number of edges and F the number of faces. Imre Lakatos had written a sparkling history of Euler's theorem in broadly Popperian terms, against the then current assumptions in the history of mathematics (Lakatos, 1976). David Bloor had criticised Lakatos, putting a strong programme spin on the history framed in Mary Douglas's ideas of grid and group (Bloor, 1978). Ray and I then came in with an account rooted in methodological developments. Sadly, Leeds University Occasional Papers did not enjoy a wide readership. Neither of us followed up this work and so far as I know *Monstrous Thoughts* has received no attention, although I for one remain rather proud of it!

Though still meeting from time to time, we then went our separate ways, but each of us remained committed to the directions set by our early work: Ray the master methodologist, me the would-be pragmatic and practical theorist-reformer. In different ways I think we were both finding the then dominant forms of sociology frustrating and disappointing, although Ray has remained a major figure in the discipline.

In the late 1980s, we both found ourselves faced with having to think about programme evaluation. Ray was involved in prison education and the evaluation of prison education programmes in Canada and the UK (Duguid and Pawson, 1998). I had accepted a secondment to the British Home Office, where my first assignment related to the evaluation of Safer Cities crime prevention projects (see Tilley, 1992, 1993a, 1993b). We both found ourselves having to think about the evaluation of crime-related programmes. It was not planned.

In the late 1980s we both attended a meeting of the Social Research Association. We could not quite believe what we were hearing. It was our first exposure to the crass treatment of programmes as variables whose association with a given outcome, as measured through a comparison with a 'control' area, was taken as the mark of rigorous evaluation. Moreover, enormous sums of money were being spent on just this. It was a kind of eureka moment. We knew that what was being done did not make sense. We could see our way to doing better. For Ray, I think this was a chance to deploy his methodological interests in a new direction. For me, it provided an opportunity to take theoretically informed applied social science forward.

At that stage, neither of us was well versed in the literature on evaluation methodology. We read and read and the more we read the more confident we became that we had something new to say that could take evaluation in a new and improved direction. At the same time we found a few others who were stressing variants in theory-driven evaluation, including a group of Americans, Gary Henry, Mel Mark and George Julnes, who were fellow realist travellers, albeit ones who were more sympathetic to the experimental and quasi-experimental methods of which Ray and I were highly sceptical (Mark et al., 2000).

Armed with our realist orientation towards improving evaluation methodology, we began to present our ideas at conferences and to apply them in our empirical work. Our first published excursion appeared in the 1992 *Yearbook of Correctional Education* (Pawson and Tilley, 1992). Subsequent studies, appearing as reports, book chapters and journal articles, followed quite quickly. These provided the basis for refining our methodology and also furnished many of the examples used in *Realistic Evaluation*. We also found work whose logic accorded with the realist position we were developing, albeit that it was not framed explicitly in our terms, and we used these as further examples (for example, Hope and Foster, 1992; Laycock, 1992). Initially ours was a *succès de scandale*. We were the bad boys of evaluation methodology. Although by then chronologically quite grown up, we wrote with a frisson of excitement. We were outsiders to the evaluation establishment challenging opposing established orthodoxies.

Simon Ross, who was then at Sage, agreed to contract us to write what became *Realistic Evaluation*. Ray had an ESRC fellowship and I had an indulgent boss at the Home Office, Gloria Laycock, who was sympathetic to what we were doing and enabled me to make my contribution. The chapters went back and forth. We talked, wrote, argued and agonised about what we were saying. We honed and re-honed the text. We struggled with Chapter 8, which remains the least convincing part of the book but was essential to its overall structure. Sage served us very well. Simon was supportive and the brilliant copyeditor he allocated to us saved us from some embarrassing errors with his eagle eye for detail. *Realistic Evaluation* came out in Spring 1997 in both hardback and paperback. It seemed expensive at the time. I recall Ray saying that we would be doing OK if it sold 1,000 copies. It was not widely reviewed. It was returned as Ray's ESRC final report and it was graded 'Excellent'. We were delighted.

Realistic Evaluation remains in print at the time of writing, after nearly 20 years. It has sold around 12,000 copies. It is also very widely cited – roughly 4,000 to date according to Google Scholar and over 1,000 in Thompson's Web of Science. For social science these are big numbers! In terms of the attention it has received *Realistic Evaluation* has far exceeded anything else I have written. Ray's work has enjoyed greater attention, but *Realistic Evaluation* is also for him the single work that has so far had most impact. Invitations to write book chapters, address conferences, bid for funds and supervise PhD students have followed. Ray has been assiduously (and rightly) picky in what he's agreed to do. I've tended to say yes and to be told off by Ray for doing so! Sage has pressed us from time to time to produce a second edition, but we have not done so in part because of a reluctance to go over old ground and in part because we were quite proud of what we had done and didn't want to publish anything that fell short in style or substance of what we'd originally produced. Moreover, we did not wish to change the basic position, even if some of the details might have been improved.[3]

Ray and I continued to meet regularly as we still do. We've written a few pieces together and talked about more that have come to nothing. Alongside our wives, we go to cricket, go on holidays, generally spend New Year together and exchange family news: domestic interests now take precedence with only occasional chats about our respective work.

Until recently, post *Realistic Evaluation*, the paths of Ray's and my work have gone in rather different directions. In concert with his enduring interests in methodology, Ray has worked extensively on realist review methods and produced outstanding work on this (Pawson, 2006b). We were both rather shocked at what appeared to be the methodological assumptions of the Campbell Collaboration, which in many ways traduce Campbell's own work. Taken-for-granted evidence hierarchies, drawn on mechanically to identify the few studies that pass muster for meta-analysis to calculate effect sizes, seemed to us both to be wrong headed. We had one collaborative outing where we tried to show how different types of evidence could be stitched together to answer crucial realist questions (what works for whom in what circumstances and how) for enlightenment and usefully to inform policy decisions (Pawson and Tilley, 2001). Thereafter Ray has taken this ahead on his own, building on all his and our earlier work.

While Ray stuck with methodology I stuck with theoretically informed applied social science, in particular as this relates to crime prevention. I have wanted practitioners and policy-makers to think in the realist terms with which Ray and I wanted to infuse evaluation methodology. In this sense the work we did together has continued to drive my work, albeit towards theory development and research use rather than evaluation and research synthesis. I was and am worried at the prospect of ready-reckoner (what do the experiments tell us about net effects?) policy and practice (Tilley, 2000, 2006). I have railed against researchers who encourage and feed that approach to research, policy and practice (Tilley, 2009a). I have been dismayed to find subtle theory married to what I deem a crass commitment to so-called 'gold standard' methods of evaluation and research review, putting randomised controlled trials (RCTs) atop the methodological pile. I have pushed for discretion informed by evidence-tested theory relating to what works for whom in what circumstances and how (Tilley, 2006). I have been shocked at the lack of or lazy formalisation and testing of theory in advance of the policy and practice within which that theory is (often tacitly) embedded, and the disasters that can follow (Tilley, 2004). I have tried to show how policy can be misled when drawing on just those types of evidence celebrated by quasi-experimentalists (Tilley, 1999, 2001).

In 2018 I find myself less a collaborator with Ray and more a user of his methodological work. UCL is the lead member of a consortium (also including Birkbeck College, Cardiff University, Dundee University, the Institute of Education, the London School of Hygiene and Tropical Medicine, Southampton University and Surrey University) which successfully bid for a large, £3.2 million grant from the Economic and Social Research Council and the College of Policing to serve the research needs of a What Works Centre for Crime Prevention that is based at the College of Policing. Among other streams of work, we have to assemble, assess, code and represent for users all extant systematic reviews of crime prevention interventions.

We have also to conduct 12 new reviews. At the time of writing these have focused, for example, on 'alleygating' (gating rear-access alleyways mainly as a means of preventing domestic burglary), tagging in shops (the attachment of tags of various kinds as a means of reducing shop theft) and electronic monitoring (the attachment of monitoring devices to offenders as a means of preventing repeat offences). Our pitch for the work combined realism and the statistical meta-analysis associated with the Cochrane and Campbell Collaborations. Ray kindly agreed to be one of our expert advisors. He also came down to give a characteristically spellbinding presentation of realist synthesis, using his work on policies relating to passive smoking in cars as his example. How and why were we trying to merge two methodologies that are ontologically and epistemologically incommensurable with one another? More particularly, how could I, who had helped work through some of the thinking behind realist synthesis and have remained an arch-critic of so-called experimentalism, sign up to this?

The answers are pragmatic. First, there is no way that we would have won the grant framed exclusively in realist terms. The scope of work would not allow it. Second, for obvious reasons, I also believed that, although stressed in the scope of work, traditional meta-analysis (even in its increasingly refined incarnations) would not be adequate to meet the needs of policy-makers and practitioners. Third, there had been some neo-realist syntheses in crime prevention, which were orientated to the needs of practitioners, and which we could plausibly point to as exemplars of research review and synthesis that have been widely read and found useful (see the papers shown at www.popcenter.org – for example, Clarke, 2002). Fourth, I appreciated that, at least for some policy decisions, some evidence-based estimate of returns on an intervention in terms of overall effect size and optimal use of limited resources was important but, for very good reasons, could not be gauged from realist syntheses. Fifth, the bid was not mine alone, but reflected also the differing views of others involved in the work (although it is very gratifying to be able to say that the realist side of the work has been very widely endorsed across the consortium). Finally, I feared that the likely winner of the bid, should we not succeed, would not do a good job and would not best serve the interests of improving crime prevention policy and practice.

We are in the throes of our What Works work as I write this. We have formulated 'EMMIE' as a means of assessing and coding reviews. EMMIE refers to Effect (size/s), Mechanism (or mediator), Moderator (or context), Implementation and Economy (returns on resources allocated to the intervention) (Johnson et al., 2015; Tilley, 2016). I know that mechanisms and mediators are different from one another, that mediators and contexts are also different from one another, that effect sizes are contingent and variable by sub-population and that the same goes for returns on the resources allocated to interventions. So, EMMIE is a bastard device. I remain (mostly!), however, unapologetic. EMMIE is orientated not to methodological niceties, but instead comprises a means of marshalling the best evidence available to meet policy-makers' and practitioners' needs. It speaks to evidence relating to considerations they perforce have to take into account in their decisions. It is the work of someone focused on getting research into improved policy and practice rather than on promulgating coherent and consistent methodology. Moreover, EMMIE challenges the growing hegemony of evidence hierarchies and associated assessment tools that take RCTs to be the gold standard, their closest cousins as next best and the remainder of social science research far below. One of Ray's greatest achievements has been to show how different types of evidence can be used to speak to the theories incorporated into policies and practices and how, out of bringing that diverse evidence to the theory, better understanding (and to me better policy and practice) can follow. The promotion of cook-book assessment tools favouring cook-book experimental methods as a means of informing cook-book policy and practice decision-making continues to be anathema to me (Pawson and Tilley, 1998a, 1998b). An alternative is to try to equip policy-makers and practitioners with realistically tested theory that they can knowingly draw on in devising, developing and implementing interventions in the ever-changing situations in which they have to act.

One other aspect of work with Ray for *Realistic Evaluation* continues to drive what I'm doing. This relates to theory elicitation, formalisation and testing. Police officers pride themselves on being practical. One senior officer said to me, in a moment of exasperation, 'I didn't join the police to think!' This doesn't mean that the police do not use theory. They are inveterate theorists. Most just don't know it. Their theory is mostly disguised and therefore remains untested. It is easy routinely to prop up the theory with confirmatory anecdotes and to 'monster-bar' (i.e. exclude as aberrant) apparent exceptions. Much of the theory is reproduced unreflectively. Some, however, is novel and imaginative. For both there is a useful job for social scientists, at best in collaboration with the police, in eliciting the theory, formalising it into suites of propositions about contexts, mechanisms, regularities and outcomes and then searching out evidence that will test the theory (Tilley, 2014). This is not so much realistic evaluation as realist research in the service of improving the foundations of police activity. Here, one of the roles of the realist, applied social scientist is to formulate and test the theory at a middle-range level of abstraction that speaks neither universally to all cases nor specifically only to one particular case. It has been fun to be involved in this. I also think it comprises an important way ahead in the conduct of theoretically informed applied social science. It would not have been possible without the foundational work with Ray.

So, where next? Let me speak here to four issues that for me have emerged repeatedly, some in occasional musings with Ray, any of which may result in work by one or other of us, both of us, neither of us, or perhaps some third party.

The first issue relates to medicine. Realist evaluation and synthesis has had a big impact in health, where Ray has latterly done much important work (in contrast to my substantive area of interest, crime prevention, where it has enjoyed much lower levels of penetration). However, Ray and I have talked about the application of realist evaluation to clinical medicine and clinical trials. Medical researchers talk and write a lot about disease and treatment 'mechanisms', where they use the term just as we do. They conduct diverse types of research to test their theories, just as we advocate in realist evaluation (see Mukherjee, 2011).

They do conduct RCTs down the line when the underlying theory has been worked through and tested, to determine whether or not on balance the treatment works within participant populations. This latter stage is quite controversial (see Peto et al., 1995; Rothwell, 2005; Flather et al., 2006) and there has seemed to us to be a useful job to do in rehearsing in realist terms the nature and sequence of the theory and empirical research and, critically, then the design of the trials to provide findings that can be used by clinical practitioners. Sequencing in research seems to me to be especially important in the production (or non-production) of cumulative findings but to have received little systematic attention.

Second, economic evaluation is clearly important in the allocation of scarce resources. Economists like clear effect sizes to feed into their models. They also like to monetise benefits and disbenefits. The numbers fed into these models seem fragile, especially when derived from RCTs and quasi-experiments. Yet limited resources are a real constraint on policy and practice and decisions have to be made about their disbursal. It is not so difficult to see how sequences of evaluations could lead to improvements in economic returns, at least to the public purse. These could be achieved as better understanding of interventions and how they work for sub-groups leads to better targeting with fewer unintended negative effects, fewer nil effects and more positive outcomes. But even this has yet to be formally worked through.

Third, our critical attention was directed mainly at evaluations that fell short, in terms of conventional evidence hierarchies, of RCTs. We paid rather less attention to RCTs themselves. Yet there is much to say critically about them as well as where, when and how they could be useful. In social settings the assumptions behind the strong internal validity claims of RCTs are rarely met (such as full randomisation, successful blinding and independence of targets of intervention and analysis). The limitations to any possible claims to external validity from individual studies are generally acknowledged, though the problems of expecting external validity to come through replication are widely overlooked.

Fourth, as indicated realistic evaluation has been widely sold and cited. Yet the legacy in terms of studies that we recognise as great examples is quite small. We have worried about 'Janet and John' efforts and have also wondered about the development of cook-books of our own. Some years ago, Ray said to me he thought perhaps only two people really understood realist evaluation (and I wasn't entirely sure he meant me as the second!). Nowadays such a quip would no longer capture any underlying reality. The contributors to this volume clearly have a rich understanding and appreciation of realist evaluation and realist review. Yet the translation of the methodological principles into research practices remains a problem that has yet to be adequately resolved.

To conclude, this has been an affectionate account of a long-term friendship, collaboration and continuing legacy. The conditions were a fortuitous meeting, a fortuitous convergence of interests and complementary but far from identical orientations to doing social science. The collaboration worked for as long as it did through a degree of mutual respect, some tough differences between fairly obstinate equals that we were eventually able to resolve, and bags of fun along the way. I would not have missed it for anything. Ray is an important methodologist. He has also been a great friend and co-worker. I wish him a happy retirement, but hope that he still finds time for at least one more book!

NOTES

1 When Ray was undertaking his early work on methodology, the main focus of the most influential sociology in Britain was on class and social mobility. It was Ray's natural example. What he said was useful in its own right, regardless of its methodological import.

2 SSK was probably the most exciting sociology at the time. It may be less exciting now, as the provocative relativism its proponents once embraced is no longer so live an issue.

3 We produced an updated version under contract by the British Cabinet Office (Pawson and Tilley, 2004), which we liked but they did not publish. An abbreviated version appeared as Pawson and Tilley (2009).

2

MAKING UP MECHANISMS IN REALIST RESEARCH

Malcolm Williams

WHAT THIS CHAPTER IS ABOUT

Realist research aims to close the gap between the real and our knowledge of it; mechanistic thinking is an indispensable approach to this. However, this chapter suggests that there is always going to be a conceptual gap between mechanisms formulated by the scientist and the 'real' mechanisms out there. It argues that this is inevitable and suggests that the researcher's 'mechanisms' are heuristics. A description of what mechanisms are, the epistemology and ontology of mechanisms, and measurement and evidence lead to a three-point conclusion. Firstly, mechanisms and mechanistic thinking are much more attractive propositions than the empiricist alternative. Secondly, the mechanisms we make up are models or approximations of 'real' mechanisms. Thirdly, if mechanisms are models, then we are at least informally adopting the principle of inference to the best explanation, a direction often embraced in natural science realism. Realist research should be guided by these three principles.

How this chapter will help you to do realist research

The chapter delves into and deepens our understanding of one of the key concepts in realist research – the mechanism. Further understanding of this concept will allow the realist researcher to conduct their investigations with an appropriate philosophical understanding, considering both the ontology and epistemology of the realist mechanism.

A practical tip: a take-home message from the chapter

Researchers should be eclectic about the use of theories and methods, and use these as heuristic tools to propose possible mechanisms. However, our theories should always be testable, so that theory is always linked to method.

Ray Pawson has done more than anyone to champion the concept of mechanisms and mechanistic thinking in social science. His elegantly simple formulation of outcomes resulting from mechanisms operating in a context is a very useful shorthand for a realist conception of a complex causal order. So, my starting point here is to support the formulation and spirit of C + M = O. My finishing point will hopefully be on message, but between I want to pose some difficult questions and propose some possibly deviant answers.

The gist of my argument is this. The ontological core of realism is that the real, whether physical or social, exists independently of our knowledge of it. However, we can come to know aspects of the real, but there will always, as Roy Bhaskar puts it, be a gap between the intransitive objects of nature and the transitive objects of science (Bhaskar, 2008).

Realist research aims to close the gap between the two and mechanistic thinking is an all but indispensable approach to this. But there is always going to be a conceptual gap between mechanisms formulated by the scientist and the 'real' mechanisms out there. Part of the argument here is to say why this is inevitable and part of it (the deviant bit) is to argue that the researcher's 'mechanisms' are heuristics, but none the worse for this. We make up mechanisms.

REALISTS NEED MECHANISMS, SO WHAT ARE THEY?

Let us begin with the alternative to mechanistic thinking. As so often, Ray Pawson has done much of the heavy lifting for us here. In his ground-breaking *A Measure for Measures*, he talks of two rival approaches to causality in philosophy (Pawson, 1989: 127–8). The first of these is a successionist approach, associated with empiricism and particularly the philosophy of David Hume. The successionist view is that we cannot directly observe causes, but only the sequence of events. The regularity of the joint occurrence of events gives us warrant to inductively infer a causal connection. Indeed this is precisely the strategy of the 'causal analysis' tradition in sociology (see, for example, Imbens and Rubin, 2015; Morgan and Winship, 2015) where the statistical relationship of several independent variables to a dependent variable(s) in a model is the basis of causal inference. Usually these are linear regression models which aim to show the cause of an outcome by 'explaining' as much of the statistical variance in the model by fitting the independent variables to the model to give the best 'fit'. Some variables will be strongly associated, others less so and some possibly not at all (or negatively associated). I will return to causal analysis later, because though I (along with other realists) believe it starts from wrong assumptions, it is nevertheless sophisticated and a possible ally rather than an outright enemy!

The trouble with causal analysis is that it divorces theoretical reasoning from the empirical. As philosophers such as Popper and Polanyi taught us, theoretical reasoning, however informal or badly specified, is inevitable. This was also understood by the logical positivists and they concluded that this requires a translation between a theoretical and empirical language. This is problematic, because the translation itself will depend upon some kind of operationalising theory (the variables do not speak for themselves – they are constructs). Secondly, even if we ignore this issue the researcher is torn between just saying that variables are associated or making some kind of inference about why they are associated. David Lewis neatly sums up the first position that 'It is the doctrine that all there is to the world is a vast mosaic of local matters of particular fact, just one little thing then another' (Lewis, 1986: ix–x). The second position of inference is adopted by those in the causal analysis tradition and is both inevitable and inconsistent with Humean doctrine, which does not admit of 'hidden variables' – that is reasoning about those things we can't see.

Science (and social science) has come a long way from a simple doctrine of observation with the senses (Pawson, 1989: 133–4). Natural scientists use instrumentation to 'observe' and 'measure' and this depends on agreed rules about what counts as a measurement of some phenomenon. Similarly, social scientists use questions in various questionnaire formats, or economic or demographic indicators, etc. In short, theorisation is unavoidable. So as David Freedman, in a paper on statistical models for causation (Freedman, 2007: 128) notes, 'Strong assumptions are required to infer causation from association by modelling. The assumptions are of two kinds: (i) causal and (ii) statistical.' For 'causal', read 'theorising causes'.

The alternative to these empiricist positions I have outlined is the 'generative' approach[1] which maintains that events or outcomes are connected at a deeper level and that there is some kind of necessity in their connection. There is, then, a process or mechanism that, when activated, brings about particular sequences of events. Mechanisms might be hugely complex or very simple. The components of the mechanism must have particular dispositions (sometimes called liabilities or causal powers) that make the outcomes possible. For example, solubility in water is a disposition. However, while it does not follow that because something can be dissolved it will be dissolved, nevertheless, as Stephen Mumford notes, 'the properties of being soluble and being dissolved would have some degree of necessity connecting them' (Mumford, 2007: 74).

Despite the apparent incongruity between empiricist doctrine and practice, as Pawson concedes, at least empiricism operates with a very clear agreed understanding of the meaning of its terms. Realists (and other post-empiricists) must employ a more holistic approach to meaning that blurs or better integrates observational and theoretical terms. Thus 'concepts derive their meaning by being viewed as components of a system' (Pawson, 1989: 135). He goes on to say:

The idea is not that we depend on an open ended system of relations which can be used to define and redefine terms but that the meaning is ascribable with a 'closed system' or 'model' in which all the terms in the discourse are derivable from an understanding of the underlying mechanisms. (Pawson, 1989: 135)

He then discusses (what we might call) the 'proto-realism' of Mary Hessé and Imre Lakatos, each of whom formulated models of scientific progress that did not depend, for the most part, on the confirmation or falsification of theories by single experiments. Rather they proposed interconnected networks of theories (treated as closed systems). As Pawson suggests, the network approach provides a different consideration of the interplay between theory and evidence. He cites Lakatos, who proposes that this is not a clash between theory and facts, but rather a clash of theories, an interpretative theory to provide the facts and an explanatory theory to explain them (Pawson, 1989: 146).

This does not dissolve mechanisms into merely webs or networks of theories – indeed Pawson himself emphasises the importance of 'realist closure' which must involve measurement – yet it is important to get the 'feel' of a mechanism as a set of complex interrelationships of theories, at different levels and evidence. The term evidence here is somewhat question begging and I will return to it below. Nevertheless, it remains that realism needs mechanisms or some kind of schema that can capture a complex causal order.

THE EPISTEMOLOGY AND ONTOLOGY OF MECHANISMS

I think it is probably true to say that realists are more wedded to mechanistic thinking than some other proponents of mechanisms are to realism. A very good example of this is the collection of essays edited by Peter Hedström and Richard Swedberg (*Social Mechanisms: An Analytic Approach to Social Theory*) (Hedström and Swedberg, 1998). While much of the content would be conducive to realist thinking, the essays are in no sense overtly realist. Indeed, one of the papers is by the well-known methodological individualist Jon Elster and entitled 'A Plea for Mechanisms'. As one might imagine, Elster approaches mechanistic thinking from quite a different angle.[2] The index of the book does not mention realism at all and the usual realist suspects (apart from one mention of Bhaskar) are absent. Now, this only matters because several of the authors, particularly the editors, in an introductory paper are at great pains to point out that mechanistic thinking (contrasted to law-like thinking) is the norm in many sciences, including biology and economics. Even though those sciences might sometimes be seen as 'proto-realist', they are rarely overtly so and mechanisms/mechanistic thinking is part of the methodological toolkit, rather than a philosophical grounding.

Mechanistic thinking provides the possibility of moving beyond the merely descriptive to explanations of why things are as they are. Most scientists and I include social scientists, want explanations but they mostly do not care whether this makes them realists, instrumentalists, conventionalists – or any other 'ists'. However, those of us who start off from realist assumptions care initially about matters ontological and epistemological and the philosophical grounding is important. There are very good historical reasons for this. The collapse of the regulatory regime of positivism in social science was welcomed by many as the possibility to embrace Dadaism and relativism and leave the science to the people in the white coats (Williams, 2000: 87–103). Social science realism was (and is) an attempt to rescue the science of the social and put it on a firmer non-positivist philosophical and methodological footing, which is why we are so concerned with the questions of what it is we are trying to explain and the nature of our explanation. I should add that the social science anti-realists are usually not decent instrumentalists, conventionalists or sophisticated empiricists (like Bas Van Frassen or Helen Longino). Rather, they are relativists or constructionists who don't think we can measure or explain anything in the social world.

Though many of us parted company with Bhaskar's later work, a cornerstone for us all can be summed up by the following quote:

Things exist and act independently of our descriptions, but we can only know them under particular descriptions. Descriptions belong to the world of society and of men; objects belong to the world of nature ... Science, then, is the systematic attempt to express in thought the structures and ways of acting of things that exist and act independently of thought. (Bhaskar, 2008: 250)

The last sentence is a pretty good description of what scientists do: an attempt to align explanations of reality with reality itself. If I say the loss of my keys was probably the result of the hole I discovered in my pocket, I do not rule out a pickpocket or the theft of my keys by goblins, but the first explanation is most plausible and might lead to their successful recovery through a search of those places I had recently visited. The principles of Occam's razor and verisimilitude remain at the heart of good science.

The social world and a great deal of the natural world are complex in the mathematical sense of the word. In other words, though there are recognisable patterns of what Robert Nozick called 'intransigence' (Nozick, 2001), these patterns evolve in non-linear ways, changing, strengthening and weakening over time. Some of these last for centuries, for example organised religions, others simply moments. I have called these 'social objects' (Williams, 2009). Many of the things we want to explain exist in specific forms for limited time periods.

It is for this reason that Merton rejected grand theorising at a meta-social level in favour of middle-range theorising (Merton, 1968). Indeed, for Ray Pawson and many more of us, Merton is a starting point for a type of theorising that attempts to capture a particular phenomenon in historical context with a view to 'cumulating' such explanations (Pawson, 2013). Yet middle-range theories, like all theories, are propositional statements. From the flux of the observed social world, often because those who make or criticise policy pay us to do so, we pick out social objects of interest and try to explain them. Over the years, for me, this has included homelessness, counterurbanisation and living alone.

We can (and I have) proposed a plausible mechanism to explain homelessness (in the United Kingdom) as resulting from a confluence of neo-liberal housing policy and its outcomes of lack of affordable accommodation and restrictions on access to what there is, high youth unemployment, changes in household structure and substance abuse (Williams, 2010). For policy-makers it is perfectly possible to produce statistical evidence for the existence of such a mechanism. However there are two problems with this: firstly, what counts as homelessness? In practice street homelessness is a very small part of a huge problem of housing need and moreover only a small hard-core of people remain on the streets for very long (Williams and Cheal, 2001). An explanation of street homelessness (as opposed to other forms of extreme housing need) suggests a different mechanism of substance abuse, leaving home or institutionalisation (Williams and Cheal, 2001). Secondly, homelessness was the focus (that was what the politicians wanted in research sponsored by government) but equally we could have begun with poor health. A major part of explanations of poor health is substandard housing, though other factors such as diet, employment (or lack of it) and income would form elements in a proposed mechanism.

Now, I'm not saying that there are no mechanisms present in the above descriptions of homelessness and I am certainly not saying these things are accidentally associated. It is possible to show that each of these elements exists, but showing the way and the extent to which they might cohere is quite another matter. Nevertheless, there is something going on in which homelessness or severe housing need is an outcome. What is probably going on is that there are a number of overlapping and interacting mechanisms that evolve over time, but whether they can be captured by the proposition of an elegant mechanistic framework is debatable. Moreover, what the mechanism looks like will depend on where you start from.

This complexity and emergence is far from lost on Pawson. In fact, in his book *The Science of Evaluation* (Pawson, 2013) a chapter is given over to complexity and emergence. He speaks of evaluations of interventions; the latter, far from taking place in a vacuum, in fact take place in an already crowded field of policy change upon policy change in communities or organisations that are themselves evolving.

At this point I should reassure the reader that I am not abandoning mechanisms, I am merely working through the implications of the view of realism and science Bhaskar proposes.

What I am suggesting, however, is that we probably need to start by thinking of mechanisms in two ways:

1. ontological – the actually existing mechanisms of 'nature' (in this case, society);
2. epistemological – the mechanisms we propose to account for the outcomes.

Obviously, we seek to match (1) and (2) as closely as we can in the spirit of Occam's razor and verisimilitude, but the fact is that we make up (2) on the basis of what we know, or think we know. And quite rightly so!

However, before I go on to talk about the ways in which we can make up mechanisms, let us go back to Pawson for advice and reassurance. In the *Science of Evaluation* (Pawson, 2013: 61–2) he sums up seven steps to critical realist enquiry. Step 6 says:

Although the social world transforms ceaselessly, this does not mean it is endlessly chaotic. Social institutions change, but not into blue cheese. There are corresponding social mechanisms that govern and limit social transformations. These too are located in the deep, underlying structures of society. (Pawson, 2013: 62)

This is the way I take this advice: the complexity of social life cannot ever be grasped, because it is too much and too fast in its change. But underlying that complexity there are ontological features which shape and limit change and give rise to the relative invariance of things that we can measure, or at least to an extent know. That means when we make up mechanisms, they are not works of fiction but will arise from phenomena that are apparent, through measurement, through reasoning or through informal observation. But there is one last ontological point to make, which is controversial for many realists (I have discussed this at length in Williams (2011) and what follows is a synopsis of that argument).

If we accept that the social world is indeterminate this has consequences both for our theory of causality and for the mechanisms, we propose. A key feature of critical realism is that of natural necessity, which Harré and Madden describe thus:

> When the natures of the operative powerful particulars, the constraining or stimulating effect of conditions and so on are offered as the grounds for the judgment that a certain effect cannot but happen, or cannot but fail to happen, we have natural necessity. (Harré and Madden, 1975: 19)

I have proposed that such necessity cannot exist in the social world. It can certainly exist in the physical world, where there is an ultimate 'grounding' of dispositions (or powerful particulars) in fundamental laws, such as gravity or thermodynamics. In the social world there is no such grounding or reduction (except in instances where the social is enabled or constrained by the physical world). The social world could or can be different, however unlikely this is. Indeed, we can express likelihood in terms of ontological probability. In the physical world natural necessity can be expressed as 1s and 0s (must be the case and cannot be the case), but in the social world, *until an event actually occurs*, the probability lies somewhere between the 0s and 1. The occurrence of that event then changes the probability of subsequent events. These probabilities change through time as a result of interactions and the apparent intransigence of much of the social world is the outcome of relative stability, not natural necessity. That does not mean there is no *necessity* in the social world, but the necessity that does exist is *conceptual necessity*, that is the dispositions of social objects, be they characteristics of office (a police officer, the President of France), rules, norms or social interactions, are what defines or makes that social object and no other social object.

This has implications for mechanisms (1) and (2). Mechanisms (1) are far from clockwork – they are in fact a changing, but relatively stable, nesting of social objects with a relative propensity to change. Indeed, to use an analogy from Karl Popper (1979), they are more like clouds than clocks. Clouds have form and shape and we can describe and explain them, but in no way are they even relatively closed systems in the way that a clock is. The implication for mechanisms (2) is that, like clouds, we can propose what a mechanism might look like and what its key characteristics are, but the best we can do is propose a resemblance – a model of (1). But it will never be a model of which we can ever be sure of accurate resemblance.

So, while we can speak of mechanisms having, in a general sense, certain properties – they have causal efficacy, they are often complex and they are dynamic – any particular specified mechanism (2) is inevitably a social construct that we hope will match in important and useful ways with mechanism (1). The mechanisms we make up are models of the world. Dave Byrne, discussing the work of Paul Cilliers, says the following:

... our models are attempts ... to grasp the *structure* [original emphasis] of complex systems. Here structure is not a static arrangement, a meaning which the common usage of the word can only too easily imply. It is the whole dynamic system in action with potential for radical change being part of the character of that system. Moreover complex systems are structured in hierarchies not of strictly defined and separate sub units but, as Cilliers puts it, of messy (with the messiness being indispensable), interpenetrating and mutable (although robust) hierarchical orders of components. Of particular significance is that these hierarchies are context dependent. (Byrne, 2011: 91)

It does not stretch this description too far to substitute 'mechanism' for 'structure' or 'system'.

MEASUREMENT AND EVIDENCE

Realists talk a lot about theory; it is omnipresent with different levels of formality. Theoretical reasoning can be applied to the testing of a theory, such that the reasoning renders that theory less or more plausible, but scientific realists need more than that if they are not to simply emulate the armchair theorising of a Giddens or Bauman. We need evidence. Evidence comes in different forms and strengths. Rarely is there one piece of evidence that is a eureka moment that clinches or falsifies a theory – at least that is rarely the case in natural science and perhaps never in social science. Most of what we do and have is messy, untidy and imperfect. We are, as Cathie Marsh observed, detectives (Marsh, 1982: 2).

Detectives look for certain kinds of evidence and, like Sherlock Holmes, they have their methods, but the methods are often informal or opportunistic (see Chapter 8 written by Geoff Wong). I think social science research is mostly like that. We have to work with the data we have or can reasonably collect and the methods we use are governed by things like ethics, access and the size and nature of samples. Many statistical techniques will have been designed for normally distributed samples, for parametric data, for minimum sample sizes, and we struggle to find a suitable statistical strategy. Sometimes we must work from previously collected survey data, in which what we would like to measure has not been measured so we must use 'proxies'. For example, where income data is not collected (such as in the UK Censuses) we can use other variables, such as where someone lives, their housing tenure and occupation, to provide an indicator that stands in for income. Indeed occasionally valuable conclusions can even be gleaned from poor research (poor conceptualisation, poor analysis, etc.). This was acknowledged by Ray Pawson in his paper 'Digging for Nuggets: How "Bad" Research Can Yield "Good" Evidence' (Pawson, 2006a).

However, the biggest challenge for realists is what we measure and how we measure it.[3] This is at the heart of 'realist closure' and I will now briefly outline the issue (see also Williams, 2003; Williams and Husk, 2013) and in the following section I will use two examples to illustrate the potential and limitations of mechanisms.

There has long been a debate in social research about operationalisation. We are good at thinking up theoretical concepts that may explain aspects of the social world, but we may be less good at turning them into measures (Cicourel, 1964). A good example is the Marxist perennial of 'alienation'. Marx described it and, for him, a lot depended on it (especially in his earlier work), but I don't think anyone has yet come up with a decent measure of it. Why? Because there are different ways to be alienated and the menu of ways to be alienated will depend on the society you live in and your place in that society plus a pretty hefty psychological component. Meanwhile, none of the things I have just listed is 'fixed' but rather is in flux. Maybe we can't crack alienation, but what about important sociological variables such as class and ethnicity? Again, Marx and other theorists write with confidence about (say) the bourgeoisie and the proletariat, but trying to measure these things with both validity and reliability (especially comparatively between two relatively homogeneous societies) is challenging and the best we can get are approximations that must make trade-offs between validity and reliability (Williams, 2003). Equally, the distribution of ethnic groups varies widely, even in particular states, and there always remains a voluntaristic aspect to declared ethnic group membership (Williams and Husk, 2013). The upshot of this is that, in trying to get mechanism (2) to look like mechanism (1), the best we can do are approximations. And remember, we do not always have control over how we measure, because a lot of the data we must work with is secondary data with predefined categories and measurements.

It is not all bad news. Three kinds of variables can be measured with relative validity and reliability. Given the caveat of possible error, we can still measure things like biological sex, age, income, housing tenure, education, etc. We can measure beliefs and we can measure attitudes, though whether the measures of these capture the aspects of the mechanism we wish to construct or test cannot be precisely known.

So where are we so far? As realists we believe that there is a reality out there that exists despite us. We notice things that matter to us: crime, poor educational attainment, poor health – the outcomes of some processes or 'mechanisms'. As scientific realists we want to discover and explain these mechanisms, but they are partly, perhaps wholly, hidden. Like clouds we may see them, have a feel for them, but they move, change shape, disappear. And our methods often fall short of what we'd like them to be but, undaunted, we use our imperfect methods to try to capture at least what is important in those mechanisms.

SOME MECHANISMS

In their research of social stratification in the United States, Blau and Duncan (1978) tried to do what I describe above, using perhaps imperfect methods to try to capture at least what is important in those mechanisms. Their methods are well summarised in the paper by David Freedman (2007) I mentioned above. I draw on this paper for the following description.

In the 1950s and 1960s, Marxists believed that the US was a highly stratified society, with status determined by family background and transmitted through the school system, yet nevertheless the system was permeable to an extent and individuals could transcend their stratum. It is a nice example of a proposed mechanism. The Outcome (O) is the *relatively* fixed strata and the mechanism proposed is one of a superstructure of education and family type, themselves the outcomes of an economic 'base'. In this research only the superstructure mechanism is explored. The contexts are the US itself, because presumably a similar mechanism could exist elsewhere, but also local contexts, which may be cultural or socio-economic.

Initially Blau and Duncan produced a correlation matrix of the following variables, measured from the 1962 Current Population Survey: Son's Occupation; Son's First Job; Son's Education; Father's Occupation; Father's Education. The measurements themselves were standardised, for example: education in number of years and occupation on a prestige scale of 0–10. A path analysis was then conducted (reproduced on page 131 of the Freedman paper) which indicates causality between (for example) father's and son's education and between father's occupation and son's occupation. The standard deviations indicated the level of permeability in the causal paths. As mechanisms go, this is a pretty crude one. We could point to the measurements themselves, the level of standardisation and, most importantly, the 'black box' of those things not measured, which presumably give rise to the large standard deviations in some of the pathways. The mechanism goes beyond description and provides some level of explanation of the key features of stratification and its permeation, but it is probably a million miles from the complexity of the 'real' mechanism (1). A modern-day realist would want to improve on the mechanism, to better titrate the permeability by exploring, perhaps at a meso or micro level, what socio-economic and cultural differences might exist to change the chances of mobility through education or occupation – in other words, construct other 'mini mechanisms' and test them on a subset of this sample (or a sample emulating it). So, for example, with the addition of a geographical variable – say there was more permeability in Boston than in New Orleans – then we would seek initially to theorise and then to test why there is such a difference. Methodologically this may well point to plurality and, while the results may not integrate in a way mixed methods advocates would like, they may well help us construct a mechanism of theoretical terms, some parts of which are supported by data (of different strengths and quality) and others remain (as yet) theoretical propositions only. In this example I have made up, I illustrate what might have been done to investigate this mechanism further, but next is my attempt (with colleagues) to explain the increase in the numbers of people living alone in England and Wales.[4]

The population of Great Britain has grown by 5 per cent over the past three decades, yet the number of households with a single occupant has grown by 31 per cent (Summerfield and Babb, 2003: 42). The 2001 Census showed that 16 per cent of all adults under pensionable age were living alone. The increase in numbers living alone is not just a British phenomenon, but is found throughout most European countries, which would seem to indicate there is a common causal mechanism at work. Indeed, a number of theorists have confidently identified such a cause as a result of changes in patterns of intimacy and interdependence (see, for example, Giddens, 1992; Beck and Beck-Gernsheim, 2002). Whatever the veracity of these claims, they are hard to demonstrate and often mutually exclusive. Whatever the mechanism, it is likely to be complex.

However, some relatively simple longitudinal analyses of linked Census data (from the England and Wales Census) punctured some theoretical myths and suggested the possibility of more than one separate mechanism. Table 2.1 shows the originating household structure of those living alone ten years later. This is for two reasons. Firstly I will pick out some trends that might indicate mechanisms, but secondly a slightly longer look at the table will show the huge complexity of moves into living alone. Like an Escher drawing, the more you look the more there is to see.

TABLE 2.1   Household structures (1991) for men and women living alone (2001) by age

Household Structure 1991	Age of men in 1991				Age of women in 1991				All
	26–34	35–44	45–54	All	26–34	35–44	45–54	All	
1 person < 65	30.7	37.0	39.4	**35.6**	30.1	26.8	30.5	**29.2**	32.4
2+ adults, no elderly	12.1	6.9	9.4	**9.5**	13.0	10.8	17.5	**14.5**	12.0
Couple, no dependent children	15.3	9.1	12.1	**12.2**	18.4	9.9	16.1	**14.6**	13.4
Couple + dependent children	19.2	22.1	7.7	**16.6**	9.5	12.9	3.9	**7.9**	12.2
Couple + dependent children + adult	1.6	4.9	4.8	**3.7**	1.7	7.0	2.7	**3.9**	3.8
Couple, no dependent children + adult	11.2	4.0	9.6	**8.2**	8.7	5.6	12.2	**9.4**	8.8
1 parent family	1.2	2.9	2.8	**2.3**	10.2	18.9	7.3	**11.6**	7.0
Complex household	7.7	12.1	13.4	**11.0**	7.0	7.3	7.5	**7.3**	9.2
Other	1.0	1.0	0.7	**0.9**	1.4	0.7	2.3	**1.6**	1.3
All n =	3,073	3,123	2,791	**8,987**	1,721	2,949	4,472	**9,142**	18,129

Source: Office for National Statistics, Longitudinal Study (Williams et al., 2008).

I have picked out three interesting observations that indicate the complexity of patterns of living alone. These, incidentally, could really only be revealed by longitudinal data:

- A large proportion of those living alone at the first census point were likely to be living alone ten years later.
- There was very little difference in the percentage of men and women in the youngest age group who continued to live alone.
- Men leaving the 'traditional' nuclear family set-up of couple with dependent children are more likely to live alone at an earlier age than women. Similarly women in one-parent families ten years before were more likely to live alone ten years later, if they were between 35 and 44 (compared to other age groups).

So what is going on?

Once people live alone, the more likely they are to continue to do so, though from the data in Table 2.1 (and other analyses not shown) we can see different patterns of living alone. For younger people, prior to marriage or cohabitation it seems likely that living alone is a lifestyle choice, but this is less the case for people, mostly men, who live alone after the breakup of marriage or cohabitation. For women, after such breakup, living alone is usually postponed until after their children leave home. Even in these relatively simple analyses we can perceive elements of choice and compulsion, as well as different experiences of living alone during the life course of men and women (30.5 per cent compared to 39.4 per cent, Table 2.1). There are at least three separate mechanisms we might propose or 'make up' (and all are indeed testable to some extent):

1. Living alone for many is indeed a lifestyle choice that is related to newer and emerging patterns of intimacy. These may develop a solidity over time that makes living alone a preferred option.
2. Living alone for younger people is elective and cohabitation/marriage is postponed (this may well be connected to the above). The reasons for such postponement may be career/job related or to do with housing options.
3. The firmest emerging possible mechanism is that of the difference in age between men and women moving from nuclear families to living alone. This seems likely to be the result of cultural practices, whereby the dissolution of relationships leaves custody of the children to women, who then live alone when the children are no longer dependent. Other analyses indicate that a large proportion of men move back from living alone into 'family' structures.

The overall message here seems to be that there are a number of what we might term first-level mechanisms present, but how they are caused by deeper level mechanisms and may indeed be related at some deeper level is but speculation.

CONCLUSION: THE IMPERFECTIONS OF EVIDENCE AND THEORY, OR WHO'S AFRAID OF CAUSAL ANALYSIS?

I want to conclude by making three points.

Firstly, mechanisms and mechanistic thinking are much more attractive propositions than the empiricist alternative, principally because theory and measurement achieve compatibility. This is a cornerstone of realist thinking.

Secondly, however, while realist reasoning can be shown to be correct through empirical closure, in specific and limited circumstances, the mechanisms we propose are models of a reality we cannot fully grasp in principle because of its very mutability and complexity through time. Our mechanisms are models or approximations of 'real' mechanisms. This point is probably not at odds with Pawson's approach at all and it might be said I have constructed a straw person here. However, a third thing, I believe, follows.

If our mechanisms (2) are models, then we are at least informally adopting the principle of inference to the best explanation, and a direction often embraced in natural science realism (Psillos, 2005).

Something follows from this, and possibly a bitter pill for my fellow realists to take: that this is pretty much what those people doing causal analysis are doing!

I quote from Hubert Blalock, one of the first of that tribe:

One admits that causal thinking belongs completely on the theoretical level and that causal laws can never be demonstrated empirically. But this does not mean that it is not helpful to think causally and to develop causal models that have implications that are indirectly testable. (Blalock, 1961: 6)

In this sentence (and a number of times elsewhere) Blalock is proposing the existence of a reality – and indeed one that is active – but he is also setting some limits to what a research programme can tell us about reality. This is not simply a Humean acknowledgement that there may be a reality but we can't possibly know it, but rather an implicit admission that reality reveals itself to us partially and imperfectly. He goes on to say:

Reality, or at least our perception of reality, admittedly consists of ongoing processes. No two events are ever exactly repeated, nor does any object or organism remain precisely the same from one moment to the next. And yet, if we are ever to understand the nature of the real world, we must act and think as though events are repeated and as if objects do have properties that remain constant for some period of time, however short. (Blalock, 1961: 7)

The sharp eyed will have picked out that my Blau and Duncan example above came from a paper that was all about causal analysis, its possibilities and limitations.

This was deliberate. I could have picked an illustration from more mainstream illustrations of mechanisms at work (there is a plethora of these in Ray Pawson's work alone), but what I wanted to show was that mechanistic thinking and causal analysis are not mutually exclusive. What is wrong with causal analysis is not its techniques but the starting assumptions that variables have a life of their own. Yet modern forms of causal analysis will accept many of the limitations and criticisms levelled at them by realists, for example that there is rarely an assumption of linearity in a regression model and the relationships are assumed to be additive, but parsimony remains a watchword so that it is not simply a matter of just fitting more and more terms to a model to torture the data into the findings you want.

What I am suggesting is that the techniques of causal analysis provide us with the most sophisticated modelling techniques and we should not conflate essentially heuristic, statistical reasoning with theoretical reasoning. Now this only works if we are prepared to accept that mechanisms (1) are at least partially illusive – hence my illustration of the complexity of even simple data on living alone. If, however, we are prepared to allow that mechanisms (2) are proposed heuristic models of (1) then we can be eclectic about our methods.

Finally, then, I would suggest our research is guided by three principles:

- Firstly, that there are underlying causal mechanisms that produce outcomes, and that we can at least partially reveal these mechanisms, though this will never be complete.
- Secondly, that we are eclectic about our theories and methods and we use these as heuristic tools to propose possible mechanisms, though our theories should always be testable so that theory is always linked to method.
- Thirdly, that a principle of inference to the best explanation is guided by parsimony, so that we should prefer models of mechanisms that either have the most empirical content or are the most testable. The very best models will be falsifiable.

NOTES

1 As Pawson notes (1989: 128) the rivalry between the successionist and generative approaches was first described thus by Rom Harré (1972).
2 Indeed the overall tenor of the book, including the introductory essay, is methodological individualism. Hedström and Swedberg set out the key features of mechanisms and mechanistic thinking to ground any account in causal agents – individual actors (Hedström and Swedberg, 1998: 12–13). Whether this is or should be the case is not central to the argument here; however, I doubt that this is always possible or desirable if we allow for institutional actors to be agents of causal change, sufficient to the mechanism we are trying to discover.

3 In this chapter I concentrate on how we can formulate mechanisms from quantitative (survey-based) data. Much of realist inference is from synthesising the results of a number of studies, both quantitative and qualitative. Though I think much of my argument applies in these cases, it is at the 'sharp' end of operationalisation and the primary hypothesisation of mechanisms where there is a particular challenge.

4 The description which follows can mostly be found in Williams et al. (2008), but several other papers were published in this research programme.

3

UNDERSTANDING MECHANISMS IN REALIST EVALUATION AND RESEARCH

Gill Westhorp

WHAT THIS CHAPTER IS ABOUT

This chapter revisits three interrelated issues in realist philosophy and realist social science: the nature of mechanisms, the nature of open systems and the relationships between contexts and mechanisms in open systems. It explains why mechanisms are 'invisible' and the implications for doing realist research. It argues that – like all things realist – the 'reasoning and resources' construct of programme mechanisms (Pawson and Tilley, 1997) only 'works' in some contexts and that other constructs may be necessary for understanding whether and how some types, or aspects, of policies and programmes work. The chapter examines for what tasks and types of evaluation research Pawson and Tilley's construct of programme mechanisms is most appropriate and explores four alternative constructs: powers and liabilities, forces, interactions and processes. Examples include self-esteem as a context, a mechanism and an outcome in youth programmes, and how public disclosure initiatives identifying 'under-performance' or 'deviant behaviour' work.

How this chapter will help you to do realist research

The chapter reminds you that there are several constructs of mechanism and that any construct can be right for your research so long as it is consistent with the fundamental realist conception of mechanisms. The key message is to ensure that your chosen mechanisms are explanatory rather than simply descriptive.

A practical tip: a take-home message from the chapter

It is not enough simply to describe that different mechanisms fire in different contexts: for true realist explanation, it is necessary to explain 'why'.

INTRODUCTION

This chapter revisits the idea of mechanisms as underlying causal processes with a view to supporting realist approaches in a wider range of policy- and programme-relevant research and evaluation. In realist evaluation, Pawson and Tilley's (1997) construct of programme mechanisms as comprising 'reasoning and resources' has attained such prominence as to overshadow other, more fundamental constructs. However, the chapter will argue that – like all things realist – the 'reasoning and resources' construct only 'works' in some contexts. Other constructs may be equally useful – and indeed necessary – for understanding whether and how some types of, or some aspects of, policies and programmes work. This chapter examines the following questions:

- For what tasks in what kinds of evaluation research is Pawson and Tilley's construct of programme mechanisms most appropriate, and for which is it not, and why?
- What alternatives are there? Are the alternatives mutually exclusive, or can they be used together to build more comprehensive understandings of whether, how, for whom and in what contexts policies and programmes are effective?

Answering these questions requires delving back into realist philosophy and realist social science to re-examine three interrelated issues: the nature of mechanisms, the nature of open systems and the relationships between contexts and mechanisms in open systems. Each of these straddle the natural and social worlds, which is important because many policies and programmes do so as well. They also straddle the relationship between policies or programmes and the contexts into which they are inserted. That relationship is a central issue in realist research and evaluation and will be revisited in this chapter.

I do not seek to undermine the 'reasoning and resources' construct of programme mechanisms. It is useful for the evaluation of particular kinds of programmes and for particular aspects of other kinds of programmes. It has also helped shift attention toward the critical role of decision-making at all stages of programme implementation – including, most critically, the decisions taken by participants – in determining programme effectiveness. The basic argument is not that the construct is wrong, but that it applies in a limited range of contexts, and that other constructs may be more useful for other contexts.

Two basic premises underpin the argument that follows. The first is that the field of 'policy- and programme-relevant research and evaluation' is much broader than just evaluation. It includes research into natural and social issues themselves, as distinct from the policies and programmes designed to address them. It includes basic and applied research in biology, physiology, geology and other natural sciences as well as psychology, sociology and other social sciences. It also includes policies and initiatives not always considered to be 'social programmes'. To reach their full utility, realist methodologies must be applicable across this wider field, and this requires that concepts and methods must make sense in those different kinds of systems and different forms of enquiry.

Secondly, realist evaluation is not simply a type of evaluation. It is a type of applied realism. That is, it is underpinned by an understanding of *how the world is* and how it works (ontology), and an understanding of the nature of knowledge (what we can know and how we can know it – epistemology). This point is sometimes missed by those who see it as a method ('just another tool in the toolkit'), rather than as a fundamentally different set of assumptions with real and persistent implications for how policies and programmes work, as well as for how research and evaluation work.

We begin by revisiting the idea of 'mechanism'.

CONSTRUCTS OF MECHANISM

The idea of mechanisms as being causal processes or powers is central to realism. Nevertheless, it remains one of the most poorly understood ideas, in part because it has been defined in different ways by different authors.

James Mahoney, writing in 2001, identified 24 different 'definitions' of a mechanism (although some are perhaps more explanations or extracts from explanations than definitions). He initially sorted these into three categories. The first two categories are clearly not realist; the third is the realist philosophy of science construct of mechanisms. Here, Mahoney draws only on the epistemological construct of mechanisms in realism: 'Causal mechanisms are posited relations or processes that the researcher imagines to exist; they do not refer to any particular set of empirical conditions' (2001: 581).

However, the notion that mechanisms are 'posited relations that the researcher imagines' misses one of the most fundamental assertions of realism: that mechanisms are real. They exist ontologically and cause effects in 'the real world'; they are not simply 'imagined'. The process of the *discovery* of mechanisms may well (may even necessarily) involve imagination, but this does not turn mechanisms into imaginary things or into mind-dependent entities.

For an explanation of the construct used in a realist philosophy of science, we turn to the realist philosophers of science and social science, among them Bhaskar, Harré and Archer.

Here the central idea is that the internal structures of things, along with the necessary relations between those structures, have the power 'to produce an effect in virtue of its nature' (Harré and Madden, 1975: 16), or 'causality is a matter of the real powers that things have, in virtue of what they are, to affect other things in specific ways' (Groff, 2004: abstract). It should be noted that the term 'things' here does not necessarily refer to material things. Social structures and relationships and systems of ideas and beliefs are just as much 'things' as are material or biological things.

The term 'stratified reality', as used in realist research and evaluation, comes from the writings of Roy Bhaskar (1997). Bhaskar argued that the world comprises the *empirical* – that which is or can be observed or experienced; the *actual* – that which exists, regardless of whether or not it is material and whether or not it is experienced; and the *real* – which includes both of the two previous categories but also includes that which causes what is to be the way it is, and events and processes to be the way they are (1997: 56). Mechanisms are 'that which causes' and lie, in this view, in the domain of the real. Described another way: that which has real effects must by definition itself be real, whether or not it is material or observable. Causes by definition have effects, so causes are real.

These levels are nested within each other. Everything that is 'empirical' must by definition be actual and incorporate its own causal forces and processes. That which is 'actual' may not be empirically observed or even observable, but necessarily involves real causal forces. Causal forces are real whether or not they are currently generating actual (or empirical) outcomes and whether or not they can be observed.

In fact, it is a common claim that mechanisms are not observable: they are 'underlying' and 'invisible' (e.g. Bhaskar, 1997; Pawson, 1989). This claim itself warrants some consideration. If it is the case, why is it the case? I argue that this is so because (a) they operate at different levels of the system than the outcome they generate; (b) they operate at different timescales than the outcome of interest; and (c) they necessarily depend on relationships and interactions between components, some of which can be observed but others cannot (or not with currently available instruments).

Let us consider briefly each of these in turn. Realism has long acknowledged that mechanisms operate at different levels of the system than their outcomes. Bhaskar noted 'the idea of some lower-order or microscopic domain providing a basis for the existence of some higher-order property or power; as for example, the neuro-physiological organization of human beings may be said to provide a basis for their power of speech' (1997: 115). It is necessary to look to the sub-systems – of what they are comprised, what they do and how they do it, and what the consequences of their operations are – in order to understand how a system – or some aspect of it – works.

However, realism also acknowledges that causation works downwards, as well as upwards:

The idea of downward causation is anti-reductionist and posits ... that influences can be expected to occur in both directions – upward from subsystems and downward from the whole; every level constrains others. (Mark et al., 2000: 156; see also Bhaskar, 1997: 112)

That is, each level of a system has its own 'powers and liabilities' which may cause effects at higher or lower levels of the system. The nature of those powers and liabilities will of course vary according to the nature and level of the system in question. By implication, reduction of the concept of programme mechanisms to the interaction between programme resources and stakeholder 'reasoning' may be insufficient. It also implies that investigating mechanisms is likely to require different methods and tools than those used to investigate programme outcomes, irrespective of the level at which those outcomes occur.

The issue of temporality – here referring to the timescales over which mechanisms work – is less discussed in realist literature. Pawson (2013) discusses time and, in particular, history as context for programmes; other than that, neither time nor temporality are listed in the indices of many famous realist references. (The notable exception is Archer's (1995) work on morphogenesis, which addresses social change over time and issues of time in some types of social analysis.) However, some have argued that mechanisms fire 'instantaneously' with their outcomes (Tilley, personal communication, quoted in Westhorp, 2008), and in some cases this is clearly close to true: the chemical interaction of the constituents of gunpowder and the bang of the explosion are close to instantaneous. However, equally clearly there are mechanisms that take years or even generations to operate: the 'short-term' outcomes of early intervention programmes may take years to manifest and the longer-term outcomes may manifest over a whole lifetime. The timescales for evolutionary mechanisms can be even longer. Many social policies and programmes require repeated action over time to be effective: what starts as one kind of mechanism (e.g. a conscious choice in response to a particular resource) may become another (habit) as a result of yet another (new pathways built into brain structure as a result of habit, through the biological process of myelination). Here too time plays a role in the operation of mechanisms.

If causal processes operate over different timescales than the outcome of interest, that too has implications for research and evaluation methods. The methodological implications will be different for prospective and retrospective studies, and for research programmes as distinct from single programme evaluations. One obvious implication is that any 'standard' programme evaluation, lacking the capacity to investigate some kinds of mechanisms as they operate over time, is likely to have to draw on a range of other research in order to be able to substantiate causal claims.

The third explanation of the invisibility of mechanisms is that mechanisms necessarily depend on relationships and interactions, some of which cannot be directly observed. This will likely be the case for interactions occurring at 'lower' levels of systems (for example, chemical and electrical interactions that 'are' the processes of thought within individual humans) and potentially at very high levels of systems (for example, interactions between political and economic systems). Even where some aspects of an interaction can be observed (say, communication between two humans), other levels cannot (say, the unconscious drivers of particular responses within that communication).

If mechanisms depend on relationships and interactions, then those relationships and interactions must be a focus of investigation. For some kinds of interactions where observations are not possible, existing research may provide aspects of the required evidence. For others, observational methods may be required, albeit supported by other methods.

So far we have identified that there are realist and non-realist constructs of mechanism and that the realist construct refers to real, underlying and probably invisible causes. We have also seen that the causes may be invisible due to the level of the system at which they operate, the time period over which they operate and their dependence on interactions and relationships. In the next section, we move forward to consider mechanisms in evaluation research.

MECHANISMS IN EVALUATION

Pawson and Tilley argued in their original book (1997) that programmes work by changing the decisions made by programme targets or participants:

Progress is made by the purposeful actions of subjects. Programmes will, in one way or another, offer a range of opportunities. Whether they are cashed in depends on the potentialities and volition of the subject. We are thus claiming ... that choice making is the agent which engineers change within social initiatives. (p. 37)

This is then summarised in the classic construct of programme mechanisms as comprising 'reasoning and resources':

Reaching 'down' to the layers of individual reasoning (what is the desirability of the ideas offered by the program?) and 'up' to the collective resources on offer (does the program provide the means for subjects to change their minds?) (p. 66)

Here, however, we strike the primary assumption that constrains the effectiveness of 'reasoning and resources' as a sole construct of programme mechanisms: it assumes that the target of the programme is individuals and individual decision-making. This is seductive not just because many programmes do indeed aim to change the decisions of individuals, but also because all policies and programmes involve humans in some way and all involve decision-making at some point.

However, it is not the case that all programmes aim to change individual decision-making. Some aim to change the decision-making of governments (think of international relations and some international development programmes). Others aim to change political structures and processes (think of processes of democratisation in many developing countries). Some aim to change power relationships within systems (for example, the various attempts to empower and depower employers, unions, workers and regulators in industrial relations systems). Many seek to change how organisations work as systems (think Lean or any other efficiency-oriented programme in large organisations (Goodridge et al., 2015)). Some aim to provide infrastructure – transport or communications systems, water and other utilities. Some aim to manage natural resources, where understanding the mechanisms of the natural systems and their interactions with human systems is critical. Individual decision-making of course plays a role in each of these interventions, but it is not necessarily the 'make or break' mechanism, not necessarily the point at which an intervention will succeed or fail. The implications are that we need constructs of mechanisms which do capture the 'make or break' change processes and that a construct which focuses only on 'reasoning and resources' will not be adequate. To remain realist, different constructs of programme mechanisms will be required, which will still need to be consistent with the underlying principles of realism.

Even this, however, assumes that evaluative research focuses on intentional policies and programmes. This need not be the case – and perhaps, if 'social betterment' is the goal – should not be the case. It is of course a rather tired truism to say that new technologies are changing the fundamental structures of the societies in which we live. Some have profound implications for political, legal and economic systems. Those technologies are eminently suitable subjects for realist evaluation: what kinds of outcomes, for whom, in what respects, in what contexts, how, why and when not, why not? Because these social changes are not being introduced by programmes or policies, but must – as any change must in realist terms – be the result of underlying mechanisms, the implication is that we need a construct of mechanisms that is independent of programmes, but which remains congruent with realist principles.

In order to develop constructs that are appropriate for these different kinds of investigations, we must first revisit the idea of open systems.

Open systems

One useful definition of a system is 'a set of interacting or interdependent component parts forming a complex or intricate whole. Every system is delineated by its spatial and temporal boundaries, surrounded and influenced by its environment, described by its structure and purpose and expressed in its functioning' (https://en.wikipedia.org/wiki/System). A key idea here is that a system is 'described by its structure'. In realist terms, this means both identifying and describing the elements that are *necessary* for the system to exist and the necessary *relations* between those elements – the ways that the elements must interact for the system to operate as it does. Some elements of systems will be described in terms of others: an adult is only a parent if he or she has a child, a property-owner is only a landlord if there is a tenant, a tenant is only a tenant if there is both a property and a property owner, and so on.

We have already seen that different levels of systems have their own powers and liabilities: higher levels of systems have properties and powers that sub-systems do not. As Elder-Vass (2004), Archer (2015) and others before them have argued, these emergent properties and powers are a result of stable organisation between the component parts of the system:

Only when this particular kind of parts is present in this particular set of relations to each other does the higher level entity exist, and only when this particular kind of parts is present in this particular set of relations to each other do they have the causal impacts that are characteristic of the higher-level entity. (Elder-Vass, 2004: 163)

To be considered a higher-level system, the system must have causal properties that are not reducible to the individual parts. Here is the crux of the issue: *the causal properties of systems are not solely reducible to the decision-making of people within those systems.* The implication for evaluation is equally clear. If programmes are indeed social systems, as Pawson and Tilley have eloquently argued, then the causal properties of the programmes are by definition not reducible solely to the decision-making of the targeted individuals. In fact, Pawson and Tilley (1997) made this argument themselves:

Social programs are undeniably, unequivocally, unexceptionally social systems. They comprise, as with any social system, the interplays of individual and institution, of agency and structure, and of micro and macro social processes ... causal powers lie not in particular objects ... or individuals ... but in the social relations and organizational structures which they form. One action leads to another because of their accepted place in the whole. (pp. 63–4)

This basic realist insight seems to have been overlooked in much subsequent writing about, and examples of, realist evaluation. In the next section, we examine alternate constructs which may 'fill the gap'.

ALTERNATE CONSTRUCTS OF MECHANISM

We have seen already two classic realist constructs of mechanism: 'the powers and liabilities of things', which is the realist construct at its most general; and 'reasoning and resources', which is Pawson and Tilley's construct of the powers and liabilities of programmes. A quick review of the examples that have been used by Pawson and Tilley and other authors to help explain the idea of mechanisms, however, reveals other ways that mechanisms might be conceptualised. These include:

- *forces*, which push or pull or otherwise exert pressure: gravity is the classic example (Pawson and Tilley, 1997: 57);
- *interactions*, which result in a transfer between elements resulting in changed states: the chemical interaction between the chemical constituents of gunpowder is another classic example (Pawson and Tilley, 1997: 58);
- *feedback or feedforward processes*, in which later stages depend inherently on earlier ones: the thermostat in an air-conditioning system is the classic example.

These material examples are used, of course, because they are straightforward and easily understood. What they do not provide is instant translation to either biological or social systems. Table 3.1 takes the five constructs of mechanism and applies them to four different levels of systems: the material levels of systems in which the mechanisms of chemistry and physics predominate; individual humans, in which mechanisms of psychology, emotion and cognition come into play; group-level systems, using families and organisations as examples, and the institutional level of social systems. Table 3.1 is populated with examples used earlier in the chapter and some additional simple examples to make the case.

TABLE 3.1 Constructs of mechanism at levels of systems

Construct of mechanism	Material	Psychological/ cognitive	Social – group	Social – institutional
Powers and liabilities	Trees can grow: e.g. photosynthesis	Humans can learn: e.g. sensitisation; motivation	Groups can make agreements	States can make laws
Forces	Gravity	Love	Peer pressure	Laws, regulations
Interactions	Gunpowder explosion	Reasoning and resources	Contracts	New technologies and market systems
Feedback or feedforward processes	Genetic inheritance	Developing attachment style	Negotiation	Stock market crash
Reasoning and resources	Neurons firing: electrical signals	Logic-in-use; affective response	'Group think'	Cultural assumptions

A few points of clarification are necessary here, in part to explain the table and in part to link these examples back to earlier discussions of the nature of mechanism.

Powers and liabilities

'Powers and liabilities' is the fundamental realist construct of mechanism. Because other mechanisms can be operating concurrently which 'cancel out' their effects, they can be operating without effects being manifest. A tree has the power to grow whether or not it does; humans have the power to learn whether or not they are currently doing so; workers have the power to work whether or not they are currently employed (Sayer, 1992: 105).

However, saying that these powers exist and giving them a name does not explain *how* they operate. The same point – that naming is not explaining – applies to all the other examples in Table 3.1 as well. In order to understand the mechanism, it is necessary to move 'down into' the lower levels of the system (think of the myriad mechanisms actually involved in a tree growing). Each sub-system will then explain some particular thing about how trees grow.

Forces

Forces (in the second row of the table) push or pull or otherwise exert pressure. However, they are not insurmountable or deterministic: they operate in some circumstances and not others. Gravity does not drag a tennis ball under water. Love pushes and pulls humans to do extraordinary things but it is not the sole determinant of outcomes. This too is typical of all mechanisms and therefore all examples in the table: mechanisms operate only when the circumstances are suitable, and always in concert and in competition with other mechanisms.

Interactions

Interactions, to operate as mechanisms, must result in a transfer between elements resulting in a changed state. The interactions represented in the third row of the table are not necessarily 'visible' in their titles. The interaction involved in gunpowder exploding is between the chemical constituents of the explosive while the changed state is the explosion. A contract is the outcome of an interaction between buyer and seller which, because it is embedded in legal and economic systems, carries with it new powers and liabilities. If today I signed the contract and paid the money to buy a house, I have as a result of that new rights (powers) and responsibilities (liabilities); the seller has greater financial resources and thus financial power but some decrease in rights and responsibilities.

Note too that 'reasoning and resources' have made an appearance in the psychological/ cognitive column of the 'interactions' row: here the interacting elements have been named but the outcome (a decision and probably behaviour) has not.

Processes

In the fourth row, mechanisms have been described as processes. Although all mechanisms are processes, not all processes are mechanisms in the realist sense of the word. Some processes happen in the realm of the empirical – that which we experience and observe – and these are not mechanisms. A teacher running a lesson is implementing a series of processes, but that does not make teaching a mechanism. Its counterpart, learning, on the other hand, is a mechanism: it is an inherent 'power' of humans, which involves a complex series of chemical, electrical and attentional processes involving sub-systems of the human brain and body.

The types of processes that are implied here are feedback or feedforward processes – where later stages depend inherently on earlier ones and outcomes would be different if the earlier stages had been different. These processes are not directly observable, at least on the level of the outcome that they generate. To use the example of genetic inheritance: genetic structure has relatively recently become observable, given the right kinds of equipment. The process of how dominant genes prevail over recessive genes or of how x and y chromosomes combine may also potentially be observable in the right kinds of laboratory experiments – but 'genetic inheritance' as an overall process is not directly observable in the actual conditions in which it happens naturally. Only its outcomes can be seen.

Reasoning and resources

In the final row, Pawson and Tilley's construct of 'reasoning and resources' is given similar, if not identical, treatment. There are material processes involved in any cognitive or affective response: given space limitations in the chart, 'neurons firing' is shorthand for those processes. At the cognitive/psychological level, 'logic in use' is closer to rational and 'affective response' is clearly emotional: either or both can shape decisions. At the social level, the mechanism 'group think' describes a process in which the pressure (or desire) for consensus outweighs individual reasoning. Cultural cognition 'refers to the tendency of individuals to conform their beliefs about disputed matters of fact (e.g. whether global warming is a serious threat; whether the death penalty deters murder; whether gun control makes society safer or less safe) to values that define their cultural identities' (www.culturalcognition.net). This overall process has been found to work through at least two mechanisms: biased assimilation ('the tendency of individuals selectively to credit and dismiss information in a manner that confirms their prior beliefs': Kahan et al., 2010: 503) and the credibility heuristic (in which individuals tend to impute characteristics of knowledge, honesty and impartiality to members of an 'in-group' but not members of an 'out-group': Kahan et al., 2010: 9). Kahan et al.'s (2010) overall description of cultural cognition is a masterly description of how multiple 'smaller' mechanisms operate together to create the 'larger' mechanism and how those mechanisms operate to generate different outcomes for groups with different worldviews:

People notice, assign significance to, and recall the instances of misfortune that fit their values; they trust the experts whose cultural outlooks match their own; they define the contingencies that make them worse off, or count as losses, with reference to culturally valued states of affairs; they react affectively toward risk on the basis of emotions that are themselves conditioned by cultural appraisals – and so forth ... cultural cognition ... helps to ... [show] how one and the same heuristic process (whether availability, credibility, loss aversion, or affect) can generate different perceptions of risk in people with opposing outlooks. (Kahan et al., 2010: 6)

Multiple constructs of mechanism

One final note about Table 3.1 is warranted. Many of the examples it contains could in fact be described using any of the constructs in the table and at any of the levels of the table. Consider the psychological/cognitive level of the powers and liabilities row: 'Humans can learn'. Learning can be described at any level including the material (e.g. the chemical and electrical processes involved in memory formation (http://neuroscience.uth.tmc.edu/s4/chapter07.html)) and the cognitive/psychological (e.g. motivational mechanisms in learning (Markman et al., 2005) and self-efficacy in learning (Schunk and Ertmer, 2000)). At the group level, research into communities of practice (e.g. Cruz et al., 2009), peer learning (e.g. Campbell and Mzaidume, 2001) and the effects of teacher–student relationships (e.g. Hamre and Pianta, 2006) each identify different mechanisms. At the institutional level, Popper and Lipschitz (1998) define organisational learning mechanisms as:

... institutionalized structural and procedural arrangements that allow organizations to systematically collect, analyse, store, disseminate, and use information relevant to the performance of the organisation and its members. (p. 170)

These structures and relationships must then be supported by 'organisational values': 'continuous learning, valid information, transparency, issue orientation, and accountability.' Thus the article describes both the observable and non-observable elements of mechanisms required for organisational learning.

Similarly, however, learning can be described as a power (capacity) of individuals, as a force, as when new learning pushes or pulls one to change behaviour; as an interaction between the learner and the learning materials, often also involving interactions between learners and teachers; as a process that occurs over time, as new learned materials are 'joined on' to existing knowledge; and as a process of reasoning and resources, as different individuals respond in different ways to the learning opportunity provided in a programme.

The question then arises: is one of these constructs 'more right' than others? My answer here is that any construct of mechanism can be right so long as it is consistent with the fundamental realist conception of mechanisms: that they are causal forces or processes which operate at a different level of the system than the outcome that they generate; that they are not observable using the same observational tools or methods that 'work' at the level of the outcome they generate; and that they involve description of at least three things: the necessary components of the system, the necessary relationships between those components and the processes (or interactions) through which those components and relationships generate the outcomes that they do. This will ensure that they are explanatory rather than simply descriptive. They may also operate at different timescales than their observable outcomes.

If this is the case, how does one decide which construct to use? Perhaps one construct is more suited to the particular questions to be addressed or the nature of the evaluand. Or perhaps one construct makes particular sense to the investigators and those who will use the findings. Philosophically speaking, I refer back to two earlier points in this chapter. One is that the great majority of policies and programmes will involve human reasoning at some point, which will almost invariably affect its effectiveness, so inclusion of either column two (psychological/cognitive) or row five (reasoning and resources) is likely to be useful. However, other mechanisms at other levels of systems are also likely to be necessary. In short, a combination of two constructs may well prove to be the most useful for many research and evaluation projects.

Similarly, is one of the levels of explanation 'more right' – or 'more useful' – than the others? Again, there are both pragmatic and philosophical elements to the answers. The pragmatic answer relates to utilisation and has been available since the origins of realist evaluation:

While the appropriateness of any level of analysis is dependent on the context, understanding will typically be enhanced of a combination of molecular [smaller, component parts] and molar [larger, system level] analyses. In evaluation, the assessment of the most appropriate levels of analyses generally depends on utilization – and increasingly molecular analyses may not enhance utility. (Mark et al., 2000: 45)

The philosophical answer lies in the truism that programmes, like other complex systems, inherently operate at multiple levels. Describing a mechanism and an outcome necessarily involves two levels of systems, because the mechanisms operate at a different level of the system than the outcomes they generate. Given that many programmes do not seek to produce outcomes at only a single level (that is the behaviour of individuals), mechanisms at multiple levels are likely to be required.

MECHANISMS AND THE CONTEXT–MECHANISM RELATIONSHIP

However, this 'multiple mechanisms at multiple levels' conclusion itself begs a question. For policies and programmes, why not simply decide to treat all levels of systems above or below the level of individual decision-making as 'context' for decision-making? Is it not the case that policies and programmes aim to influence human behaviours, thus making Pawson and Tilley's construct of 'reasoning and resources' the only *relevant* construct of mechanism for the practice of evaluation, or other policy- and programme-relevant research?

The next argument is premised on the realist assumption that the same thing can be context in one circumstance, outcome in another, and mechanism in yet another. Consider the example of self-esteem. Imagine a programme which aims to raise young people's self-esteem: in that instance, self-esteem is the outcome. Another programme aims to assist young people to obtain employment and does so, in part, by raising their self-esteem. In that instance, self-esteem is operating as a mechanism (and an interim outcome as well). A third programme aims to develop young leaders and is found to work best for those who had higher self-esteem prior to the programme: in that instance, self-esteem is a context.

We now replace self-esteem with Pawson and Tilley's 'reasoning and resources' construct for programme mechanisms. Because multiple kinds of reasoning can be triggered by, or interact with, the resources on offer in a programme, multiple mechanisms can be described which explain how different outcomes are generated. Let us call these Mechanisms 1, 2 and 3 (M1, M2 and M3).

Critically, however, neither describing these mechanisms nor describing the contexts in which they fire explains *why* the explanations are different in different contexts or for different sub-groups. Identifying outcome patterns for different contexts or sub-groups only tells us *that* people in those groups or contexts respond differently. Explaining *why* context generates different responses in turn requires understanding *how* context affects mechanism. The word 'how' in that last sentence in fact implies another mechanism, the outcome of which is the 'reasoning and resources' mechanism (M1, M2 or M3 respectively). This is the equivalent of self-esteem having moved from outcome to mechanism in the example above. The explanatory structure here is not just the famous 'In this context, this mechanism generates that outcome', but 'C1 *generates* (or contributes to or constrains) M1 which in turn *generates* (contributes to or constrains) O1'. This means that there is a mechanism (or a set of mechanisms) operating in the context that causes the programme mechanism to fire (or constrains its firing).

Pawson's own work provides examples in which mechanisms in the context enable or disable programme mechanisms. One will suffice for the purposes of illustration. In his brief realist review of 'naming and shaming' (Pawson, 2006b: Chapter 7), a series of public disclosure initiatives are identified, each of which is intended to work through a broadly similar process of identifying 'under-performance or deviant behaviour', naming and publicising the miscreants, public sanction and recipient response. Mechanisms operate at each stage of the intervention, and alternate mechanisms can fire at any stage. At the 'recipient response' stage, the intended mechanisms include 'the subjects being shamed, regretful, penitent, contrite, restrained, reintegrated' (p. 153). However, other mechanisms can also operate, including 'the individual or institution under sanction … accepting the label and amplifying deviant behaviour, or … ignoring and rejecting the label and continuing existing behaviour, or … reinterpreting the label and adopting a perverse modification to behaviour' (p. 153)

Let us then treat these end point 'recipient response' mechanisms – intended and unintended – as being M1, M2 and M3. Pawson describes five examples of 'circumstances' (contexts) which can affect whether and how the programme mechanisms operate. These include the moral authority of those calling out the guilty parties and the susceptibility of the named parties to shame, the nature of the sanction, control over information flow, control over the media and the political clout behind the sanction. The nature of public opinion is discussed in relation to the first of these: it can range 'from moral panic … to "there but for the grace of god" … The review needs to examine the balance of norms and values operating around the social problem addressed, and consider how formidably they gather in support of shaming sanctions' (p. 154).

Here, norms and values are clearly being discussed as context for the intended programme mechanisms (as indeed they are), but equally clearly, those norms and values have their effect by operating as social forces which cause, or contribute to, outcomes – that is, by operating as a mechanism.

This example has focused on 'higher' levels of the system (social norms) operating concurrently as context for, and mechanism shaping, programme-level norms (shame or pride in being named). That is norms exist in context so they are part of the context for the programme mechanisms. When they generate outcomes in their own right they operate as mechanisms (albeit not programme mechanisms). Given that causation operates both upwards and downwards, it is equally feasible that the contextual explanation of a programme mechanism may lie at a lower level of the system. The obvious examples are when structures and processes inherent to the human brain structure shape decision-making. Examples here might include people's attachment styles (Bowlby, 1982; Berlin et al., 2007) or the ways that scarcity shapes decision-making (Shafir and Mullainathan, 2013). These are, perhaps, more commonly understood as 'lower-level mechanisms' or 'subsidiary mechanisms' contributing to higher-level mechanisms. In philosophical terms, however, whatever enables or disables *the current mechanism of interest* operates as context for that mechanism. If the mechanism of interest is a policy or programme mechanism, then everything that affects it is, from one perspective, context. It is when we seek to examine *how* the context affects that mechanism that we invoke the 'mechanisms in the context shape (activate, generate, influence) programme mechanisms by … ' format of explanation. That is, whether something 'wears the label' of context, mechanism or outcome at a particular moment in any analysis does not depend on its intrinsic nature. Self-esteem is self-esteem, whether it is currently functioning as outcome, mechanism or context. Rather, the label relates to the function it plays in explanation of a particular finding or event.

To summarise: the explanation of *how* C1 generates M1 lies in the internal structures and processes of the relevant aspect of context. Or, put another way, mechanisms inherent to the context shape, enable or disable the mechanisms inherent to the programme. Consistent with all other realist explanation, this explanation usually lies at a different level of a nested system than does its outcome. At this stage of the argument, our intermediate outcomes are programme mechanisms M1, 2 or 3: they are sets of reasoning, and they cannot themselves be explained at the level of reasoning. The same argument applies when considering 'higher-level outcomes' that follow after the 'reasoning' of programme implementers or participants: these are new causal processes and they may not be best described in terms of reasoning and resources. In both instances – 'below' or 'before' the 'reasoning' involved in a programme mechanism, and 'above' or 'after' it – we need ways of conceptualising these mechanisms other than 'reasoning and resources'. This is where the other formulations of mechanism – as powers and liabilities, forces, interactions or processes – will come into their own.

And why does this matter to policy- or programme-relevant research or evaluation? The answer is the same as that for explaining the mechanisms inherent to programmes themselves. Explanation of how and why (rather than simply a description of 'that') is necessary in order to know whether or how to adapt the programme to context. The theory for 'how' context affects programme mechanisms is as important as the theory for 'how' programme mechanisms generate programme outcomes.

CONCLUSION: DESCRIBING MECHANISMS IN REALIST RESEARCH AND EVALUATION

This chapter is of course too brief to do justice to the nature of mechanisms and has not sought to address every difficulty that arises with their use in policy-relevant research and evaluation. However, it has sought to make three main points. The first explored why it is that mechanisms are 'invisible': because they operate at different levels of the system than the outcome under investigation, they operate over different timescales, and they necessarily involve interactions that might not be observable. Each of these factors has implications for research and evaluation design and methods. The second is that mechanisms operate at all levels of all systems all the time; every level of a system has its own 'causal powers and liabilities'. The construct of 'human reasoning and programme resources' works well for explaining decision-making in response to programmes, but it cannot explain causal powers and liabilities at other levels of systems. Consequently, we need ways of conceptualising mechanisms that can be applied at other levels of systems. Those offered here are powers and liabilities, forces, interactions and feedback or feedforward processes. Finally, the interaction between mechanisms in contexts and programme mechanisms was re-examined. It is not enough simply to describe 'that' different mechanisms fire in different contexts: for true realist explanation, it is necessary to explain 'why'. Here it was argued that mechanisms inherent to the *context* shape, enable or disable the mechanisms inherent to the *programme*. Understanding these interactions is as important as understanding how and why programme mechanisms generate patterns of outcomes.

4

MAKING CLAIMS USING REALIST METHODS

Brad Astbury

WHAT THIS CHAPTER IS ABOUT

One of the most pressing challenges for policy-makers and practitioners is the issue of external validity or how to translate a policy or a programme from one jurisdiction to another across time. This chapter traces the debate about internal and external validity. The focus of the chapter is an emphasis on generalisation through explanation. This chapter explores the potential of middle-range theory development as a means of providing modest forms of generalisability for programmes and interventions. Drawing on a case study of an early intervention programme for families in crisis it illuminates how descriptions of programmes as logic models cannot explain causality, but if combined with ancillary methods – such as stakeholder theories, a commitment to embracing existing theory, the capacity to pitch this at a middle-level of abstraction and to target specifics within policies or programmes – then transferable lessons through which we can learn cumulatively can be produced.

How this chapter will help you to do realist research

The chapter provides an account of the labour or 'tricks of the trade' required when developing coherent and plausible theoretical explanations of how programmes work, for whom and in what circumstances. Programmes are tried, tried and tried again. This leaves an evidential trail that can be harnessed alongside primary research to develop middle-range explanations of programme or policy mechanisms.

A practical tip: a take-home message from the chapter

Developing theories of causal mechanisms should be systematic not mechanical. It requires theoretical sophistication, methodological dexterity and analytical prowess – in other words, a significant degree of intellectual leg work.

INTRODUCTION

Social programmes are conceptualised by realist evaluators as dynamic mini-systems introduced into complex systems. These systems interact and are open in the sense that boundaries are permeable, movement is free and, importantly, participants are not easily shielded from multiple and contingent causes. In contrast, laboratories strongly resemble closed systems where undesired causal noise is forcibly excluded. Yet almost all social and evaluative research takes place in real-world, field settings. The doyen of experimental evaluation, Donald T. Campbell, recognised this enduring complication and went to great lengths to point out that social experiments are designed to answer specific causal-descriptive questions of the following kind: Did the intervention, at this place, with these participants, on this occasion, taken as a whole, cause the observed effects? In other words, experiments probe highly localised causal connections between programmes and effects.

The fact that programme X was effective in locality A does not guarantee that success will be repeated when rolled out to localities B, C and D with persons E, F and G. Campbell's appreciation of the practical limits of experimentation can be seen in his meticulous rela-belling of internal validity to local molar (pragmatic, atheoretical) causal validity. This new terminology is more accurate but less catchy. Somewhat presciently, he stated that the label 'would probably not survive this chapter' (Campbell, 1986: 69). And so, like much else in the history of evaluation methodology, Campbell's careful thinking on experimental design has largely been lost on present-day randomistas. Enthusiasts riding the evidence-based policy wave are increasingly using randomised controlled trials (RCTs) to make general claims about 'what works?' The leap from 'it worked' to 'it works' is appealing to politicians and policy-makers who desire quick off-the-shelf solutions. Experiments fit with a habit of mind that seeks out universal regularities from a singular counterfactual observance of the succession of two events: if programme A is present, we see results Y; if programme A is not present, we don't see results Y. Therefore programme A works. This reasoning is an induc-tive fallacy.

When outcomes do not materialise in other locations – and invariably this is the case – programme delivery staff are typically the first to receive blame. Failure was due to lack of faithful replication. Important elements of the innovation were missed or, worse still, deliberate subterfuge was at play. In common parlance, taking what works to 'scale' requires fidelity to core components and a compliant workforce to assemble and deliver the right dosage of treatment packages. This conception assumes that strict duplication of the observable machinery of programme activities is the divine path to transferabil-ity. Expectations that the same intervention will produce the same effects in different contexts are naive. To use a realist mantra, social programmes do not work always and everywhere. Programmes produce quite different outcomes when introduced to differ-ent persons in different settings at different times. Instead of trying to find definitive answers to what works, Byrne (2013) argues that we should focus on a more variegated set of questions:

- What has worked?
- How has it worked?
- Which is to ask: what causal mechanisms have operated?
- Where has it worked?
- When has it worked?
- Can it work elsewhere?
- Can it work elsewhen?

Developing answers to all of these questions in a single study is a Herculean task, some might even say Sisyphean, so much so that David Byrne also addresses these questions in Chapter 6. Even so, a range of measures have been developed to tackle the problem of generalisability. Of course, there is no universal agreement. Methods and techniques remain hotly contested. This is because referents and framings of generalisability vary depending on the researcher's philosophical stance, disciplinary perspective and methodological bent. For example, external validity is the preferred nomenclature of experimental evaluators, while qualitative and case study researchers talk about transferability and naturalistic generalisation. Survey researchers extrapolate from samples to populations, psychologists reproduce and replicate and ethnographers elucidate thick descriptions. On one end of the epistemological spectrum, positivists search for universal covering laws, while on the other end radical constructivists claim that 'the only generalization is there is no generalization' (Lincoln and Guba, 1985: 110).

The principle of generalisation that I want to examine in this chapter is causal explanation.[1] The goal is to demonstrate the merits of a modest form of theoretical generalisability, especially as applied in the context of evaluation research involving social interventions. The perspective advanced here draws primarily on Pawson and Tilley's (1997) realist evaluation and Pawson's (2006b) realist synthesis, although there are affinities with Merton's middle-range theorising as well as ideas outlined by the new analytical sociologists (Hedström and Swedberg, 1998). A core concern in each of these is the centrality of substantive theory and social mechanisms. The logic of enquiry involves building and testing an account of how and why an intervention or family of interventions work, for whom and in what circumstances. Although the resulting programme theory will always be partial and corrigible, the explanation produced can facilitate generalisation beyond the persons, settings and time of a discrete one-off evaluation project. At the very least, identifying causal mechanisms provides an alternative to mindless mimicry of the surface features of a programme from one location to the next (Bardach, 2004; Tilley, 1996).

Indeed, because many supposedly novel interventions share common underlying mechanisms, focusing on mechanisms instead of specific interventions may be our best hope to learn cumulatively from one programme to another and from one evaluation to the next. But what does one do when carrying out a realist study that seeks to address the 'will it work elsewhere' question? Bearing the above in mind, the goal of this chapter is to render the realist toolkit by demonstrating tactics that help federate local evaluation findings. The chapter is organised in the following way. The next part concentrates on the historical context of methodological debates, particularly how theory-based evaluation emerged from contestation surrounding internal and external validity. Following on from this an example of realist evaluation in practice is highlighted, focusing on generalisation at the level of mechanism and middle-range theory. Discussion then turns to specific tricks of the trade in realist evaluation before some concluding remarks are offered.

HISTORICAL CONTEXT

In *Realistic Evaluation* Pawson and Tilley (1997) present a short history of evaluation and conclude by paying homage to Peter Rossi and Lee Cronbach – two evaluation theorists 'whose insights we aim to modify and develop' (p. 29). Rossi, of course, is a central figure along with Chen in the early years of theory-driven evaluation. Rossi saw theory-driven evaluation as a way to integrate the contrasting perspectives of Campbell and Cronbach on the relative priority given to internal and external validity (Chen and Rossi, 1987). Internal and external validity tend to be inversely related. This is because the various controls that are exercised in order to increase internal validity often come at the cost of decreased external validity.

In an ideal world, evaluation studies would have high internal and external validity, but this is not the case – trade-offs are inevitable. Campbell, however, maintained that internal validity should take precedence as the *sine qua non* of evaluation research because there is little use in replicating programmes that fail to demonstrate causal connections. First, we need to know whether something works on average, then we can dig deeper to find out why, for whom and in what contexts. In sum, Campbell would like evaluators to start by addressing questions of causal description, such as 'Did the program work here?' They then move on to questions about causal explanation, such as: 'Does/would the programme work in other settings, times, places, populations, etc.?'

Although he saw much to like in Campbell's advocacy of experimentation, Cronbach's later works, including two seminal books published throughout the 1980s, were 'against the writings of Campbell and his team-mates' (Cronbach, 1982: xiv). Essentially, Cronbach disagreed with the order of priority, emphasising the greater importance of external validity in applied settings. He repeatedly expresses a preference for achieving a marginal decrease in uncertainty in relation to the most important questions (bandwidth) over achieving great decreases in uncertainty in relation to unimportant questions (fidelity). High on his list of unimportant questions is the local molar causal question that Campbell values most highly. For Cronbach, internal validity is 'a property of trivial, past-tense, and local statements' (1982: 137). He dislikes evaluation that is solely for the purposes of accountability and repeatedly emphasises the need to look forward, not backward. Policymakers need knowledge of causal mechanisms and contingencies to support present and future application:

Knowing this week's score does not tell the coach how to prepare for next week's game. The information that an intervention had satisfactory or unsatisfactory outcomes is of little use by itself: users of the study need to know what led to success or failure. Only with that information can the conditions that worked be replicated or modified sufficiently in the next trial to get better results. (Cronbach et al., 1980: 251)

In Cronbach's system, a given study contains variations in units, treatments, observations and settings (utos). Where units are typically individuals or groups, treatments are the intervention as applied, observations are the outcomes measured and setting is the local context. These elements of 'utos' are samples from a larger population referred to as UTOS. According to Cronbach, external validity in its most prized form involves theorising to situations that manifestly differ from those sampled (referred to as *UTOS). This is because 'there is no direct way to convert findings about schools in California into a prediction about schools in New Jersey; only by bringing to bear concepts about kinds of communities, or curricula, or taxation systems can the transfer be made credible or criticized' (Cronbach, 1982: 175).

There are some distinct parallels to realist evaluation. One of Pawson's principal tasks for the realist evaluator is to facilitate the transfer of knowledge by developing a theory of the intervention. We are reminded that 'what are transferable between cases [i.e. different settings] are not lumps of data but sets of ideas' (Pawson and Tilley, 1997: 123). Accordingly, Pawson maintains that 'Cronbach is undoubtedly correct in his overall sensibility to the importance of external validity', yet argues that his elaborate UTOS schema never caught on because 'it describes the problem rather than setting in motion the solution to the issue of external validity' (p. 28). For realists, generative explanation is the engine that drives solutions and the CMO formula represents the catchy mnemonic. Intriguingly, it is Campbell the experimental villain from *Realistic Evaluation* that receives attention and praise in Pawson's next major works, *Evidence-Based Policy: A Realist Perspective* and *Science of Evaluation*. One gets the sense this should have been Cronbach. After all, it was Cronbach's initial questioning of the utility of experiments and emphasis on generalisation through explanation that provided a keystone for developments in theory-driven evaluation that have occurred on both sides of the Atlantic.

CONDUCTING REALIST EVALUATION: AN ILLUSTRATION

This edited collection focuses on the practicalities of doing realist research and evaluation. There is certainly demand for information that specifies how to operationalise realist methodology. Recent publications on standards, protocols and training materials have been embraced eagerly.[2] The need has arisen partly because the approach is still relatively new, and partly because foundational texts, like *Realistic Evaluation*, do not provide material tools for practice. As one astute observer has noted, Pawson's writings are 'unashamedly intellectual' and 'theoretically ambitious' (Stern, 1997). It is unlikely, for example, that researchers would read Pawson's quartet of books and say: 'Now that I know about the importance of stratified social ontology and underlying generative mechanisms I can write up an evaluation plan and prepare interview schedules.'

To borrow a phrase from Shadish et al. (1991), the 'abstraction is persuasive; the tools for its implementation are not' (p. 372). Much like Cronbach, for whom this statement was originally intended, Pawson has not furnished us with a four-volume series of cookbooks. This makes those who seek a convenient recipe uncomfortable. My own view is that realist evaluation involves a flexible and creative mind-set, in much the same way that another rough-tongued brawler[3] once put it:

Be a good craftsman: Avoid any rigid set of procedures. Above all, seek to develop and to use the sociological imagination. Avoid the fetishism of method and technique. Urge the rehabilitation of the unpretentious intellectual craftsman, and try to become such a craftsman yourself. (Mills, 1959: 224)

In light of this book's emphasis on practice, I describe an example of my own efforts to apply realist strategies. The case has been selected, not because it constitutes an exemplar (if there is such a thing), but in the hope that it demonstrates two things: firstly, that evaluators with a modest budget and timeframe can still aspire to 'ask big questions of small interventions and to use small interventions to test big theories' (Pawson and Tilley, 2001: 322); secondly, that collective long-term efforts are required to chip away at the problem of programme generalisability. The narrative may also be instructive for readers new to realist approaches that are worrying about getting started. While reading books can aid preparation, they are no substitute for learning a craft. Following Howard Becker's (1998) notion of tricks of the trade, I conclude the section with some insights on the practice of realist evaluation.

THE SET-UP

Several years ago I was invited to participate in a small-scale evaluation of an early intervention and prevention programme located in Melbourne, Australia. The initiative was part federally funded by the then Commonwealth Department of Family and Community Services. The grant was running out and sponsors were keen to determine whether it was worth extending. The programme, at the time, was known as 'Families in Crisis' and sought to achieve a range of positive outcomes for kinship families caring for children who have been abandoned and/or orphaned as a result of parental illicit drug use. The intervention still exists today in a modified form and is delivered by the Mirabel Foundation (Mirabel), a philanthropic agency that bases its activities around a vision that every child deserves a childhood, and a mission to break the destructive cycle of addiction. This guiding philosophy is embedded throughout the service delivery model and underscores the organisational aim of minimising the negative effects of parental drug use on children while strengthening the capacity of kinship carers to provide a stable and nurturing environment[4] (Mirabel, 2016).

The evaluation was informed by a realist approach to understanding what it is about the programme that works to generate desired outcomes for children, kinship carers and the broader community. I very consciously use the word informed, as the evaluation parameters were mostly determined before I joined the study. Even so, there was scope to include realist strategies as part of the brief under the broad purpose of programme clarification and improvement. The realist strand used primarily qualitative data to develop ideas about how and why the programme works, for whom and in what circumstances. Major sources of data included: internal programme documents and administrative records, staff interviews, focus groups and interviews with a representative sample of kinship carers, observations of the programme in action and in-depth case studies with a small purposive sample of kinship families.

A programme logic model was initially developed as a first step towards elaborating in realist terms the mechanisms responsible for generating outcomes (see Figure 4.1). The model provided a useful visual depiction of the relationship between programme inputs, activities and desired outcomes for children, kinship carers, organisations and communities.

While development of the initial logic model was useful in describing how the various components and activities of the programme fitted together, it did not reveal any detailed insight into causal mechanisms. Preliminary interviews with staff, however, provided an early clue that there is something quite powerful about bringing people who have a common experience together. It was not until engaging directly with kinship carers during focus group sessions and interviews that a clearer picture of what appears to be a clustering of mechanisms emerged. When asked to elaborate on *what it was about programme activity x or y that was beneficial*, kinship carers responded in a surprisingly consistent way. Their responses can be grouped and summarised as follows:

- 'I'm not the only one/I'm not alone.' The realisation that there are others in the community who are also caring for children as a result of parental illicit drug use. Children similarly realised that there are many other kids whose parents have drug problems and this is why they are now living with extended family. The opportunity to compare one's own situation with similar others appeared to be a 'normalising' experience for many.
- 'There are others worse off than me.' Attendance at social outings, support groups and so on provided an opportunity to hear from other (often less fortunate) kinship families. This seemed to enhance perceptions of well-being and improve emotion-focused coping.
- 'If they can do it, then so can I.' Opportunities for interaction with kinship carers, especially those who have been with the programme longer and are seen to be managing well. This appeared to provide a sense of hope that things will get better and was sometimes used as inspiration for self-improvement.

These findings led to an exploratory investigation of the social science literature on group interventions and, eventually, to social comparison theory as an organising framework for understanding how and why activities provided through the Families in Crisis programme might work to generate desired outcomes for kinship carers and children.

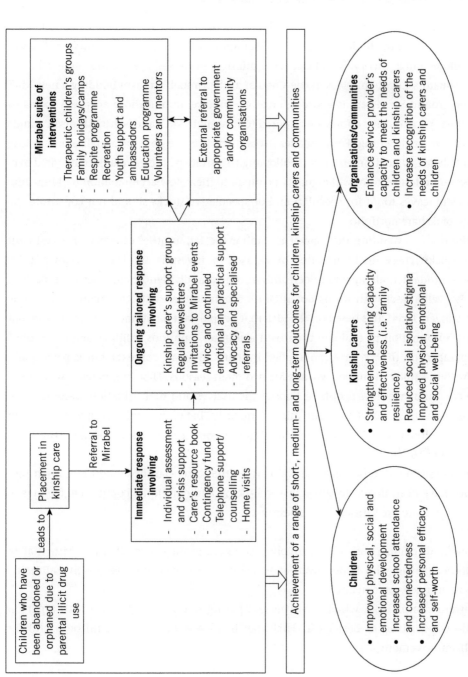

FIGURE 4.1 Initial logic model for the Families in Crisis programme

Children who have been abandoned or orphaned due to parental illicit drug use

Leads to

Placement in kinship care

Referral to Mirabel

Immediate response involving
- Individual assessment and crisis support
- Carer's resource book
- Contingency fund
- Telephone support/ counselling
- Home visits

Ongoing tailored response involving
- Kinship carer's support group
- Regular newsletters
- Invitations to Mirabel events
- Advice and continued emotional and practical support
- Advocacy and specialised referrals

Mirabel suite of interventions
- Therapeutic children's groups
- Family holidays/camps
- Respite programme
- Recreation
- Youth support and ambassadors
- Education programme
- Volunteers and mentors

External referral to appropriate government and/or community organisations

Achievement of a range of short-, medium- and long-term outcomes for children, kinship carers and communities

Children
- Improved physical, social and emotional development
- Increased school attendance and connectedness
- Increased personal efficacy and self-worth

Kinship carers
- Strengthened parenting capacity and effectiveness (i.e. family resilience)
- Reduced social isolation/stigma
- Improved physical, emotional and social well-being

Organisations/communities
- Enhance service provider's capacity to meet the needs of children and kinship carers
- Increase recognition of the needs of kinship carers and children

ENTER MIDDLE-RANGE THEORY

Much has been said elsewhere in this volume on the nature and relevance of Robert K. Merton's theories of the middle range for realist inquiries. The important lesson from Pawson is that middle-range theory (MRT) can serve multiple purposes in evaluation research. Too often, evaluators cast themselves in the singular and formidable role of building a new MRT from the ground up. There is a strong creative impulse among those attracted to realist endeavours. Yet extensive efforts are required to formulate MRT and Merton himself admits that often we get it wrong. For a smaller investment it is possible to capitalise on existing MRT to federate evaluation enquiries. Following this strategy, the generalisability yield over the medium to longer term will arguably be much higher. Slow accumulation of 'blue-chip' theories still leaves room for speculation. But speculative stocks should not constitute the majority of a share portfolio.

At the risk of extending the market metaphor too far, another category of investment is value stocks. These stocks are often overlooked by investors and trade at a lower price relative to fundamentals such as price/earnings ratio and dividend yield. Social comparison theory is a value stock with strong potential for evaluation research. Originally proposed by Leon Festinger (1954), it is based on the idea that people have a natural tendency to seek out objective information to evaluate their own attributes, opinions, abilities and situations.[5] Social comparison theory has been applied in many different contexts, but is particularly relevant to the study of support groups for two main reasons. First, comparison with other people can influence how people feel about themselves and their situation. Second, comparisons have been found to occur most frequently 'between similar people or between people with similar problems and self-help groups consist of just such people' (Dibb and Yardley, 2006: 1603).

There are two main types of social comparison that can occur in support group settings, and both have been linked to subjective well-being and emotional coping (i.e. feelings of positive mood and life satisfaction). These are:

- downward comparison, which involves comparing one's own situation with that of another person who is perceived as worse off. This may improve positive affect by increasing self-esteem; and
- upward comparison, which involves comparing one's own situation with a person who is perceived as better off. This may instil a sense of hope and be useful for self-improvement.

Refinements to classical social comparison theory suggest that the interpretation of social comparisons is more important than whether the comparison is with someone in a better or worse situation (Buunk et al., 1990). The way in which a person interprets a comparison is influenced by a range of individual, social and situational factors. For example, women appear to be more likely to seek out information for social comparison than men and optimistic individuals are more likely to interpret social comparison information positively. According to Dibb and Yardley (2006) this suggests that social comparison mechanisms are much more complex than originally thought, and may lead to positive or negative outcomes depending on how a situation is interpreted:

When we see others who are better off than ourselves, we could feel optimistic that we could be like that too, or we could feel pessimistic if we believe we could never be like that person. Conversely, downward comparison could result in feeling lucky that we are not in the situation of the target or anxious because we might be in their situation one day. (p. 1603)

Applying social comparison theory to one component of the Families in Crisis programme, kinship carer support groups, suggests there are at least four mechanisms that may be triggered by participation in group sessions:

1. upward comparison interpreted positively (i.e. 'when I see other kinship carers who are experiencing fewer problems than I am, I am pleased that things can get better');
2. upward comparison interpreted negatively (i.e. 'when I see other kinship carers who are doing better than I am, I find it threatening to notice that I am not doing so well');
3. downward comparison interpreted negatively (i.e. 'when I see other kinship carers who are doing worse than I am, I experience fear that my own situation will decline'); and
4. downward comparison interpreted positively (i.e. 'when I see other kinship carers who experience more difficulties than I do, I am relieved about my own situation'[6]).

The most common mechanism triggered by the Families in Crisis support groups was *positively interpreted downward comparison*. As the following selection of comments illustrates, the activation of this mechanism typically generates positive changes in the way kinship carers think and feel about themselves and their situation:

We came to the meetings feeling sorry for ourselves and came away feeling lucky as a lot of people were a lot older, with more children and greater financial needs. (KC 24[7])

It's good to meet people with the same problems and realise others are worse off. (KC 3)

You hear other people's problems and feel more comfortable. (KC 1)

I love going to the meetings each month. You think you are badly off until you talk to other people, then you realise that you are luckier than others. (KC 21)

To meet other people in the same situation – it's a reality check. You see people worse off and you realise how lucky you are. (KC 5)

It is important to point out here that kinship carers did not appear to actively seek out downward comparisons with those who they saw as being worse off (as this may give the impression that kinship carers were intentionally gaining pleasure from someone else's misfortunes). Instead, comparisons seemed to occur passively and were used 'as a form of emotion-focused coping, aimed at alleviating the negative emotions that stress produces by contrasting their situation with that of others who are worse off' (Buunk and Gibbons, 2007: 8). Kinship carers believed that this form of passive downward comparison can be beneficial for children as well:

Our granddaughter has been well protected so is not involved with the drug taking which other children have been exposed to. We are probably one of the most fortunate people. Our granddaughter is realising that as she talks to others. (KC 16)

And:

Debra went on a bus trip to the movies with Mirabel and she realised that there were other children with their mothers in jail. She doesn't feel different anymore. She also sees that some are in a worse situation. Debra has never witnessed a lot of the things that others have seen, such as picking up syringes. Mirabel has done this for her – they have put Debra on the right track. (KC 23)

In these comments we can see clearly that it is not programme activities like going to the movies or attending a monthly support group that mediate results, but the underlying response mechanism that a particular activity generates under certain circumstances. In other words, it is the way the resource offered by the intervention influences the recipient. Of course, social comparison mechanisms are context-sensitive and generate different effects, or even no effects, depending on how individuals respond to social comparison information. This means that kinship carer support groups produce varie-gated outcome patterns. For example, while most kinship carers spoke positively about support groups, some found that attending group sessions was 'depressing', indicat-ing the operation of negative upward and/or downward comparison. Several carers also reported feeling uncomfortable in a group setting. This suggests kinship carers with low social comparison orientation may not gain much benefit from group programmes (Van der Zee et al., 1998).

Figure 4.2 summarises the cluster of social comparison mechanisms and illustrates the role of context in shaping their operation. The two upper quadrants are important because they represent comparison mechanisms linked to desired outcomes for kin-ship carers identified in the logic model. The two lower quadrants indicate mechanisms leading to negative outcomes. Crucially, activation of positive comparison mechanisms depends on various features of the context, some of which are listed on the right side of the diagram.

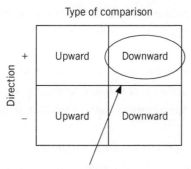

Type of comparison

Context can influence the way in which comparisons are 'interpreted'

- Role of facilitator
- Heterogeneous vs homogenous groups
- Gender
- Low emotional state
- Low social comparison orientation

Most common form of comparison identified among the sample (a mixed blessing?)

FIGURE 4.2 Context and social comparison mechanisms

While most kinship carers engaged in downward positive comparison to enhance subjective well-being this may be 'a mixed blessing as a coping strategy, if exclusive reliance on downward targets serves in the long term to deter self-improvement' (Wills and Mendoza, 2004: 408). One implication for programme development is the need to explore ways to promote upward positive comparison given the significance for longer-term well-being. It would also be helpful to understand better what features of the context facilitate positive downward (and upward) comparisons, as these appear to be associated with improvements in the social and emotional functioning of kinship carers.

Two contextual factors are particularly salient. First, the composition of kinship carer support groups influences the range of comparisons that are possible. While support groups for kinship carers are likely to be beneficial in their own right for belonging, normalisation and information exchange, homogenous groups provide fewer opportunities for positive upward or downward comparison than a heterogeneous group (Carmack-Taylor et al., 2007). Second, programme facilitators and group members are likely to play an important role in promoting positive interpretations of comparisons. Kinship carers with lower emotional states, for example, may require extra support to ensure that comparisons are interpreted positively rather than negatively.

This is roughly where the evaluation terminated. In reality, the line of thinking detailed briefly above constituted but a minor part of a larger evaluation report dutifully delivered to the sponsors. The programme was re-funded and to my knowledge still exists in a modified form. This is by no means unusual. By dint of practical necessity, evaluators are rarely asked to look beyond the requirements of the here and now. This is the Achilles heel of realist evaluation. Further development of context-mechanism-outcome configurations would provide more detailed knowledge to support programme improvement and generalisation. This might involve testing specific hypotheses for this particular intervention. For instance, when a facilitator attuned to comparison cues is present (context), does this increase activation of positive upward comparison (mechanism) leading to sustained emotional well-being of kinship carers (outcome)? There is also value in pursing more general work that tracks the fortunes of the same mechanism across different policy domains. This is because group-based interventions are ubiquitous. Support groups are a good example of what Pawson (2006b) refers to as an intervention family. They have been used to assist with drug and alcohol addictions, mental illness, terminal cancer, anorexia, gambling and victims of crime to name just a few. To add further contextual complexity, support groups can be delivered face to face or online, peer led or professionally facilitated, structured or unstructured, and so on.

However, this does not mean that every support group is totally unique. To say that context matters is not the same as concluding that interventions are context-bound. Knowing, for example, that social comparison mechanisms are likely to manifest whenever group-based interventions are implemented may help to develop, test and refine these kinds of programmes in more effective ways. Elaborating an MRT of group interventions provides a 'reusable conceptual platform' for mounting future enquiries, as opposed to starting every evaluation from scratch (Pawson, 2013). In sum, building a knowledge and theoretical base about families of interventions rather than treating all programmes as completely novel may help avoid policy amnesia and constant reinvention of the wheel. Or so Pawson's theory of evaluation science goes. This, of course, implies that the propositions entailed in such an endeavour also need to be scrutinised closely and refined over time (Astbury, 2013).

TRICKS OF THE REALIST TRADE

Rapidly increasing interest across health and international development (see Marchal et al. in this edited collection) as well as many other sectors has created more opportunities than ever before to conduct realist enquiries. But opportunity has also brought with it several challenges in applying realist evaluation methodology. Perusing discussion threads and posts on the RAMESES listserv can seem a little like peering into a group therapy session. How can realist evaluation be used for complex, large-scale policy reform? What exactly is a mechanism and how do I find one? I can't seem to distinguish between context, mechanism and outcome? How do I collect and analyse data in a realist way? What's the difference between critical realism, transcendental realism and Pawson's realist evaluation? What role do values play in realist enquiry? How do realist evaluators adjudicate between rival programme theories? The list goes on. My hope here is to stimulate further dialogue and debate regarding the tricks of the realist trade (Pawson and Manzano-Santaella, 2012).

Howard Becker (1998) defines tricks as ways of thinking, sometimes specific procedures and operations, that provide a way around common difficulties or problems encountered by artisans of a trade. Becker suggests that tricks are often usefully presented as rules of thumb derived from experience. Below I summarise four tricks that were helpful in solving problems encountered during the evaluation case example discussed above: (1) bracketing; (2) dual theorising; (3) abstraction; and (4) concentrating fire.

The first strategy responds to the problem of confusing programme activities with mechanisms. The issue often arises because it is difficult to 'see' the intervention when focusing on context, mechanism and outcome configurations. The trick itself is nothing exceptionally innovative. It involves *bracketing* the C + M = O formula in the first instance, and using a descriptive logic model as a platform to support deeper analysis of underlying generative mechanisms. This tactic has traditionally been under-utilised by realist evaluators, perhaps because of scant attention to logic models in Pawson's writings. Then draw on available evidence to develop a diagram that summarises the way in which the components of the programme fit together in a simple logical sequence. There are literally dozens of ready-made templates available, but strongly resist the temptation to assemble a generic list of inputs, activities, outputs and outcomes. Invite a variety of stakeholders to critically assess the plausibility of the model. Above all, remember that boxes and arrows are not causal explanations. Look beneath the visible machinery of programme operations. What is it about an intervention that makes it work? By what means are changes in participants' internal cognitive and affective states triggered? Mechanisms are real but elusive, and are usually not directly observable. Remember that 'it is not the lofty sails but the unseen wind that moves the ship' (Bierstedt, 1960: 9).

The second tactic addresses the limitations of using only information from stakeholders to develop explanations of how programmes work. Carol Weiss (1997) reminds us that local sources of information about pathways to outcomes can be plain wrong, or, at the very least, partial and incomplete. Realist evaluators should not rely exclusively on stakeholder hunches and reify these with catchy labels. This can lead to mechanism neologism. Blaikie (2007) offers the following caution:

> Perhaps at this stage in the development of the social sciences it is necessary to exhaust the explanatory capacity of known types of structures and mechanisms before launching too far into the difficult territory of discovering new ones. Possible mechanisms can be gleaned from existing theories. (pp. 87–8)

One remedy involves integrating stakeholder theory with formal theory (aka substantive or research-based theory). Chen (1990) calls this *dual theorising*, while others use metaphors like theory knitting, weaving or stitching (Leeuw and Donaldson, 2015; Punton et al., 2016). Start by learning as much as you can about the beliefs of those close to the programme – the designers and developers, the administrators who oversee and manage, the staff who deliver services and the beneficiaries. This reduces the possibility of imposing your own pet theory on the programme. An inventory of explanations can then be developed and presented to programme insiders for confirmation, refutation and refinement. It is often possible to connect these candidate mechanisms to formal theory, even if the theory itself does not explicitly refer to a mechanism. Sometimes relevant theories are quite obvious given the nature of the intervention. For instance, health education programmes typically draw on theories of reasoned action and planned behaviour, while many situational crime prevention initiatives are designed using opportunity reduction and routine activities theory. Frequently though, the theoretical base is not clear and only emerges as the study progresses.

Theory selection presents another challenge for realist evaluation. How should evaluators choose given the vast number and diversity of existing social science theories? While there is no easy solution, Merton's (1968) technique of *abstraction* provides useful guidance. In the example presented above, the component of the programme engaging kinship carers was perceived as an instance of a more general class of interventions called support groups. Likewise, mechanisms analytically inducted from themes in the qualitative data pointed toward the centrality of group interaction for facilitating comparison. At this stage of the analysis, abstraction enabled the 'casing' of evidence and ideas to connect the empirical and theoretical realm.[8] A literature search using these concepts led to a stock of knowledge regarding group-based interventions. From here, searching articles for theory led to Festinger's work as a conceptual lens for explaining how these kinds of interventions work.[9] Of course, the interplay of general and particular, of conjecture and evidence, is more complex than implied here. The practice of realist evaluation involves acuity for spotting nuggets of stakeholder wisdom, while at the same time possessing working knowledge of a fairly large repertoire of theories and basic mechanisms.[10] This entails simultaneously working upwards from local data and downwards from formal theory to provide a pincer movement on mechanisms.

For the last trick of the trade it seems only fitting to draw on concluding counsel from the main progenitor of sage realist advice, Ray Pawson. An enduring challenge of conducting theory-driven enquiries is determining which aspects of the intervention theory to evaluate. Realist evaluators soon realise the impossibility of tracking each micro-step in the implementation chain, tracing the minutiae of all programme activities and transactions, and targeting every single causal sequence. In a lively little plenary for the European Evaluation Society meeting in Seville, Pawson (2003) recommended *concentrating your fire* on aspects of the intervention that seem most crucial for success (what he calls the 'juicy bits'). Each component and activity of the Families in Crisis programme could have been interrogated in greater detail and at much greater length, possibly leading to the identification of other mechanisms relating to referral and assessment processes, case management and inter-agency collaboration and so on (see Figure 4.1). There were two main reasons for subjecting group activities to closer realist analysis. A fundamental underlying premise identified in the early phase of the evaluation was that there is something quite powerful about bringing people who have a common experience together. Zooming in on data that spoke to this part of the intervention map revealed that the 'something' entailed comparison mechanisms. From a pragmatic perspective, selecting this part of the programme package also fitted well with the commissioner's information needs, as considerable time and resources were allocated to group activities under the programme's service delivery agreement. From the organisation's perspective, growing demand for services also required reflection on how to establish the support group model in new locations.

CONCLUSION

A central purpose of this chapter has been to illustrate some of the practicalities of implementing realist enquiry, especially in the context of evaluation research involving social interventions. Realist evaluation is a theory-driven approach that grew out of and built on attempts to resolve early debates about the relative importance of internal and external validity. It shares many similarities with Lee J. Cronbach's approach to programme evaluation, which emphasises mechanisms and causal explanations of programmes in context. There are also strong affinities to Merton and the new analytical sociologists who focus on social mechanisms as basic building blocks of middle-range theory. While there are terminological and substantive differences between these writers, one shared ambition is to position theory and generative explanation at the centre of efforts to progress and accumulate knowledge.

The practice of realist evaluation, at least as I understand it, must be rigorous and systematic but never mechanical. Theory construction is iterative and involves making conjectures about plausible underlying generative mechanisms, identifying the contexts that influence their operation and the different outcome patterns that follow. Imaginative guesswork and deliberative judgement is required to distinguish mechanisms from programme activities, to select and combine various types of theory and evidence and to decide where to concentrate empirical efforts, all the while trying to maximise the utility of the evaluation for immediate stakeholders as well as strive for longer-term enlightenment. Concerns among some circles that realist evaluation is being misapplied seem justified, but there is a danger that the tendency toward protocols and standards may stifle innovation. My inclination is to view realist methodology as a resource that imbues a way of thinking. Inevitably this will lead to variation in application. To paraphrase an old saying, realist evaluation is 'like a blank cheque: its potential value depends on the user and his use of it' (Cohen, 1968: 1).

Finally, it would be foolhardy to guarantee that the intervention case example detailed here would necessarily meet with success if implemented at different places with different people at different times. Understanding of social comparison mechanisms and their interaction with context remains incomplete. Given the complexity of open systems it comes as no surprise that evaluation researchers 'are not so good at "fortune telling" – offering guidance on whether the "same" programme will work in another place and on another occasion' (Pawson, 2003: 472). Explanations also have a shelf-life. Propositions entailed in programme theory will not last into perpetuity because generalisations have a habit of decaying over time (Cronbach, 1975). There are further reasons to be cautious of the extent to which mechanism-based reasoning solves the problem of generalisability. In any particular study, plausible but incorrect mechanisms may be proposed while relevant mechanisms remain unidentified. Mechanisms can also produce paradoxical and unanticipated effects (Howick et al., 2013).

Policy-makers seeking simple answers are unlikely to find these in the conditional conclusions of realist enquiries. There are no universal truths or proven programmes to borrow or steal from other jurisdictions and then replicate blindly. Realist evidence does not arrive in a vacuum-sealed package. Instead, heavily contextualised guidance is offered to inform (not make) policy decisions. For example, Program A appears to produce outcomes B, C and D but not E. It seems to do this by influencing processes J, K and L, but only in contexts M, N and O. We know very little about whether it will work in P, Q and R. These causal recipes provide a bridge to support extrapolation from here to there. Combinations of relevant ingredients linked to outcomes are like a 'highway code' that alerts policy-makers to the difficulties they might expect to confront and some of the safest ways to deal with them. Realist advice is like a road map, not a programme blueprint: it 'does not tell you how to drive, but how to survive the journey' (Pawson, 2006b: 170). While there are no magic solutions to the problem of generalisability, causal explanation is an important part of the armoury of responses to the 'will it work elsewhere' question.

NOTES

1   An alternative perspective is provided by Cook (1990, 1993) and later Shadish et al. (2002) who situate causal explanation as one of five principles required to support generalised causal inferences. The other four principles are: (1) surface similarity; (2) ruling out irrelevancies; (3) making discriminations; and (4) interpolation and extrapolation. There are some parallels and differences to the realist perspective on causal explanation, particularly in relation to how context and mechanism are conceptualised. It is beyond the scope of this chapter to enter these debates. Interested readers are strongly encouraged to consult the above sources.

2   See the RAMESES Projects website at www.ramesesproject.org.

3   This refers to a comment by Edward Shils (1960), who described C. Wright Mills as a 'solitary horseman – who is in part prophet, in part a teacher, in part a scholar, and in part a rough-tongued brawler' (pp. 77–8). Like Mills, Pawson's irreverent and jocular style has evoked strong reactions among some quarters of the mainstream evaluation community.

4   For more information see www.mirabelfoundation.org.au. For an account of the origins of the organisation see Clohesy (2006).

5   There are some intriguing aspects of the development of thinking around social comparison processes, including connections to Merton's theory of the reference group that Pawson admires so much. This history is not central to the arguments in this chapter, but interested readers might wish to consult Hyman's (1960) 'Reflections on Reference Groups' and Goethals' (1986) 'Social Comparison Theory: Psychology from the Lost and Found'. Although many credit Hyman for coining the idea, it was Cooley (1992) in *Human Nature and the Social Order* who provided what is possibly the first antecedent outline of reference group theory. One of the clearest elucidations is still Merton and Kitt's (1950) 'Contributions to the Theory of Reference Group Behaviour'. Interestingly, Merton's collaborator on this essay, Alice Kitt, married Peter H. Rossi in 1951. As we have seen, Rossi is one of Pawson's favourite sociological scholars who went on to make important contributions in the field of evaluation.

6   The descriptions have been adapted from the social comparison scale developed by Van der Zee et al. (2000).

7   The term KC = Kinship Carer and the number identifies the individual carer who participated in an interview. Where names are used in direct quotations these have been changed to protect participant anonymity.

8   For a pertinent description of casing as applied here see Ragin (1992) who states that: 'As researchers our primary goal is to link the empirical and the theoretical – to use theory to make sense of evidence and to use evidence to sharpen and refine theory. This interplay helps us to produce theoretically structured descriptions of the empirical world that are both meaningful and useful. Casing is an essential part of this process; cases are invoked to make the linking of ideas and evidence possible' (Ragin, 1992: 225).

9   Booth and Carroll (2015) provide advice on systematic processes for theory-searching and selection that may help avoid accusations of 'stumbling' on theories that seem to fit the data or 'cherry-picking' from fields that the evaluator happens to be familiar with.

10 By basic mechanism, I mean something like the types and levels of mechanism outlined by Hedström (2005). For other examples of attempts to categorise mechanisms see McAdam et al. (2001), Bennett (2013) and Elster (2007). These efforts are far from satisfactory. Even so, they indicate the potential value in working toward more exhaustive explanation.

5

THEORY AND REALIST METHODS

Bruno Marchal, Guy Kegels and
Sara Van Belle

WHAT THIS CHAPTER IS ABOUT

This chapter discusses common pitfalls that applied realist researchers encounter and how these can be avoided. First, the differences and commonalities between three fundamental concepts for realist studies are explored: middle-range theory, programme theory and context-mechanism-outcome (CMO) configurations. Then, the main avenues to eliciting initial programme theory (identifying programme assumptions using interviews and document reviews, exploratory research and literature reviews) are illustrated with examples from evaluations of programmes and interventions implemented in health systems in resource-constrained settings of low- and middle-income countries like Ghana, Uganda and South Africa during the last 15 years. Secondly, the challenges of using configurational analysis and how contexts, mechanisms and outcomes can be tied together during the analysis are discussed. Finally, the chapter concludes by reminding researchers that clearly demonstrating how the empirical findings relate to initial programmes or middle-range theory is essential to provide plausible and actionable explanations.

How this chapter will help you to do realist research

Common problems often occurring during the initial phases of realist projects include the difficulty of distinguishing between middle-range theory and programme theory but also choosing the 'right' theory or theories to start with. This chapter offers clear guidance on how to deal with theory that you can apply to your own investigations.

A practical tip: a take-home message from the chapter

In realist research, the term 'theory' means several different things. These can and should be ascertained, developed and made explicit.

INTRODUCTION

About 20 years ago, a number of authors called for developing research and evaluation designs to better deal with complexity in health (Ragin, 1999; Wolff, 2000; Fulop et al., 2001; Kernick, 2002). In the field of medical research, the UK Medical Research Council produced its first guidelines for research into 'complex' (multi-component) interventions in 2000 (MRC, 2000). These were criticised for adopting a narrow perspective on complexity (Hawe et al., 2004) and consequently the guidance was updated (Craig et al., 2008; Moore et al., 2015). Meanwhile, alternatives to the randomised controlled trial design, considered the gold standard for producing evidence in health care, emerged. Outside the discipline of health, approaches including realist evaluation (Pawson and Tilley, 1997), qualitative comparative analysis (Ragin, 1998), contribution analysis (Mayne, 2001) and process tracing (George and Bennett, 2005; Waldner, 2012) addressed causal complexity.

In the emerging discipline of health policy and systems research (HPSR), the notion that health systems are in essence social and thus complex systems has gained currency. In this view, people are at the core of the health system: out of dynamic social relations, social action and change emerge (Gilson et al., 2011). Health policy and system researchers also acknowledge the uncertainty that arises when one deals with the relative unpredictability of events in social systems and recognise the subsequent methodological challenges (Bennett et al., 2011). Calls were made for better use of methods from the social sciences and, more specifically, realist evaluation was identified as an approach useful to deal with complex issues in HPSR (Gilson, 2012).

Realist evaluation is, indeed, well suited for the study of (social) complexity (Westhorp, 2012; Byrne, 2013; Pawson, 2013), because it considers causation to be generative in nature: actors have a potential for effecting change by their very nature. Accepting as such the role of actors in change (agency), realist evaluation considers structural and institutional features to be contingent on the actors and researchers. Both actors and programmes are rooted in a stratified social reality (see David Byrne in this volume), which results from an interplay between individuals and institutions, all with their own interest and objectives. If all human action is embedded within such a wide range of social processes, then causal mechanisms reside in social relations and context as much as in individuals. It is people not programmes that change situations or solve problems and these people's choices are far from entirely predictable, hence realist evaluation by definition deals with social complexity.

It is therefore no surprise that during the last ten years, realist research has been making inroads in the field of health policy and systems research (Marchal et al., 2012), where it is being applied in research at all levels of the health system, from clinical care to policy-making.

In this chapter, we discuss the use of realist research in health policy and systems research, some common pitfalls realist researchers encounter and how these can be avoided. We will focus first on the middle-range/programme theory, and how the initial theory can be developed. In a second part, we will discuss the challenge of the configurational analysis, or how context, mechanism and outcome can be tied together during the analysis. We will illustrate the challenges with examples drawn mainly from realist research carried out in the resource-constrained settings of low- and middle-income countries.

USING REALIST EVALUATION IN HPSR IN LOW-RESOURCE SETTINGS

During the last 15 years, we have been involved in realist studies mainly in low-resource settings, evaluating programmes and interventions implemented at diverse levels of the health system:

1. Studies at the *micro-level* focused on relations between providers, patients, health service managers and citizens. Themes include the role of management in motivating volunteers (Vareilles et al., 2015a; Vareilles et al., 2015b), adult HIV patients' adherence to treatment (Mukumbang et al., 2016a) and adherence of children infected with HIV to a new treatment formula (Nebot Giralt et al., 2017).
2. Research at the *meso-level* looked into organisational issues such as capacity development of health district management teams (Prashanth et al., 2012; Prashanth et al., 2014a; Prashanth et al., 2014b), effective district leadership (Kwamie et al., 2014; Kwamie et al., 2015), the link between management and organisational commitment (Marchal et al., 2010a, 2010b), supervision of first-line providers (Hernandez et al., 2014) and organisational accountability (Van Belle, 2014; Van Belle and Mayhew, 2016).
3. At the *macro-level*, issues of systems design and policy were explored, including user fee policies (Robert et al., 2012) and governance (Van Belle, 2014), but also intersecting issues such as the implementation of fee exemption policies (Marchal et al., 2013b), decentralisation (Kwamie, 2016) and the implementation of intimate partner violence policies by primary health care providers (Goicolea et al., 2013; Goicolea et al., 2015b; Goicolea et al., 2015c).

In all these studies, we have encountered a number of methodological challenges. The first group of challenges relates to the complex nature of the topics under investigation. Researchers often justify the use of realist evaluation in HPSR arguing that it addresses the complex nature of their research topic. The process of studying any complex issue, whichever methodological approach is used, always includes capturing unpredictable, emergent phenomena. This requires a study design that allows for alterations to the planned intervention by the actors involved, as well as parallel events or context elements that may affect the implementation and the outcomes. The study design should also enable the research team to identify the social interaction that leads to emergent behaviour. The realist approach fits this bill, and as a consequence, in many realist research projects, a key challenge is how to deal with the difficulties of describing the complex processes and making sense of them in terms of causal attribution. This requires an open mind on the part of the researcher as well as flexible research designs (McDaniel et al., 2009) – including the willingness to accept uncertainty and unknowns. In practice, narrowing the scope of the study is an often used strategy to deal with perceptions of overwhelming – or unmanageable – complexity.

A second set of difficulties relates to the realist evaluation approach. These have been described by Pawson (2008, 2009a), Pawson and Manzano-Santaella (2012), Marchal et al. (2012) and Wong et al. (2016) and include the long-discussed issues of what constitutes a mechanism, the difference between intervention modality and mechanism, and the risk of conflating context with mechanism. Furthermore, there is the challenge of moving from simply describing context, mechanism and outcomes to developing a configurational analysis that ties all elements together to show how the outcomes came about (Pawson and

Manzano-Santaella, 2012). Finally, causal configurations (CMOs), programme theories and middle-range theories pose problems for novice realist researchers in terms of how to choose the right level of theory development (Pawson, 2009a).

Since some of these issues have been discussed at length in other chapters of this book, we focus here on the difference between middle-range theory, programme theory and context-mechanism-outcome configuration, the development of the initial theory and the configurational analysis. We refer the reader to the chapter by Brad Astbury in this volume, who focuses on generalisation at the level of mechanism and middle-range theory.

WITH WHICH THEORY TO START?

A problem often occurring during the initial phase of our realist research projects is the difficulty of distinguishing between middle-range theory (MRT) and programme theory (PT). Health policy and system research faces the challenge of complex causation par excellence. Researchers often focus on one level of the system but need to take into account the interaction between actors, institutions and other forces at other levels. This compounds the challenge of choosing the 'right' theory or theories to focus our investigations on: at which level should one look for explanations? To help answer these questions, we explore the differences and commonalities between middle-range theory, programme theory and context-mechanism-outcome (CMO) configuration.

Pawson and Tilley (1997) adopt Merton's definition of middle-range theory: 'theories that lie between the minor but necessary working hypotheses [...] and the all-inclusive systematic efforts to develop a unified theory that will explain all the observed uniformities of social behaviour, social organization and social change' (Merton, 1968: 38). Programme theory is commonly defined as the set of assumptions of programme designers (or other actors involved) that explain how and why they expect the intervention to reach its objective(s) and in which conditions. The CMO configuration is the heuristic suggested by Pawson and Tilley and used by some realists during analysis to identify the causal links between context, mechanism and outcome.

Middle-range theories and programme theories operate at different levels of abstraction and one could perhaps best describe the relation between these concepts as follows. Middle-range theories are formal theories. They often provide a bridge to a wealth of existing research and knowledge about a topic. They are invariably more abstract than programme theories, which seek to explain how and why different outcomes are generated by a specific programme in different contexts. Importantly, however, both 'programme theory' and 'middle-range theory' share the potential to bridge between different cases. Indeed, they both allow for a level of abstraction that goes beyond the local situation. Programme and middle-range theories enable the researcher to move from case-specific single-loop learning to double-loop learning: by comparing the findings and explanations found in different cases through the lens of the initial theory, the specific context of each case can be transcended. Systematically examining how the results of different cases relate to the more abstractly formulated programme theory thus allows for gradually improving the modest forms of theoretical generalisability of findings (see Brad Astbury in this volume). In addition, the opportunity to test theories between cases allows for the judging and further refining of theories, leading, we suggest, to more robust theory development.

At the start of the research or evaluation project, suitable initial middle-range theories are identified. Often, the programme theory of the designers of the intervention (how they think the programme is going to achieve the desired outcomes in a particular context) is described in parallel. The result is an elicited initial theory that will be tested and that informs the design of the study and the data collection.

HOW TO ELICIT THE INITIAL PROGRAMME THEORY

While Cole (1999) noted that clear guidance on how the initial programme theory can be developed is scarce, there are at least three main avenues to do this. First, the assumptions of the programme designers and implementers (what Pawson and Tilley call the 'folk theories') can be elicited using interviews and document reviews. A number of techniques can be used to make sense of the data. For example, 'cause mapping' and 'concept mapping' (Rosas, 2005) may help to clarify how the key actors understand the intervention by identifying their assumptions and their reasoning. This results in the identification of the key elements of the problem or intervention and, in the latter case, of the expected short- and long-term outcomes as described by the stakeholders. This resembles 'pattern matching' (Trochim, 1989), whereby the stakeholders are interviewed and the pattern of the theory proposed by them (or by extension derived from prior theory) is compared with the observations made by the researchers. Also, the 'argument analysis' technique can be used to draw useful propositions from data sources such as interviews, project documents and reports. Used in philosophy, argument analysis searches for the 'warrant' (or generally accepted causal principle, the 'because' part of the argument). As these 'because' parts are often not made explicit, such 'warrants' need to be inferred by the researcher doing the analysis (Leeuw, 2003).

A second avenue to develop initial PT is through exploratory research (Lipsey and Pollard, 1989). In their study of the link between management practices and performance in hospitals, Marchal and colleagues (2010a) carried out an exploratory case study of a well-performing hospital to bolster their initial programme theory, which was based on a rapid review of the literature, discussions with colleagues and personal professional experience. On the basis of document reviews and interviews, the researchers described the management and leadership practices at the hospital, the interpretation of these practices by the staff and the local context. Quantitative data on hospital performance was also collected.

The analysis indicated high levels of trust between health workers and their management team and of organisational commitment, which were related to a comprehensive set of management practices ranging from structuring command-and-control practices to commitment-eliciting practices. The analysis led to a 'consolidated' initial programme theory which was subsequently tested in a series of case studies. Similar exploratory research was carried out in other realist studies, including Goodridge et al. (2015), who also studied leadership practices. In Box 5.1, Aku Kwamie (2016; Kwamie et al., 2015) explains how she also used exploratory research to refine the initial programme theory underlying an intervention to address maternal and children's health.

BOX 5.1 SWIMMING THROUGH THEORIES – MRT VERSUS PT: WHERE TO START AND WHERE TO END?

We undertook a realist evaluation to understand the context of decision-making by district managers in implementing maternal and newborn health programmes. We specifically focused on how a leadership development programme (LDP) designed by an international agency 'worked' to improve managerial decision-making when introduced into Ghanaian districts (Kwamie, 2016; Kwamie et al., 2015). We found that the LDP, as in many other such interventions, assumes universal validity of its presumptions and that it does not foresee differential impacts in various contexts. We therefore began our study with an exploratory phase to uncover possible theories of how the programme might work in our particular context. We engaged in a case study of a single health district, in which we conducted participant observations during a ten-month period, semi-structured in-depth interviews and a document review. This allowed us to draft a context-specific theory of managerial decision-making as it happened before the LDP was initiated, which helped to develop a plausible explanation for how the LDP would bring about change given the context.

Developing our initial programme theory on the basis of empirical research proved useful because it uncovered the context-dependence of the success of the LDP and, critically, the temporal-specificity of context. We confirmed that context can have a differentiating effect on a given intervention over time. This was indeed subsequently observed in the gap between the LDP's short- and medium-term outcomes. Starting with a 'localised' PT also underscored the fact that in complex systems, the context always matters. The pre-existing context in this case triggered a mechanism that stood in the way of sustainability of the LDP's impact.

This is significant for two main reasons. First, interventions are often selected on the basis of their success in the short term, and this points us to the need to lengthen

(Continued)

(Continued)

time-horizons to understand how interventions and their outcomes mature. Second, the context-neutrality of the programme theories of many programme designers may be a cause for concern because they cannot account for observed differences in different contexts.

Source: Aku Kwamie

Finally, a realist synthesis (Pawson et al., 2005) or another appropriate literature review method designed to capture complexity can identify relevant theories used in the field in question or in other disciplines. We refer to Chapter 9 in this volume in which Andrew Booth and colleagues elaborate a more detailed discussion of realist synthesis.

When eliciting the initial programme theory, it makes sense to combine data collection approaches in an iterative process. Byng et al. (2005), for instance, constructed the middle-range theory on the basis of a literature review, a description of the intervention and discussions with facilitators involved in the programmes they were studying. Wong et al. (2010) used brainstorming, browsing the specialist literature, discussions with colleagues and snowballing of references to identify relevant middle-range theories on the effect of Internet-based education programmes. Mason and Barnes (2007) and Mukumbang et al. (2016a) similarly combined different avenues of enquiry.

Vareilles and colleagues focused on the motivation of Red Cross volunteers. The authors combined a number of techniques, in different steps, to identify potential programme theories. First, they interviewed Red Cross volunteers and programme managers working in Sierra Leone, Burundi, the Philippines and Argentina. This was followed by interviews of experts on volunteering at the International Federation of Red Cross Societies (IFRCS). This step aimed to elicit the general assumptions regarding volunteering and motivation. Subsequently, exploratory research was carried out in Kampala (Uganda) in two study sites with contrasting management practices. Data collection tools included a context analysis, document review, conversations with Ugandan Red Cross volunteers via Facebook and a survey of Uganda Red Cross staff (Vareilles et al., 2015b). Finally, the authors carried out a realist synthesis of community health volunteer performance (Vareilles et al., 2017). This yielded a long list of candidate MRTs. Through discussion among researchers, Red Cross staff and occupational psychology experts, self-determination theory (SDT) was tentatively identified as the theory with the highest explanatory potential. SDT is best considered as a grand theory, which over a period of more than 30 years has evolved from focusing on intrinsic motivation to become a theory of self-motivation, social functioning and well-being (Ryan and Deci, 2000). Within this theory, the psychological needs of perceived autonomy, competence and relatedness are considered to be the main drivers of intrinsic or interiorised motivation and behaviour change (Deci and Ryan, 1985). These drivers made sense in terms of explaining the motivation and behaviour of volunteers and thus provided the kernel for a middle-range theory that could be tested in empirical studies. The MRT of this study stated that management practices that effectively address these three groups of needs would enhance the 'autonomous' motivation of volunteers if the organisational culture of the Red Cross matches with the volunteers' expectations and if adequate resources are available for the volunteers to carry out their tasks. Subsequently, this initial MRT was tested in a case study (Vareilles et al., 2015a).

In summary, there are three broad approaches to eliciting the initial programme theory: identifying the assumptions of the programme designers and managers, exploratory research and literature reviews. The nature and complexity of realist studies make it difficult to prescribe sequence or ideal components since how these are to be combined will depend to a large extent on the existing knowledge, resources and experience with the issue under investigation.

BATTLING WITH CONFIGURATIONAL ANALYSIS IN REALIST STUDIES

Context-mechanism-outcome (CMO) configurations offer case-specific and fundamental building blocks of realist explanation. These hypotheses provide the most plausible explanation of the outcomes observed in the study. They facilitate the further refining of theory, in what Pawson and Tilley call a process of specification (Pawson and Tilley, 1997: 86). CMO configurations are real only when they offer the most adequate explanation of the changes generated through an intervention. They may contribute to the increasing refining of theories, which may progressively reach higher levels of abstraction through an accumulation of studies where similar or different configurations of context, mechanism and outcome are encountered.

Realist researchers typically use the CMO configuration as a heuristic technique during data analysis to elicit the generative causal processes underlying the outcome. However, often lists of outcomes, context factors and mechanisms are produced without attempting to develop causal configurations that link these elements into an explanatory account (Pawson and Manzano-Santaella, 2012). Furthermore, researchers often confuse how the intervention is carried out (intervention modalities) with the 'mechanism', and 'mechanism' and 'context' are also easily conflated.

In an effort to unpack the CMO configuration and provide researchers with practical guidance for analysis, modifications have been proposed by many realist investigators, for instance Willis et al. (2014), Dalkin et al. (2015) and Jagosh et al. (2015). This proliferation of modifications illustrates the limitations that heuristic techniques per se can encounter when confronted with the complexity of the issues under study. For example, Jackson and Kolla (2012) proposed an analytical strategy that emphasises identifying not factors, but relationships between context, mechanism and outcome ('linked dyads and triads'). In our practice, we found it useful to systematically add 'intervention' and 'actors' to the configuration (see, for instance, Van Belle, 2014), expanding the CMO to 'ICAMO'. Adding 'Intervention' to CMO stimulates the researcher to describe the intervention as it actually was implemented (or not) and to differentiate it from 'context'. Adding 'Actors' focuses the researcher's attention on identifying the different groups of subjects targeted by the intervention and assessing how they responded to and adopted the intervention (or not). This focus on actors can make it easier to tie mechanisms to specific groups of programme users and stakeholders in specific contexts. For example, in the evaluation of an ART adherence club intervention, using ICAMO as a heuristic quickly pointed to the different effect on sub-groups of patients, service providers and programme managers (Mukumbang et al., 2017). This revised configurational analysis strategy also has the potential to force the realist researcher to take into account the agency–structure interactions and the patterns these may lead to. In a realist research project on accountability of health actors in a rural health district in Ghana, Van Belle and Mayhew (2016) used the ICAMO heuristic to explicitly describe the key actors and their accountability practices. They then explored the web of relationships and the social context of the small rural town where they all worked and lived to assess whether, how and in what conditions the actors were accountable for their actions to the public.

While the ICAMO modification can help in the within-case analysis of the causal configuration, in health policy and systems research we often compare multiple cases or events. Here, we found qualitative comparative analysis (QCA), developed by Ragin (1998, 1999), useful. QCA belongs to the case-based methods and explicitly adopts a complex causation perspective (Byrne, 2005). It is argued to be compatible with the realist rationale of analysis because both approaches share 'a complex notion of causality, a generative perspective, a theory-driven approach to empirical observation and a limited scope of generalization' (Befani et al., 2007: 173). QCA uses comparisons of configurations of attributes of cases to identify necessary and sufficient conditions and thus infer causality.

Goicolea et al. (2013) used QCA to help in making sense of the findings of 15 case studies. This realist research project focused on how the Spanish national policy on intimate partner violence was adopted and implemented by primary care teams in four regions. The initial programme theory was developed on the basis of exploratory literature reviews and policy analysis, and adapted after the first case study (Goicolea et al., 2015b). This initial theory was tested in three case studies and led to a refined PT, which included the mechanisms of self-efficacy, perceived preparation, woman-centredness, teamwork and knowledge (Goicolea et al., 2015a). A truth table, a tool used in QCA to assess conditions in terms of necessity and sufficiency, was drafted on the basis of the programme theory. The authors added mechanisms, context conditions, intervention elements and outcomes as headers in the columns of the truth table and populated it with empirical data from the three initial studies and 12 more cases. While QCA cannot per se identify mechanisms or context conditions, it can help in identifying which combination of presumed elements of the ICAMO may explain the outcome. The initial analysis identified several patterns explaining the outcomes of the cases. Further analysis indicated that self-efficacy and perceived preparation were found to be necessary for triggering good team responses to IPV, but none of the mechanisms were found to be sufficient to explain good performance. The implementation of IPV protocols (intervention) and a good team climate (context) were found to be important intervention and context factors respectively. Ultimately, the programme theory was modified to reflect these findings (Goicolea et al., 2015c).

Configurational analysis of causation is at the core of realist evaluation and the above examples show how realist researchers and evaluators either adapt the CMO heuristic or use additional tools and approaches to demonstrate how the observed outcome can be explained through a configuration of intervention, mechanism and outcome. We have already mentioned process tracing and contribution analysis, and approaches such as these may provide additional inspiration to further develop methods for causal analysis in realist research. While the configurational approach is one of the main reasons why many health policy and system researchers are attracted by realist research – besides its capacity to elicit, test and develop theories (Van Belle et al., 2017) – it comes with the challenge of identifying the relative contribution of the intervention to the observed outcome and the conditions required for it to trigger the mechanism. Methodological innovation in this field is the new frontier in realist research.

CONCLUSION

Health policy and system researchers increasingly adopt a realist evaluation approach and one can almost say it is becoming a fashion in the world of health policy and systems research. To avoid it becoming a fad, realist researchers and evaluators need to deal with the challenges presented in this chapter of positioning theory at the heart of explanation. A stratified account of the real assumes, ontologically, that we cannot understand an intervention from the accumulation and analysis of empirical data alone. Key to high-quality realist research is adopting a configurational mode of analysis that seeks to explain the observed outcomes and how the actual intervention triggered mechanisms in actors in specific contexts to lead to these outcomes (or not). Clearly demonstrating how the empirical findings relate to initial programme or middle-range theory is essential. Only if realist researchers manage to elicit, test and refine theories (be it programme theories or theories of the middle range) that provide plausible and, crucially, actionable explanations will their results be perceived to exceed the level of banality or common sense.

ACKNOWLEDGEMENTS

We would like to thank Aku Kwamie (Ghana Health Service Research and Development Division) for her contribution to this chapter and the fruitful collaborations over the years.

6

RESEARCHING COMPLEX LARGE-SCALE NESTED INTERVENTIONS

David Byrne

WHAT THIS CHAPTER IS ABOUT

Drawing on the case of housing market renewal, the focus of this chapter is complex realism. The case shows how the world is made up of material practices, decisions to build or not build housing stock, and causal processes that cannot be readily identified in empirical research, but then have their expression in the bricks-and-mortar shaping regeneration. This chapter provides a practical example of what complex realism looks like, the ways in which social policy, private markets, geographical and global processes, institutional structures and human agency interact. It elaborates the emergent properties of this complexity that are neither linear nor determined and demonstrates the multi-layered, multi-faceted social system with long and interwoven chains of causality that are resistant to resolution in any complex system. But as this chapter shows, even these wicked problems can be partially explained using the methods of realism.

How this chapter will help you to do realist research

Very many of the problems we research are complex puzzles, the interaction of structures, agency and outcomes that cannot be explained by the practices and processes we can measure. This chapter offers practical resolution through a complex realist approach.

A practical tip: a take-home message from the chapter

Replace CM = O with Mechanism(s) & Context => Outcome

INTRODUCTION

The purpose of this chapter is twofold. It is an attempt first to explicate the meaning of the term 'complex realism'. Second, it will attempt to see how engaging with the framework of understanding what is complex realism, which is not a theory but rather a way of understanding the world in ontological terms, enables us to understand what is going on in large-scale interventions in real complex systems. Evaluation will be considered here, not only in relation to the absolutely legitimate purpose of evaluation itself, i.e. to understand what works, but also in a realist frame of reference what works when and where in what context. An examination of evaluation in large-scale urban programmes which are part of the 'regeneration' agenda in formerly industrial and now post-industrial urban systems will also be used to illustrate both the methodological issues involved in dealing with large complex social systems and the way issues of power and interest matter when we move into domains where there is no consensus. The example which will be used to illustrate and carry my argument is that of Pathfinder – the UK's Housing Market Renewal initiative of the early twenty-first century.

Most realist evaluation has been undertaken in relation to programme interventions which operate in relation to one form of action or a set of related actions which is introduced into a complex system often in the form of an organisation understood as a complex system. That way of thinking is perfectly appropriate and has almost always been informed by a clear understanding of any complex system as embedded within and intersected with other causal systems which have causal powers in relation to the system of interest and themselves are subject to the causal powers of that very system. The point of this chapter is to review this kind of approach through the lens of what Reed and Harvey defined as 'complex realism' (1992) – that is, as a synthesis of Bhaskarian critical realism as a philosophical ontology and non-linear complexity science as a scientific ontology.

Complex realism is a frame of reference which endorses Bhaskar's conceptions of the nature of our scientific descriptions of reality being the empirical organisation of observations through social processes – that is, as both constructed by the practices of science and informed by reality itself. What we can observe is the actual, the way reality is as generated by underlying causal mechanisms at the level of the real. In Reed and Harvey's framing the complexity element takes the form of recognising that social systems at all levels are far from equilibric and complex in form. In other words, they are not to be understood by reduction to components in an analytical fashion but the processes within them are massively interactive. Moreover, social systems are nested. For example, individuals are themselves complex systems but live within households which exist in spatial areas, are surrounded by institutional forms and are affected by markets (which are *not* to be understood through reduction to individual economic actors) and so on. It is very important to recognise that to say that systems are nested is not to imply a downward hierarchy of causation. In contrast, all systems at all levels are intersected with other systems and causal powers flow in all possible directions. Of course, social structures have causal powers for individuals but individuals, sometimes as sole actors if charismatic and/or massively economically powerful, may have causal powers for structures and collectivities, themselves emergent, have potentially massive causal powers. Reed and Harvey wrote within a sociological tradition profoundly influenced by Marxism and therefore for them the relations of capitalist production always had the status of a generative mechanism at the level of the real.

Pawson and Tilley's proposal of 'Realist Evaluation' (1997) with its paradigmatic formula of:

Context + Mechanism = Outcome[1]

which was firmly located in the realist, if not critical realist, ontology fits well with much but not all of the general approach of Reed and Harvey. The idea of mechanism accords with the Bhaskarian conception of an underlying order of reality which generates the nature of reality as the actual in context and where what we observe can be understood as the empirical.

The point of an evaluation in this frame of reference is to identify a mechanism for achieving a desired change and establish the context(s) within which that mechanism could operate to achieve that outcome. Pawson in particular has firmly associated this approach in applied social science with the Mertonian conception of theories of the middle range, theories which are neither grand overarching general social theories of the order of those associated with the canonical figures of social science nor restricted hypotheses as understood in classical formulations of the hypothetico-deductive method. Let me make it plain that I have no quarrel with this when it is applied to specific and highly defined interventions which, while in no way corresponding to the protocols of the randomised controlled trial (RCT), particularly in their acknowledgement of the significance of human action and the need to take account of this in any process of evaluation,[2] nonetheless operate at a level of some-what defined specificity and in a relatively restricted context. The majority of evaluations cast within the realist evaluation paradigm have been carried out in health, penal or peda-gogical contexts where, while context and other systems matter, there is still a fairly high degree of precision in relation to specification of the system within which the intervention is intended to operate.

LARGE-SCALE INTERVENTIONS

What I want to consider in this chapter is interventions on a much larger scale where the boundaries of systems are highly permeable and causal chains run in all directions.

Typical of such interventions are the large-scale urban programmes which operate under the heading of 'regeneration'. These programmes have usually been located in urban sys-tems which were formerly centres of major industrial activity but which have lost most of both their industrial employment and 'value added' in the form of industrial production. The causal drivers for this transformation from industrial to post-industrial character have been a combination of massive increases in industrial productivity – fewer people make more – and the global relocation of production from the old 'advanced industrial states' to elsewhere, pretty much to every nation state outwith the old industrial nations which has a functioning economic and social system and cannot be classified as 'failed'. In this the development of the shipping container and of port and related container transport systems has probably been the most important technological factor. Shipping containers massively reduce the transport cost component of manufactured consumer goods and make production far removed from the site of purchase and consumption a viable propo-sition. This global shift in material production of course extends beyond the consumer goods sector to incorporate all aspects of industrial production. It has happened and it is causal to a phase shift transformation in the urban systems of the old industrial, now post-industrial, nations. In a recent paper (Byrne, 2016) I have examined what we might call the political economy as context issues which surround efforts to understand what has happened and is happening in such urban systems. That piece was explicitly informed by a realist frame of reference but did not focus on evaluation. That task is what I am attempting here.

I have had pretty much a working life engagement with this issue and with interventions designed to address its many social consequences. From 1974 to 1977 I was Research Director of the North Tyneside Community Development Project (CDP), one of the 12 CDPs initiated by the UK Home Office and modelled on the Ford Foundation Grey Area Projects described by Marris and Rein (1967). Actually, the CDPs were not so much designed to address the issues caused by deindustrialisation as discoverers of it as the crucial causal factor in a range of social problems which were associated with deprived neighbourhoods in urban systems towards which they were targeted. The local project final reports and particularly the inter-project report, *The Costs of Industrial Change* (1977), were the first systematic identifiers of the significance of deindustrialisation in UK urban systems. The CDPs were not the first Area Based Initiatives (ABIs) in the UK. The Educational Priority Area Programmes (EPAs) which preceded them in the 1960s had that status. However, the CDPs were the first general set of programmes which had very wide social objectives across a broad area of outcomes.

Despite efforts to force them into an experimental mode of evaluation, an approach which the experience of the Ford Foundation Grey Area projects had demonstrated to be wholly useless, the CDPs essentially produced reports which did not evaluate their specific work in any formal sense other than by a narrative of experience across domains of intervention.[3] Most CDPs articulated their understanding with reference to grand social theory in a broad sense by drawing on the Marxist frame of reference[4] as a basis for defining the driving causal forces which lay behind the social realities within which the teams were operating. That of course is in accord with the exact realist ontology of generative mechanism, the capitalist mode of production – base, the social order – the actual, and observed account – the empirical. At the time Bhaskar's formulation was not available but like so many the CDP teams were realists ahead of the availability of the term.

DEFINING BOUNDARIES

The first methodological issue for the CDPs and other large-scale urban programmes was that of defining the boundaries of the systems with which they were engaged. At one level, in almost all urban programmes this is done by limiting the operations of the programme to a defined geographical area, either an area within an administratively defined municipality, a whole municipality or a defined set of municipalities. However, such administrative definitions, while having a crucial reality in terms of the impact of governance and particularly resource allocation mechanisms, are not the whole story with any urban system. Cilliers' take on the boundaries of complex systems is particularly helpful to us here:

The propensity we have towards visual metaphors inclines us to think in spatial terms. A system is therefore often visualized as something that is contiguous in space ... Social systems are obviously not limited in this way. Parts of the system may exist in totally different spatial locations ... there are two important implications to be drawn from this. The first is that non-contiguous subsystems could be part of many different systems simultaneously. This would mean that different systems interpenetrate each other, that they share internal organs. How does one talk of the boundary of the system under these conditions? A second implication of letting go of a spatial understanding of boundaries would be that in a critically organized system we are never far away from the boundary. If the components of the system are richly interconnected, there will always be a short route from any component to the 'outside' of the system. There is thus no safe 'inside' of the system, the boundary is folded in or perhaps the system consists of boundaries only. Everything is always interacting and interfacing with others and with the environment; the notions of 'inside' and 'outside' are never simple or uncontested. (2001: 141–2)

In the same article Cilliers developed an account of how we understand complex systems in a way which resonates absolutely with the general framing of a realist ontology:

Boundaries [of complex systems] are simultaneously a function of the activity of the system itself, and a product of the strategy of description involved. In other words, we frame the system by describing it in a certain way (for a certain purpose) but we are constrained in where the frame can be drawn. The boundary of the system is therefore neither a function of our description, nor is it a purely natural thing ... We often fall into the trap of thinking of a boundary as something which separates one thing from another. We should rather think of a boundary as something that *constitutes* that which is bounded. This shift will help us to see the boundary as something enabling rather than confining. (Cilliers, 2001: 141)

Not only does this resonate with realist ontology but it also, as we should expect if we engage in any form of science where reality has a voice, corresponds closely to Ragin's answer to the question he has continually set himself and others: what is a case?

... cases – meaningful but complex configurations of events and structures – singular whole entities purposefully selected ... not homogeneous observations drawn at random from a pool of equally plausible selections. (Ragin, 1994: 125)

... consider cases not as empirical units or theoretical categories, but as the product of basic research operations. (Ragin in imperative mode, 1992: 218)

So we make the things we engage with but we make them from something rather than nothing. Moreover, whenever we are engaged as actors in relation to the context within which the programmes we are evaluating are operating, and in realist evaluation we are always so engaged, then we are part of the processes generating that context in all its complexity to however meagre a degree.[5]

The Community Development Programme was explicitly engaged in Action Research, which meant the team members together with other actors within the communities were out to change things. The Home Office Civil Servant Derek Morrell who was largely responsible for the establishment of the programme endorsed a notion of functional conflict and expected the programmes to shake things up. In complexity theory terms he wanted disturbance introduced into rather moribund systems of governance and community engagement in order to change the character of those systems. Of course, the CDPs were not by any means the first actors in their contexts nor were they the only governance actors engaged in trying to achieve change. All new policies as implemented were about achieving change. In particular, 'planning' was about changing places and in the 1970s there had been an important and recent shift in policy for dealing with areas of older housing away from demolition and replacement and towards 'improvement' and retention. At this time UK local authorities had large and ambitious programmes for change across a range of their activities. The change from selective to comprehensive secondary education was largely complete but very recent. There were programmes for council house building on a large scale. Social services had been reorganised following the Seebohm report (Seebohm, 1968). Lots of things were happening in the system even within the domain of governance rather narrowly defined. We were not yet at the stage recognised by Pawson when he was asked to evaluate a particular urban intervention after the plethora of area-based interventions which followed on from the CDPs. Areas had become palimpsests on which successive interventions had been written and it would be impossible to sort out the impact of any new one without considering all those that had gone before *and* other interventions which were happening at the same time. Nonetheless, there was lots of action in the system from other governance actors in the 1970s.

Even the spatial boundaries were fuzzy. In governance terms both the then metropolitan county and regional levels were important planning actors. Journey to work areas, a commonly used operational definition of locality, were wide. People resident in the CDP neighbourhoods worked not only in other adjacent localities but actually globally given the significance in North Shields at least of maritime employment. Tyneside is a long thin estuarine city with excellent public transport, including a metro system and a good road network, and North Shields is part of a port which was a major residential locale for the merchant navy.

One crucial aspect of the Context + Mechanism = Outcome (CMO)[6] formulation is the necessity for defining outcomes in a reasonably precise fashion. If we are dealing with an outcome that can be measured in terms of impact across a target population this makes absolute sense. So, for example, the work of Blackman et al. (2013),[7] although not a prospective evaluation, dealt with the success of Local Strategic Partnerships – LSPs being governance entities intended to create 'joined up governance' across the whole of a local authority area and involving in particular local health systems as well as local authorities in Spearhead Areas (the most deprived 75 areas) in England – in closing the gap in health inequalities between their own area and national trends across a range of relevant indicators. These included premature deaths from cancer and cardiovascular disease and the rate of teenage conceptions. So the outcome set here could be defined since that was formulated in terms of measurable and measured quantitative indicators. The 'reduce health inequalities' initiative was certainly an area-based one since it was targeted at and organised within defined local authority areas, but it was uncharacteristic in terms of the clarity of the outcomes it was seeking to achieve.

Far more common in terms of either specific area-based programmes/projects or policy sets of a more general kind directed at spatially organised governance systems are much broader objectives of the form of 'regeneration' and/or 'cohesion'. Sometimes these objectives are associated with vague specifications of aspects of the system which might be measured. Often these are cast in employment terms as jobs created and/or protected, although in fact these indicators are very difficult to measure and in reality are almost never measured as such. Implicit in the objective setting is something on the lines of what I have proposed as defining an effect in complex systems (Byrne, 2011) – that is understanding effects as states of a system and understanding programmes as designed to change the state of a system to something different to what it is now. Regeneration as an objective certainly has that character. Measurements, if they are understood as I argued when discussing 'what are we measuring when we measure' (Byrne, 2002) as traces of the state of a system rather than as extraneous causal variables separate from the system, can be very useful as descriptors of the system state and hence of system change but they are by no means the only useful sort of such description. Any qualitative description also has value and we should note that such qualitative descriptions are often categorical in form. They describe differences. Likewise, perhaps, the most useful quantitative techniques are those which engage in numerical taxonomy. In one way or another[8] we sort things into kinds. Tracing the trajectories of systems by making time-ordered classifications – that is, classifying them at different time points and both seeing how cases change kind and the very classificatory systems themselves change – is a very useful approach.

TRACES OF THE CONDITIONS OF A SYSTEM

When we turn to attempts to transform the state of whole urban systems or even of sub-localities within those systems, we inevitably move into the terrain of social conflict. Let us examine this by reflecting on the meaning of the term 'regeneration'. To regenerate is to make again in a new form but the issue is always *cui bono*, for whose good, is this new form intended. So we might think that to regenerate our urban systems, which have all become much more unequal with the transition from industrial to post-industrial character, would mean that we restore at least the degree of equality that prevailed before. Or we might think that that regeneration requires us to find a new mode of creating value to replace the mode of capitalist industrial production which has so radically declined in these places. We might think of regeneration in terms of cultural renewal, not culture understood as a means to value creation, but rather as something radically different and incorporating essentially non-monetary values in terms of social norms and ways of being. Actually, the key focus of most regeneration is precisely value: the essence of the approach is summed up by the term monetise. So most urban regeneration schemes across the whole of the post-industrial world are property led. In Marxist terms after Lefbvre, it involves the attempt to extract value from a secondary circuit of accumulation.[9] There is little doubt that much nominal money value has been created by property-led regeneration but this is both subject to very rapid fluctuations in valuation and has been associated with the growth of a flexible employment market predicated on low wages and job insecurity.

Of course, one of the reasons governments and other agents of governance engage in urban regeneration is that there are problems of social order in these urban systems. The normal manifestation of these which draws attention to the issues in the systems takes the form of riots. Riots, unlike revolutionary actions, are best understood as manifestations of anomic dissociation. The UK riots of the early 1990s, including one in North Shields, and the more recent riots of 2011 were classic examples of this kind of disturbance. The phrase 'broken Britain' was used extensively in commentaries on these events. So one objective of regeneration is sometimes considered to be some form of community cohesion which in this context is understood as the re-establishment of a stable moral order. For example, the Denham report (2001) describes this as:

an integrating agenda, that incorporates, but strives to go beyond the concepts of race equality, social inclusion and social mix, the stated aim being to help 'micro-communities to gel or mesh into an integrated whole'. (p. 70)

Some urban programmes have had more precisely defined objectives. The Pathfinder scheme across a range of English cities was meant to regenerate supposedly failing housing markets. This involved the compulsory purchase of housing which certainly was fit under any sanitary regulation as a basis for selective demolition and new build and was bitterly contested by many residents, and in particular working-class owner-occupiers, in the locales affected by it. In principle this was a scheme which should have been relatively easy to evaluate. It should have been possible to establish a baseline description of the state of the local housing markets in Pathfinder areas and to see what it was like after the impact of Pathfinder. The problems in doing this were well described by the Audit Commission:

Housing Market Renewal is a radical approach to addressing the problems of neighbourhoods which have suffered long-standing deprivation. It is also a high risk approach. Five years in and with £2.2 billion committed, low demand is now less severe in pathfinder areas, the gaps between these areas and their surrounding regions have started to close and there have been clear physical improvements in many neighbourhoods. However, the extent to which pathfinders' intervention itself has led to the improvement in the problems of low demand is unclear, and while intervention has improved housing conditions for some, for others it has led to heightened stress. And there is no guarantee that intervening in the housing market in this way will address the causes rather than the symptoms of the problems experienced in these neighbourhoods. (NAO, Housing Market Renewal (HC 20 2007–2008), 9 November 2007, summary para. 15)

This is actually a good example of implicit realist formulation. Problems are actual manifestations of a real generative mechanism which is causal to them.

In 2009 the then Department of Communities and Local Government published a paper outlining *Wider Performance Measures for the Housing Market Renewal Programme* as the basis for a national evaluation of housing market renewal Pathfinders. This outlined the various ways in which particular Pathfinder projects were attempting to describe change in their areas of operation. All the models described were based on the collection of sets of data which were supposed to represent the state of the project area as an urban sub-system. For example, the Manchester/Salford Partnership used the following indicator set across four domains:

Housing:

- Mean house prices
- House prices compared to the Greater Manchester average
- Empty properties
- Turnover
- Demand
- Tenure
- Council tax band

Crime:

- Vehicle crime rate
- Domestic burglary rate
- Distribution of anti-social behaviour orders (ASBOs)

Education:

- Attainment at KS (Key Stage) 2 (age 7–11)
- Attainment at KS3 (age 11–14)
- Attainment at KS4 (age 14–16)

Wordlessness:

- IB/SDA (Invalidity Benefit/Severe Disability Allowance) claimant levels
- IS (Income Support) claimant levels
- JSA (Job Seeker's Allowance) claimant levels
- Wordlessness rate

Something similar was done in all Pathfinder areas in the form of specification of a set of indicators. In complex realist measurement terms this kind of indicator set can be understood as a set of traces of the condition of a system or sub-system. This is a perfectly sensible approach *if* it is combined with comparison, preferably through using the indicator set in the construction of a numerical typology in which the locales of interest can be compared with other locales in the urban systems of which they are parts. Then interventions can be understood as the causes of differences, following MacIver's (1942) key dictum that for every difference there is a cause. Of course, the complication is that causes may not be singular but may be complex configurations, to use the very handy term which comes from qualitative comparative analysis (Ragin, 2000).

The 2009 document was appropriately sanguine about the difficulties of disentangling cause and effect in complex systems:

Impacts can be seen in a narrow sense as achievement of outputs, and in a wider sense as the achievement of outcomes. The latter is a more difficult task as it involves making judgements about the extent to which housing market changes have been caused by pathfinder interventions, or even simply by the existence of the programme, as distinct from other factors – such as changes in the availability or attractiveness of buy-to-let mortgages. One of the initial conclusions of the national evaluation's review of pathfinder objectives was that it would be very difficult to disentangle the impact of HMR programme interventions from other factors, both those related to public policy interventions and those related to the operation of the market or the result of decisions by individuals or organisations in the private sector. (p. 9)

After Pathfinder was prematurely terminated in 2010 as a result both of austerity and public opposition in many locales which attracted national attention, a final overview report, *The Housing Market Renewal Programme in England: Development, Impact and Legacy* (Leather et al., 2012),[10] dealt not so much with outcomes as with outputs defined in terms of dwellings built, improved and demolished. The only comparison made was in terms of house prices.

The real outcome considered was the ratio of house prices in Pathfinder areas to regional median prices where there was some but not much improvement, and of course this could be in large part due to the prices paid for new construction in the Pathfinder areas. That document makes no mention of the wider outcome indicator sets outlined as objectives in

2009, although the actual document identifying these is referenced. In other words, there is an account of what was done and some discussion of housing markets but no assessment of the wider picture.

Pathfinder was very widely criticised at the time of its implementation and through-out its lifetime (Cameron, 2006; Webb, 2010). Cameron in particular noted that there was little actual evidence of 'housing market failure' in most of the locales where Pathfinder operated and that the actual justifications offered for it by those implementing it shifted from market failure to a renewed desire to eliminate areas of 'obsolete housing' even if that housing was in every way fit and actually affordable by low-income households and prices within the areas were actually rising. His account also illustrates the tensions which existed between housing renewal as an intervention and other elements in the broad set of urban programmes which placed much more emphasis on community engagement, in particular elements in the Urban Programme and New Deal for Communities.

Webb's contribution is particularly interesting. He argues precisely about the way in which academics and policy-makers influenced by them were the most powerful actors in developing and implementing the housing renewal agenda. For him their claims to science and objectivity were crucial to the whole process. Webb engages with the language of complexity in his analysis arguing that for those engaged with Pathfinder:

Complexity is made visible by reducing the potential for multiple explanations and competing narratives to emerge. Researchers become empowered to provide the interpretation which frames the dominating narrative. Romantic researchers cannot avoid having to make conclusive decisions about how to approach the mass of potential information before them and how to interpret what their synthesis then yields. In the case of the HMRI [Housing Market Renewal Initiative], these conclusive decisions are made in a politically-charged environment and from a point of view which conceptualizes housing through the existence of sub-regional markets. To a significant extent, this environment determines the nature of the dominating narratives which emerge from their research. (2010: 316)

... A crucial factor sustaining the HMRI network is a belief in the objective 'rightness' of the evidence on which it is based. But the notion that this evidence is objective is a facade. The research narratives are a product of a specific neo-classical societal perspective, interpreted through a romantic approach to complexity and produced in a highly political environment where outputs of a certain kind must be recommended to partner-actors made interested in delivering them. The veil of objectivity shields inherent values and assumptions from democratic scrutiny and displaces opposing narratives. Ultimately, the claim is a modernistic one: that restructuring housing markets will prevent abandonment in the interests of all. (2010: 324)

Certainly those engaged in promoting and enacting Pathfinder believed that they knew what they were doing and they knew because they had expert knowledge. In this respect they very much resembled the 'evangelistic bureaucrats' described by Dennis (1973).

However, in one very important respect they were different. The evangelistic bureaucrats were essentially state employees engaged in housing and planning processes which were a matter of state action. In Sunderland, the locale of Dennis's study, what was happening was determined in large part by the promotion of Washington New Town between the Tyneside and Wearside urban areas at the expense of old inner-city working-class areas. Those pushing this line genuinely believed that the New Town was a better thing for the people affected by the changes they were seeking to improve, whatever those people themselves thought about this change. It is rather easy to understand policy in the early 1970s as operating in the service of North East of England industrial capital and industrial development, but actually this was not necessarily to the detriment of industrial working-class households.

In contrast, Pathfinder did not even pretend very much to be in the interests of those who lived in the areas affected. Rather, it was about the system of urban house prices, a very important component of the secondary circuit of capital accumulation, *and* although some of the key actors were originally academics and many of those who implemented Pathfinder programmes were state employees, the programme was also a playground for private-sector interests, particularly in the form of consultants who were part of the property development system in the UK. In particular, many of the consultancy reports on particular schemes were prepared by private-sector consultants with a chartered surveyor background.

For Webb the lack of community engagement in Pathfinder was primarily because it would get in the way of expertise:

It is clear from these early HMRI documents that the role of community involvement has always been thought of as confined to the delivery phase rather than as having any influence over the nature of how to prioritize, understand and respond to low demand. For those adopting this position, alternative realities, values and priorities represent a danger of distancing delivery from the HMRI rationality, they are a threat to the scientistic nature of the HMRI, and must be risk managed. (2010: 325)

This is certainly part of the story but it was also because real community engagement, and in particular any degree of community control, would get in the way of profit accumulation both through the actual Pathfinder private-sector operations and subsequent housing developments.

The term scientistic is appropriate for Pathfinder's intellectual content, particularly in relation to the proposed but not really enacted frames for evaluation. To call them scientific would have been far too generous. Frankly, the understanding of the urban systems within which Pathfinders were located was primitive and often even descriptively inaccurate – for example, in many Pathfinder areas there was no evidence of housing market failure, no plethora of boarded up and abandoned houses and every sign of a functioning housing system. At a technical level, the approaches suggested for evaluation were simplistic. There was of course nothing wrong with using a set of appropriate indicators to describe the state of Pathfinder areas as sub-systems of the city region urban systems of which they were part. Although additions could have been made, the indicator sets suggested in Department of Communities and Local Government (2009) were a decent start on such a set of indicators as traces. However, it is noteworthy that little if any reference was made to them in the valedictory assessment of Pathfinder presented by Leather et al. (2012) after the abandonment of the programme. The indicators were about the whole state of the sub-systems. Pathfinder was about house prices and that was what was measured and used to indicate outcomes. But of course Pathfinder was operating in what in formal terms were local democratic systems, most of which were controlled by the Labour Party, a party relying on local working-class electors, particularly in the municipal wards which contained Pathfinder programmes. The programmes had to appear to be about the formal interests of those electors, even if – particularly for those whose dwellings were seized through compulsory purchase and who received compensation which was not adequate to pay for an equivalent replacement – they manifestly were not. Social conditions in Pathfinder areas deteriorated through the course of the project's implementation but this cost was never assessed as a cost falling on local residents. Improved cohesion and relative position in the urban system would have been a real gain but that was not the point.

It is enlightening to compare Pathfinder with the 'health inequalities reduction' programme examined by Blackman et al. There was no intrinsic level of conflict of interest in relation to health inequalities. Reducing them was consensual for all politicians, administrators and professional practitioners. Importantly the local strategic partnerships (LSPs) were not told how to reduce health inequalities. They did not have a mechanism presented to them, in marked contrast to Pathfinder where the mechanism was substantially prescribed in terms of a mix of clearance, some improvement and new housing inserted into the Pathfinder areas. All the LSPs were told to do was set in terms of objectives rather than mechanism. They did what they did differently and Blackman et al. were able to use systematic comparison to explore what different configurations of interventions had produced better outcomes. With Pathfinder such comparative exploration would have been pointless at a first-order level because what was done did not differ enough for the generation of a causal account based precisely on differences. At a second – and frankly overwhelming – order level, what Pathfinder did was so embedded in and related to other systems and processes operating in the same places at the same time that disentangling any impact it had, even if its outcomes were to be defined as narrowly as they ultimately were, would have been impossible.

CONCLUSION

To argue for a more nuanced approach to the evaluation of large complex programmes in large complex systems is not to abandon the language of mechanism operating in context. Rather, it is to recognise that in interventions of this kind, where agency, power and competing real interests are all in play, we cannot have either one evaluation or a prior specification of mechanism. Blackman et al. used an abductive approach exploring how differences had been generated by different social actions, the essence of the comparative approach as it has always been employed in the social sciences. With a programme like Pathfinder, identifying the mechanism and the contexts was easy but the issues under evaluation are much more about differential power. Actually local residents were not powerless. Cole (2012) uses the common language through which policy-makers and analysts identify social complexity by referring to wicked issues and goes on to suggest that a weakness of Pathfinder was that partnership was incompatible with its mechanism of demolition. Any move to partnership let in locals as potential actors and although the actual partnership element in Pathfinder in practice was very much as described by Webb (2010), even just the rhetorical approach opened up a political space in which criticisms in a context of austerity scuppered the programme overall. That is a causal account. If the kind of system descriptor indicator sets outlined in 2009 had been used in a fully comparative mode, then we might have had some sort of evaluation of Pathfinder outcomes, but they were not and so we do not know as of now if this programme did anything at all in relation to the kind of social regeneration objectives towards which its outputs were asserted to be means rather than ends in themselves. In reality the outputs became the objective outcomes.

So what I have been trying to do here is to understand how we might sensibly think about large multi-layered and multi-faceted complex social systems where we have long and interwoven chains of causality in relation to the impact of any intervention we make in those systems. Let me assert at once that I am not proposing an abandonment of any attempt to evaluate the impact of such interventions. Rather, I am arguing for very careful thinking about what is going on in the systems and about how we might understand if our intervention has made any difference and if so in what direction. After all, these are certainly 'wicked systems' and, as we know, interventions sometimes, indeed often, make things worse when we play with them. Two things emerge from this discussion. The first is the need to specify outcomes in terms of system state and, above all else, not to confuse outputs which may contribute, in whatever direction, to that system state with outcomes understood as system state. The second is the value of the & as indicated in note 1 in modifying Pawson and Tilley's original formula for CMO to read:

Context & Mechanism(s) => Outcome

There are actually three modifications here: the & to stand for interaction with rather than simple addition to; the s to indicate the possible of a plurality of mechanisms in operation; and the directional => rather than = to indicate the directional path of causation rather than the non-directional character of an = sign in an equation. All this in no way challenges the fundamental values or premises of realist evaluation. It just argues for complex realist thinking as an important adjunct to that programme.

NOTES

1 I prefer to write this as: Context & Mechanism => Outcome with the ampersand standing for interaction and a clear direction rather than the reversibility implied in mathematical convention by the = sign.

2 As Pawson puts it, 'a critical feature of all programmes is that, as they are delivered, they are embedded in social systems. It is through the workings of entire systems of social relationships that any changes in behaviours, events and social conditions are effected' (2006b: 30).

3 North Tyneside, for example, produced reports covering interventions in housing and planning, in welfare rights, in relation to women's work, and around play and youth activities. This CDP more than others had worked through local action groups and community organisation.

4 The CDP teams did not sign up to 'a Marxist theory' in a strict and limited sense. There was then, to a greater degree than now, a massive and largely unproductive set of arguments about what was the right Marxist theorisation of a social order.

5 Cilliers was very firm in asserting that the only ethical way to engage with any complex social system is from within it.

6 See note 1 for my take on this.

7 It might be argued that the logic of abductive reason is more appropriately applied post hoc, i.e. after an intervention, when it is possible to establish just what mechanisms of causation were actually in play. The notion of agreeing on a mechanism of intervention in advance seems contra to the proper insistence on the significance of social action. Qualitative comparative analysis in association with process tracing (see Byrne, 2016) is a good way of doing this.

8 The two most commonly used means for creating numerical taxonomies are variants of cluster analysis, which means that the techniques can be described in mathematical form, and neural net-based methods based on training a neural net algorithm. An interesting illustration of the force of reality on our scientific observations is that these very different approaches often generate remarkably similar typologies.

9 Much of the origins of the contemporary financial and hence economic crisis lie in the layering of a quaternary circuit of accumulation in financial speculation on top of this secondary circuit in the form of mortgages and commercial loans packaged as securities and then subject to the development of derivatives.

10 The Audit Commission did produce a final *Housing Market Renewal – Programme Review* in 2010 which is referenced in Leather et al. (2012) and elsewhere but I have been unable to locate this on government websites.

7

USING REALIST APPROACHES TO EXPLAIN THE COSTS AND COST-EFFECTIVENESS OF PROGRAMMES

Rob Anderson, Rebecca Hardwick, Mark Pearson and Richard Byng

WHAT THIS CHAPTER IS ABOUT

This chapter examines the potential synergy between economic evaluation and realist evaluation. Using a worked example from a realist synthesis of shared care, it illustrates two ways in which realist evaluations might better capture the resource requirements and resource consequences of programmes. These are: (1) articulating the costs of the resources offered by the programme and the cost implications of changes to stakeholder reasoning and behaviour in response to these programmes; and (2) surfacing the ways in which new interventions seek to be more cost-effective than existing care, thus identifying 'cost-effectiveness programme theories'.

How this chapter will help you do realist research

It outlines the methodological and practical challenges of reconciling realist evaluation with economic evaluations and suggests strategies researchers can use to address them. It illustrates how to think about the cost implications of programmes in realist terms. This will enable researchers to theorise and collect relevant data to examine the cost implications of different context, mechanism and outcome configurations which explain how programmes work, for whom and in what circumstances.

A practical tip: a take-home message from the chapter

There is scope for greater synergy between realist evaluation and economic evaluation. However, to be realised it requires that evaluators more explicitly theorise and capture the resource requirements and consequences of hypothesised programme mechanisms, outcomes and contexts.

INTRODUCTION

[The] core hypothesis [of every programme] is always as follows: if we provide these people with these resources it may change these behaviours. (Pawson, 2003: 472)

... greater attention to how, why and for whom interventions work can help strengthen the validity of a study, by specifying the links between inputs and outcomes, and improve generalisability, through a better understanding of the context in which a particular intervention is likely to be cost-effective. (Byford and Sefton, 2003: 99)

Economists compare the value of what goes in (the resources) with what comes out (the outcomes). If you can specify the inputs and outcomes with sufficient clarity to ensure that changes in resource use and benefits can be measured and valued, then it is not necessary to understand how the intervention works. (Shiell et al., 2008: 1282)

The three quotations above succinctly capture the simultaneously contradictory and complementary position that realist evaluators and economic evaluators (often economists) currently find themselves in. On the one hand, both realist evaluators and a growing number of economic evaluators recognise the paramount importance of context and the need to understand *how* and *why* interventions 'work' as the primary strategy for producing generalisable knowledge about whether they are likely to work – or be cost-effective – elsewhere. On the other hand, some economic evaluators, perhaps adhering to purist definitions of efficiency or evaluation, maintain a stance in which the 'black box' of interventions can remain black (closed) – that is, we need not understand *how* the specific combinations of resources, costs and altered outcomes that are both consumed and produced by a programme or intervention are causally interrelated; we just need to estimate and compare what 'goes in' (resources, investment) with what 'comes out' (altered outcomes, benefits). Despite more widespread recognition that economic evaluations are often poorly generalisable, should take better account of the role of context and population variations and should better recognise the conceptual challenges of evaluating complex interventions and become more theory-based, the actual methods of economic evaluation have made very few advances in these directions (Anderson and Shemilt, 2010).

The aim of this chapter is therefore to draw out and make explicit these contradictions and complementarities, these similarities and differences, between realist evaluation and economic evaluation methodology. We first provide an argument that most economic evaluations – at least as they are conducted in health care – are archetypal 'black box' evaluations, with minimal interest in how and why a particular configuration of resources (a programme) changes outcomes, and this has important consequences for the generalisability and usefulness of their findings. It then briefly summarises what health economists see as the main challenges of evaluating complex interventions and some of their suggested solutions. We then use examples of programme theory from a recent realist review of shared care for chronic conditions to illustrate two ways in which realist evaluations might better capture the resource requirements and resource consequences of programmes, and thereby produce better explanations of how they are linked to outcomes (i.e. realist explanations of cost-effectiveness). Finally, we propose some likely main features and practical challenges of 'realist economic evaluation' and argue that explanations of resource use and cost-effectiveness can be integrated within realist evaluations.

Like other theory-driven evaluation methodologies, the starting point for realist evaluation is to identify and express *how* and *why* the outcomes of social interventions or programmes are caused (Pawson, 2013; Pawson and Tilley, 1997, 2004). That is, such approaches tend to be based on expectations and explanations of greater effectiveness than alternative programmes or current service arrangements. Yet, to be successfully adopted and implemented, policy-makers, service managers and practitioners also want interventions and programmes to be affordable and cost-effective (in their locality, with their organisational structure, their staff mix and within their budget, etc.). The established evaluation methods which assess cost-effectiveness or the efficiency of interventions are economic evaluations (Drummond et al., 2005).

The primary question that drives realist evaluations is typically *what works for whom, under what circumstances and why*, and we believe the approach can be just as salient to answering questions about costs and cost-effectiveness (Anderson, 2003; Anderson and Shemilt, 2010). Realist evaluation makes prominent the role of invisible or intangible mechanisms, and we propose that the central realist conception of mechanisms as being both reasoning *and resources* implies that a potential focus on 'economic' mechanisms, contexts and outcomes – and/or a focus on the economic or cost-driving aspects of each of these – is consistent with the overall approach.

While our research experience (and our worked example of shared care) draws on our backgrounds as health services researchers and economic evaluators, we hope that the arguments and illustrations made in this chapter are accessible to evaluators in other sectors. Similarly, we hope that the chapter will be interesting and accessible to both health economists curious about the implications of realist evaluation for enhancing the generalisability of their economic evaluation findings, and to realist and other evaluators interested in extending their evaluations to explain cost differences and cost-effectiveness.

WHAT ARE REALIST EVALUATIONS?

Realist evaluations are a form of theory-driven evaluation that aim to explain how policies, programmes and interventions work, who they work for, in what circumstances and why (Pawson, 2013; Pawson and Tilley, 1997, 2004). Recognising that no one policy, programme or intervention will always work, all the time, for different groups or in different settings, realist approaches seek to explain this pattern of outcomes through building programme theories about how an intervention (policy or programme) is meant to work (often according to programme architects or policy-makers or participants), and then 'test' whether and how this programme theory plays out in the real world using empirical data.

Within realist approaches, policies, programmes and interventions are not just a 'treatment', they are *theories incarnate* (Pawson and Tilley, 1997). The theories are the assumptions, perspectives, hunches and hopes in the policy-maker's head about how the programme should lead to better outcomes, but often this theory is not articulated and remains hidden in the 'black box' of the intervention. Black-box evaluations make no attempt to uncover or elucidate the causal connections between the inputs and tangible components of an intervention and its expected outcomes (Lipsey, 1993). Theory-driven evaluations, in contrast, including realist approaches, seek to 'open up the black box' in order to 'identify the causal processes that theoretically intervene between programme treatment and outcome' (Astbury and Leeuw, 2010). In this way, realist evaluation moves from describing what works to explaining who it works for, in what context and why. Realist evaluation becomes an extended act of theory development and refinement.

Realist evaluation is based on a generative model of causation, that is there are underlying mechanisms which bring about change, that exist independently of us being able to see them, but when circumstances are right, we see their effects, and from those observations we can deduce what might be causing the change.

The methods used in realist evaluation are plural, as the focus is on developing and refining programme theory. Often quantitative data (e.g. from randomised controlled trials or surveys) are useful for describing the pattern of outcomes, while qualitative data are useful for understanding in more detail why something did or did not produce the expected outcomes.

WHAT ARE ECONOMIC EVALUATIONS?

In health care and other public service sectors, economic evaluation is an umbrella term which encompasses a range of different evaluation methods, including cost-benefit analysis and cost-effectiveness analysis (Drummond et al., 2005; Layard and Glaister, 1994). As the hyphenated labels imply, all these evaluation methods involve the simultaneous comparison of both the costs and the value/impacts of the programmes or interventions being evaluated.

Another defining feature is that economic evaluations should involve the comparison of two or more programmes or interventions. They are fundamentally a decision-informing method or option appraisal tool, usually for a particular jurisdiction or policy-maker at a given time. While in lay language it is possible to say something 'is cost-effective', to economists and economic evaluators an intervention or programme can only ever be cost-effective relative to some other intervention or programme, or to doing nothing (although doing or changing nothing usually still has costs and other consequences).

HOW ARE THEY DIFFERENT FROM REALIST EVALUATION?

The approach of realist evaluation and the methods of economic evaluation could not be more different. Economic evaluation has evolved as a highly pragmatic decision-informing form of quantitative summative evaluation. While it is mostly conducted by people with training in economics, it only partially draws upon a few key economic concepts and principles. The basis of economic evaluation methods in mainstream economic theory, in particular in welfare economics, is often claimed but also contested (Drummond and Maguire, 2001; Garber, 1996). Welfare economics is the branch of economic analysis which has developed principles and methods for informing societal (e.g. government) decisions that aim to maximise welfare at a societal level. For a good introductory description of welfare economics and of the ways in which health economic evaluation methods are based on it, see the chapter by Tsuchiya and Williams in Drummond and Maguire (2001). However, for a contrasting view, that economic evaluation actually developed more pragmatically as a technique of applied engineering and decision analysis, Garber has said that 'only recently have economists sought to graft cost-effectiveness analysis to theoretical roots in welfare economics' (1996: 26).

We have compared the main features of realist evaluation and economic evaluation in Table 7.1. Looking at these many differences, it is unsurprising that any combined or even complementary use of the two approaches has only rarely occurred.

TABLE 7.1 Economic and realist evaluation compared

	Economic evaluation	Realist evaluation
Ontology and theoretical basis	Theoretical foundation is ostensibly welfare economics. In practice, more pragmatic, and makes selective use of core economic concepts (e.g. cost-benefit principle, opportunity cost, marginal analysis). Ontology is not explicit; implicitly positivist and empiricist	Ontology: realism:* reality is both observable and external, and how it is interpreted. The programme theories relevant to a programme may be either substantive social science theory or simply the ideas and rationales of those providing or participating in the programme
Conception of causality	Not generally known or discussed (but, implicitly, successionist causation: i.e. A causes B; seeking empirical regularities that intervention A is or is not cost-effective)	Generative notion of causation: outcomes are contingent on a range of underlying mechanisms, occur at different levels of reality, and will only ever manifest as outcome patterns
Research aim	To produce estimates both of costs and effectiveness in a specific context (e.g. alongside a specific effectiveness study) or a particular decision-making jurisdiction (model-based economic evaluation)	To develop and refine programme theories (i.e. potential explanations) about how and why interventions work (i.e. produce beneficial outcomes), including how and why they work differently in different contexts
Policy aim	To inform specific decisions among a defined number of alternatives	To inform decision-makers about the way that the intervention produces its effects, and what modifies or influences that effectiveness
Type of data included/ collected	Quantitative (especially: resource use, unit costs, final (e.g. health) outcomes). Secondary research data only as part of decision modelling	Quantitative and qualitative depending on the specific knowledge gaps. Often quantitative to establish the outcome pattern, and qualitative to determine how and why this pattern occurs. Secondary research (e.g. realist reviews) may complement primary research (e.g. for theory development stage)

	Economic evaluation	Realist evaluation
Preferred study design?	*Either:* Experimental evaluation (e.g. randomised controlled trial) *Or:* Decision analytic (simulation) modelling, synthesising assumptions and cost and effectiveness evidence from variety of sources	Pluralist – no strongly preferred method or design (research question dependent) (although for some realist researchers randomised experimental methods are seen as incompatible with the realist conception of causation and mode of explanation)
Generalisability/ transferability?	Emphasis on transferability of results (e.g. similar cost-effectiveness) contingent upon key features of context (country, patient group)	Generalisation is through progressively applying the programme theory to other contexts. Realist approaches recognise that the explanations developed from a realist evaluation are always open to further development and refinement.

*Originally, in Pawson and Tilley (1997: Ch. 3), the basis of realist evaluation was described as scientific realism. In the preface of his 2013 book, Ray Pawson explains how his terminology has evolved to be 'some type of realism', while others may see realist evaluation as more closely aligned to, for example, critical realism.

Measurement vs explanation/theory-building

Perhaps the most notable difference between economic evaluation and realist approaches to evaluation is that realist approaches aim to build generalisable causal explanations of particular programmes, policies or services, whereas economic evaluations essentially aim to measure or estimate the cost-effectiveness of introducing a particular programme. In the context of a trial-based economic evaluation, this difference is most marked. The 'economic evaluation component' of a randomised trial will tend to only (a) collect data on the types and amounts of resource use (e.g. staff time, equipment, medicines, additional training) involved in providing the different interventions, and (b) collect data on any altered resource use associated with changed outcomes (e.g. patients with improved health should need less medication and fewer hospital or primary care visits). This is why some health economists have criticised current methods of economic evaluation as unhelpfully intervention-focused and outcomes-driven, often to the exclusion of considerations of context (Birch, 2002; Birch and Gafni, 2003).

Creating localised vs generalisable knowledge

There is a key difference between the goals and purpose of economic evaluation and realist evaluation. Realist evaluation seeks to produce generalisable knowledge about how context shapes the causal mechanisms through which a programme produces its outcomes. In contrast, model-based economic evaluations are always based on informing a well-specified policy choice in a given locality, country or other jurisdiction. Similarly, trial-based economic evaluations only yield a cost-effectiveness estimate in relation to the types of patients, interventions and settings included in that study (Sculpher et al., 2006). The generalisability of the findings of economic evaluations is known to be highly constrained by a wide range of contextual and other factors, and not least because resources cost different amounts in different places and times, and because the opportunity cost of particular resources will vary according to the decision context (and therefore the alternative potential use of those resources) (Anderson, 2010; Sculpher et al., 2004).

In summary, economic evaluations, as currently designed and conducted, are largely atheoretical exercises in measuring or estimating the inputs (resources and costs) and outcomes (effectiveness) of interventions and their comparators (Anderson, 2010; Birch, 2002; Lessard, 2007; Sculpher et al., 2004). While their full description of interventions and comparators is improving, they are often – in the health field at least – experimental and dominantly positivist in approach; they can easily be characterised as so-called 'black-box' evaluations. That is, very few have any definite interest – or therefore any planned data collection – in the intervening causal mechanisms or relevant contexts that are thought to produce the expected improvements in outcomes or generate changes in resource use – *or link them to each other*. Thus, where there are several economic evaluations of 'the same' complex intervention or prevention programme, there is usually neither a clear result that one programme is consistently the most cost-effective in all contexts, nor any adequate evidence that can explain how and why the cost-effectiveness of intervention X or programme Y varies from context to context. This is what Pawson and Tilley referred to as 'the Martinson problem' – that nothing works (or is cost-effective) consistently – writ large (Pawson and Tilley, 1997: 30). A number of respected and experienced health economists share these views about the explanatory weaknesses of conventional economic evaluation methods, and also point to the need for more overtly explanatory, context-sensitive, theory-driven approaches as the likely solution (Birch, 2002; Birch and Gafni, 2003; Coast et al., 2000; Drummond, 2010).

However, some economic evaluations are based on quite elaborate simulation models of long-term costs and outcomes of alternatives (decision models or decision analytic models). While decision model-based economic evaluations are an apparent exception to the criticism that economic evaluations are 'black-box' and atheoretical (because such simulation modelling at least provides an explicit framework of the supposed main causal pathways and key trade-offs involved in a particular policy choice), they are not generally recognised as a form of theory development or theory-testing. This is in part because relations within model-based economic evaluations are mathematical expressions of assumed relationships rather than causal propositions that could be discretely tested. Until the development of all decision models is based on more comprehensive and distinct processes of theory development, and perhaps can accommodate causal connections in non-mathematical ways and better capture the influence of contexts, then it seems to us they will only ever be a partial reflection of the theory-driven approach of realist evaluation.

Unsurprisingly, those health economists who have begun to confront the explanatory limitations of current methods of cost-effectiveness analysis, are those who have experience of conducting economic evaluations of complex interventions (such as models of service delivery, health policies or public health programmes). We summarise the various challenges identified by health economists in evaluating complex health interventions in Box 7.1.

BOX 7.1

Conceptual challenges:

- Inevitability of multiple outcomes, including greater importance of some intermediate outcomes[a] or non-health benefits.[c] Some important outcomes may not be expected or known at the beginning of an evaluation or may occur at the system rather than individual level.[e]
- Difficulty attributing outcomes to interventions and/or transferring findings to other settings or populations with confidence.[d]
- Greater difficulty in defining appropriate alternatives for comparison (in particular, the issue of whether new services should be evaluated as alternatives to or additional to existing service arrangements).[a]
- Greater importance of issues surrounding the scale of services. For example, in order for some types of community-based services to 'become' cost-effective, they may have to handle enough patients for the alternative hospital service to be downsized.[b]

Practical challenges:

- The use of established (e.g. clinical) outcome measures often not feasible (perhaps because important outcomes such as equity or accessibility can only be captured at the group or whole service level).[a, d]
- Incomplete identification of relevant costs, e.g. omission of capital costs.[a]
- Timing of evaluation of (newly introduced) services or programmes.[b] Evaluation too early and service operating under full capacity may underestimate effectiveness. Conversely, new or pilot projects may have higher levels of funding or staff enthusiasm/champions (e.g. investing extra time freely).[b]
- Interventions in complex systems may only create step-changes in outcomes after long periods.[e]
- The cost of whole services or public health programmes often falls on different budgets. Cost savings in one area cannot always easily be reinvested elsewhere.[d]

Key to sources: a – Godber et al. (1997); b – Coast et al. (2000); c – Payne et al. (2013); d – Weatherly et al. (2009); e – Shiell et al. (2008).

In summary, most health economists have seen the challenges of evaluating complex interventions as ones which can mainly be tackled by either more comprehensive data collection or more sophisticated decision modelling or statistical techniques (Payne et al., 2013; Payne and Thompson, 2015; Sculpher, 2001). A few others, however, have acknowledged that the lack of conclusiveness and poor usefulness of economic evaluations is more deeply rooted in a dominantly positivist or clinical-epidemiological conception of how interventions generate outcomes, an approach which poorly recognises context, complexity or the active role of programme participants in producing outcomes (Birch, 2002; Byford and Sefton, 2003; Coast et al., 2000; Shiell et al., 2008). When health economists have suggested that greater use of theory might be part of the solution, they have typically advocated using complex systems theory in a broad sense rather than expanding the use of programme theory of the specific intervention type being evaluated (Lessard, 2007; Shiell et al., 2008).

WHAT WOULD MORE EXPLANATORY ECONOMIC EVALUATION LOOK LIKE?

The following proposal for a more theory-driven approach to economic evaluation is based on discussions and presentations about this idea over the past five years, and also on the experiences of conducting a realist review of a complex intervention – shared care for chronic conditions – conducted by the present authors. In some ways it extends to empirical evaluation some of the realist-inspired ideas about conducting reviews of economic evidence suggested earlier. Our experiences suggest two main extensions to existing guidance on the design and conduct of realist evaluations.

First, we propose that the conception of mechanisms within realist evaluation, as a combination of both the *changed resources* offered and the *participant's reasoning/responses* to those resources, be more fully and consistently articulated. This is because all mechanisms are to some extent economic (in the sense that they entail altered resources) but not all of these changes in resources have salient or substantial economic consequences (i.e. not all will involve opportunity costs or require monetary investment). This first extension to the approach of realist evaluation is an endorsement of Dalkin et al.'s recent call to more fully disaggregate resources and reasoning when uncovering programme mechanisms (Dalkin et al., 2015), and that a realist evaluation that does this should go some way towards yielding explanations of cost and cost-effectiveness as well as effectiveness.

The notion that altered or new resources are an integral element of programme theory is borne out by the quotation from Ray Pawson at the beginning of this chapter. Also, importantly for a form of enquiry which is based on the often tricky business of distinguishing mechanisms from contexts, precisely identifying the mechanisms of action of a programme and the associated resources required (or that are drawn in) to foster change in a given setting can help define what the intervention or programme *actually is*. This is where some economic evaluators are already working in parallel ways to realist evaluators: by comprehensively tracing not just what tangible or purchased resources are required for the different programme components to exist, but also identifying (and valuing) what pre-existing and intangible resources are *contributed from the programme's setting* – for example, the time and personal knowledge of informal carers. In other words, because a full assessment of what resources are required in order for a programme to exist and work involves detailed tracking of who spends time doing what with whom, in what setting, etc., the detailed costing of a programme will often drive a clearer specification and understanding of all the procedures, protocols and people that constitute the programme. This process of investigating and enumerating the resources involved in a programme will not directly suggest all the relevant mechanisms of a programme, but it does provide another useful focus for theory generation. It forces consideration of the question: What do these resources *do*? Or, what do these resources offer to different participants, and how do we think they alter reasoning or behaviours?

Conversely, the realist evaluator's focus on working back from intended or expected outcomes to identify the underlying causal mechanisms can also help economic evaluators. This focus may help identify those resources which – although apparently part of the programme – actually play no part in fostering the mechanisms by which outcomes are believed to be produced. Such discoveries could play a key part in redesigning more cost-effective programmes. For example, to preview our main example of shared care, if realist evaluations reveal that the improved care outcomes of shared care mainly arise from the improved inter-professional relations and trust between primary care generalists and disease specialists/consultants in a region, and that this mainly arises through the initial social process of developing and agreeing a shared care protocol (rather than use of the protocol per se), then it may be that the enhanced electronic communications component of some shared care models is effectively redundant (and therefore an inefficient use of resources).

In summary, most 'inputs' to programmes have resource requirements, and even for intangible ones (like carer time or professional experience and competence) it is sometimes possible to estimate and value them. Also, while Pawson and others have emphasised the invisibility of mechanisms in realist explanations (i.e. you cannot directly observe changes in people's reasoning), many mechanisms have resource implications or associations (Pawson, 2013). For example, the mechanism of patient-centred decision-making between practitioners, patients and carers in the context of intermediate care probably requires longer care planning meetings, perhaps involving more people (Pearson et al., 2015). There are also those situations where the intended mechanism of action is inherently economic – for example, the provision of discounted or free nicotine patches, free domestic smoke alarms or free bicycles in city centres. These interventions are economic in the sense that if someone is receiving or consuming free, new products then someone is paying (and there are therefore benefits foregone). And how consumers and manufacturers respond to discounts or to increased taxation on harmful products (tobacco, alcohol) may be predicted by economic theories.

Finally, programme outcomes, especially those that are genuinely altering people's well-being, functioning or social situation, will inevitably lead to increased or reduced use of services, carer time, reoffending, drug use, etc. So it seems likely that all three key elements of realist theory-building – contexts, mechanisms and outcomes – might separately lead to associated changes in resource use which we could better capture in our analyses.

Second, we propose that there may sometimes be value in identifying underlying 'cost-effectiveness'-specific programme theories. By this we mean programme theories which explicitly seek to explain cost-effectiveness or altered costs. This will often be the case when, for example, a new model of care delivery (like shared care) is not necessarily believed to be *more effective* than current care, but rather is advocated because it is expected to be less costly while *not affecting effectiveness or safety etc*. In these situations, programme or service change designers will often express a number of ways in which they expect the new programme or service to be less costly or more efficient. These can often be captured as more generic programme theories, which we illustrate with the examples in the following section.

PROGRAMME THEORIES OF COST-EFFECTIVENESS – A WORKED EXAMPLE

To illustrate the feasibility and value of developing cost-effectiveness-specific programme theories, we present selected findings from a recent realist review of the cost and cost-effectiveness of shared care we have conducted (Hardwick et al., 2013). While this was not a prospective realist evaluation of shared care, it demonstrates our main proposal that: (a) discrete programme theories of cost-effectiveness can be identified in relation to a particular type of programme or health service; (b) these can sometimes be expressed in terms of mechanism-context-outcome configurations; and (c) it is possible to identify what outcomes, contexts or changes would need to be assessed in order to prospectively evaluate how and why a new shared care programme is or is not cost-effective.

Shared care is a way to manage the care of people in relation to a particular health condition, when the level of severity and/or stability of their condition means that optimal care requires the planned involvement of both primary care and specialist care professionals and services (Hickman et al., 1994; Smith et al., 2007). It has been most used for patients with long-term chronic conditions such as asthma, diabetes, arthritis, high blood pressure and depression. A shared care programme will typically comprise the following components:

1. An agreed shared care protocol for the defined group of patients (which defines: the roles and responsibilities of primary care (e.g. GP) and disease specialist care professionals, and of patients and carers; the frequency and nature of monitoring or follow-up; and the rules or criteria for referral to different services or professionals).

2. Enhanced information exchange between disease specialists and generalists/primary care health professionals (computerised, paper or telephone).
3. Care coordination (computer systems and/or dedicated person).
4. Extra education and/or training (e.g. for GPs in the specific chronic disease, or patients in self-care).

This can be summarised graphically as a flow diagram – including some speculative causal pathways between the core components of shared care and potential intervening 'mechanisms' which link the components to expectations of optimal care for a given patient group (Figure 7.1).

To identify programme theories of the effectiveness and cost-effectiveness of shared care, we conducted a review of several seminal descriptions of shared care and other descriptive and evaluation studies of actual examples of shared care. Typically, claims and assertions about how and why shared care was expected to be more effective or more cost-effective than usual care were given in the introduction or discussion sections of empirical evaluation studies. Two main programme theories of the effectiveness of shared care were identified: the systematisation of high-quality *care processes* and the fostering of positive and reciprocal *working relationships*. A three-part programme theory relating to expected efficiency gains due to introducing shared care (i.e. cost-effectiveness) was expressed as follows:

For defined types of patient, if care is shared in a systematic way between particular organisations or clinicians working in primary (generalist) and secondary (disease specialist) care, then there are efficiency gains within the health system due to:

a   shifting care to less costly settings and/or less expensive practitioners
b   better tailoring of resources to need
c   enhancing use of patient and carer resources (and thereby substituting for formally provided care services).

These programme theories of the cost-effectiveness of shared care could therefore be labelled as 'shifting' (to less expensive care settings), 'tailoring' (to lowest needed or optimally cost-effective level of care) and 'substitution' (to care which is effectively 'free of charge' to the health system).

These three programme theories of shared care can be expressed graphically, as shown in Figures 7.2 to 7.4. Each graph shows total clinical contact minutes per year (i.e. staff resource consumption) against the severity of a patient's chronic disease (running from high severity at graph origin to lower severity – and where severity is really shorthand for any aspects of a patient's condition that justify more specialist input). The absolute values are not meant to be accurate but merely to illustrate some interrelationships.

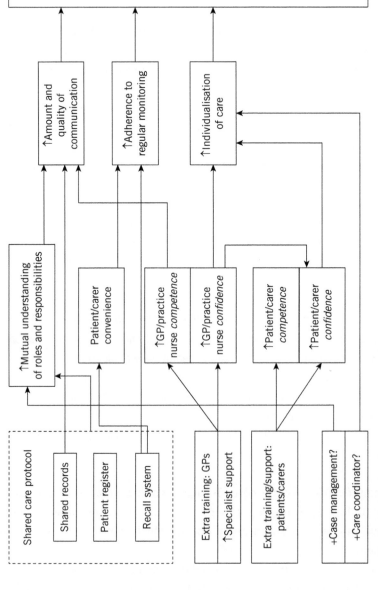

FIGURE 7.1 Provisional 'causal map' of shared care components, mechanisms and outcomes

Under *usual care* (Figure 7.2), there is typically a positive association between disease severity and the amount of clinical contact time a patient receives – on average, the more severe or unstable a patient's condition, the more clinical contact time they should receive. Also, above a particular threshold level of severity it is assumed the patient's clinical care for this chronic condition would shift from being wholly managed in primary care to being wholly managed in secondary/specialist care (e.g. regular hospital outpatient/ambulatory care visits to a consultant diabetologist, respiratory physician or psychiatrist). This diagram also assumes that being wholly under specialist clinical care would entail more clinical contact minutes during a typical year (perhaps because routine GP or practice nurse appointments are usually shorter than the typical hospital specialist outpatient appointment, and/or because more severe or unstable patients may require more frequent follow-up).

With the programme theory of *shifted* care, we theorised that there is a group of patients perhaps with moderately severe disease who under usual care would be cared for only by disease specialists, but for whom this level of wholly specialised care is assumed to be unnecessary. Instead, the implicit assumption of shared care is that for these patients optimal care should involve mainly primary care clinical visits; but, with the care protocols, enhanced information exchange and care coordination that would allow less frequent but more necessary contact with disease specialists. These less frequent contacts with specialists might be either planned (e.g. following initial referral/diagnosis and for initial treatment planning, or at regular review intervals) or unscheduled instances where symptoms change or treatment needs reviewing for other reasons (e.g. referred 'back' to the specialists according to criteria in the shared care protocol). In turn, if specialist appointments are provided by more highly paid clinicians (e.g. hospital consultants) or in more expensive settings (e.g. hospitals) than GPs/nurses working in primary care, then this shift in the combination of resources used would lead to cost-savings (at least on the basis of changes in staff mix/clinical care setting, and ignoring any additional costs of introducing and supporting shared care). So assumptions about how cost differences between programmes arise are often inextricably linked with assumptions about how programmes are thought to be more effective.

The programme theory of shifted care also highlights the importance of context to understanding whether shared care will be more costly or less costly than usual care in different situations. At the level of the health system, the salary gap (if any) between hospital-based disease specialists and primary care doctors will play a part in determining the actual cost difference associated with a shift in appointment patterns between these two types of provider. However, it will also depend on the actual staff mix delivering care – it may be that in some hospital outpatient settings the majority of care for certain diseases is nurse-led or conducted by junior doctors rather than more highly paid doctors, and this may then make hospital outpatient appointments cheaper than primary care appointments. Another contextual factor is the 'scale' of the disease-specific knowledge and experience gap between hospital specialists in a specific disease and GPs in primary care; the bigger the gap, the more additional GP training, more protocols and more avenues of specialist advice provision will need to be part of the shared care package. So, the shared care of survivors of childhood cancer (still a relatively small patient group for GPs) might require more resources and more regular access to specialist care than shared care for asthma or diabetes (for which a great amount of clinical expertise and experience already exists in primary care). And finally, of course, usual care itself will almost certainly vary and in some cases may already involve relatively high levels of communication, good levels of trust and regular sharing of patient data between hospital specialists and primary care. In these situations the anticipated benefits of shared care (and the associated cost-savings) may be minimal.

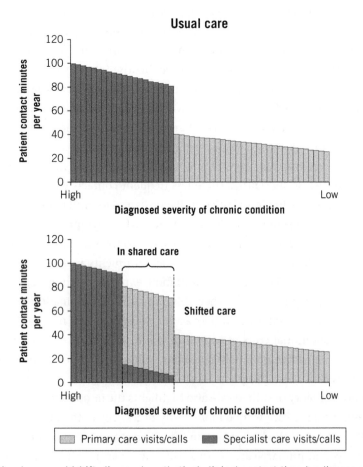

FIGURE 7.2 Usual care and 'shifted' care: hypothetical clinical contact time by disease severity

The programme theory of shifted care represents a crude service-level form of tailoring of care to need. It contains the basic idea that there is probably a group of patients for whom receiving primary care only would lead to 'under-met' need, while wholly specialist care for their chronic condition would be 'over-met' need, therefore a mix of specialist and primary care generalist input would be optimal. However, shared care may be a more cost-effective use of resources by tailoring care in two other, more specific ways. Firstly, shared care may *tailor care* to need by better matching the specific mix of specialist and primary care input, according to the different needs of individual patients, for example in relation to the particular level of severity or stability of their disease. In this way, shared care may provide anything between most clinical care being provided by disease specialists to most care being provided by the GP or other primary care practitioners. Secondly, as well as tailoring care to variations in need *across individuals* in relation to their disease severity/stability, shared care may also provide more cost-effective care by more flexibly tailoring the level of specialist care input according to variations *over time* in the same patient. Some chronic conditions, for example some mental health conditions, may require sudden step-changes in the level of specialist appointments or the level of specialist input to primary care consultations in response to sudden deteriorations in health (van Straten et al., 2015).

Note that the graph depicting tailored care (Figure 7.3) only shows the staff time resource aspects of this possible mechanism. In the longer term, the cost-effectiveness of tailoring also depends on the degree to which greater input from disease specialists actually leads to more effective treatment monitoring and decisions in relating to changing or complex clinical needs.

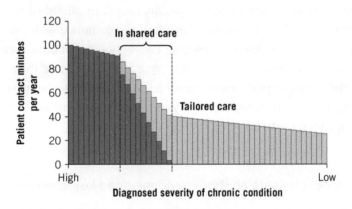

FIGURE 7.3 'Tailored care': clinical contact time by disease severity

Our third programme theory to explain the potential efficiency gains of shared care asserts that greater self-care and self-monitoring by patients would reduce the need for formal care and monitoring appointments from a health professional (i.e. *substitution*). If such resource substitution takes place and the evaluation aims to assess costs to the health or public sector, then there would be directly reduced costs of care services. This shows the potential savings due to increased self-care in addition to those of shifted care. It also shows such substitution as only affecting those patients under shared care, but of course there might be 'spillover effects', if some of the extra support and improved skills for self-care and home monitoring are given to all patients under the care of the same GPs or primary care practices.

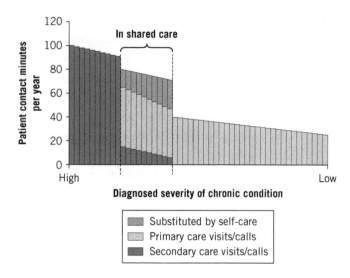

FIGURE 7.4 'Substituted care': clinical contact time by disease severity

Refining the theories of cost-effectiveness

In this section we describe what evidence we discovered in published economic evaluations of shared care in relation to two of these three programme theories: care shifting and care tailoring. While this evidence comes from conventional economic evaluations which were not explicitly theory-driven or realist in approach, we believe these worked examples usefully illustrate how prospective studies could generate relevant data to refine such programme theories in a particular health systems setting and patient group, and with a particular specification of shared care.

Cost-effectiveness by care shifting – evidence and key contexts

The shifting of care to less costly care professionals or to less costly clinical settings might occur in two main ways within shared care. Firstly, many shared care protocols stipulate a recommended frequency of routine follow-up tests and visits to monitor a patient's health and, where necessary, adjust treatment. This typically involved nearly all follow-up appointments in primary care with a GP or practice nurse rather than regular follow-up with a hospital-based specialist. So, for example, in a cost-effectiveness analysis of shared care for people with hepatitis C in Queensland, Australia, the usual specialist-based follow-up required 15 hospital appointments over a period of a year (Anderson and Haas, 2001). Under shared care, there were still 15 follow-up visits scheduled, but nine of them would be with the patient's GP. If attendance at appointments is beneficial and GP appointments are considerably cheaper than hospital specialist appointments (as is often the case), then such savings are effectively 'hard-wired' into the shared care protocol.

Note the possible intermediate mechanism of adherence to attending appointments, which may modify the cost differences due to shifting care or increase effectiveness if greater follow-up appointment adherence leads to more effective monitoring and treatment. In the evaluation of shared care in Queensland, interview evidence strongly suggested that follow-up by more geographically local (and possibly better known or trusted) GPs had led to substantially higher levels of follow-up and adherence to treatment. Such regular follow-up was especially critical given the potential psychiatric side-effects of the drugs being taken by the patients with hepatitis C.

The cost-effectiveness studies of shared care also suggested another extension of the underlying programme theory of shifting care, which involves a shift in the balance of planned versus unplanned care. As part of the planned shift to primary care appointments, other supporting aspects of shared care such as a patient register and recall system often increase planned attendance for monitoring and follow-up overall. This should, in theory, lead to better monitoring and any necessary treatment changes, and therefore a better managed condition. This in turn can lead to fewer or less severe acute episodes (e.g. asthma attacks, hypoglycaemic episodes, episodes of depression) and an associated reduction in unplanned or urgent primary care appointments or hospital appointments. The hypothetical causal chain of this more specific version of the care-shifting programme theory is shown in Figure 7.5 below.

But does the evidence from economic evaluations support this theory? For the economic evaluations of shared care in the UK in the 1990s, this seemed to be the case. While there was no evidence relating to all of these steps in all studies (most did not distinguish planned from unplanned visits), where the comparator was usual hospital care then with shared care, primary care visits increased while specialist appointments decreased (see bar charts in Figure 7.5).

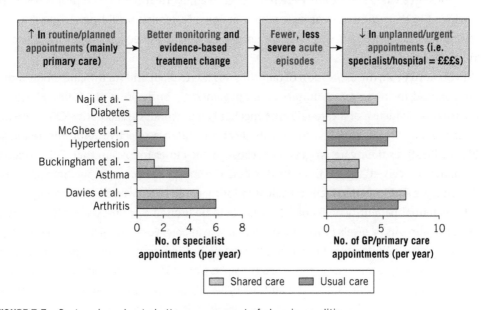

FIGURE 7.5   Cost-savings due to better management of chronic conditions

These lower numbers of specialist or emergency care appointments, probably through better planned monitoring and treatment changes, might lead to considerable cost-savings, especially if any urgent treatment for acute episodes also usually occurred in hospital or with specialists. But the differences between the cost of a specialist appointment in hospital and a GP appointment were not always large, so this might reduce the cost-savings associated with these shifts in appointment patterns.

Sometimes, however, shared care represented a shift towards *more* rather than *less* disease specialist involvement; in these cases shared care was meant to provide higher access to specialists for patients from primary care and thereby greater costs. This was often the case with shared care for depression in the United States (often called 'collaborative care'), where the comparator in evaluations was typically the usual primary physician care. Unsurprisingly, this was associated with higher costs – albeit often with improved outcomes (between 30 per cent higher and double the cost of usual care in such studies (Pyne et al., 2010; Rost et al., 2005; von Korff et al., 1998)). Thus, in the context of previously *under-met* need for disease specialist care, shared care was often cost-increasing.

Cost-effectiveness by tailoring care – evidence and key contexts

In two of the evaluations of shared care for mental health in the United States, better tailoring of care to needs was an explicit aim of shared care (Rost et al., 2005; von Korff et al., 1998). In Rost et al. this was expressed more as what could be called 'temporal tailoring'; more regular scheduled contact with patients was primarily to encourage 'continued treatment adherence when symptoms were resolving, to adjust treatment if symptoms were not resolving, and to terminate treatment which patients in remission did not require' (p. 8). These studies suggested this was especially important for the effective treatment of people with depression.

In von Korff et al., the expression of tailoring was less explicit and (in the care model aims) more couched in the terms of 'improved management' (von Korff et al., 1998). However, there was also evidence of a care-tailoring mechanism at work: 'Collaborative Care patients were more likely to be switched to new medications, often a selective serotonin reuptake inhibitor [SSRI], as their care progressed because of the closer follow-up that Collaborative Care patients received' (p. 145). So, in this case (assuming the previous medications were older, cheaper and less effective than SSRIs) tailoring could be viewed as 'tailoring up'.

The potential patient benefits of tailoring could be limited or non-existent if the actual range of treatments or levels of treatment were not available. For example, in the Pyne et al. study, treatment tailoring was limited to altering medication, without any opportunities for offering psychological or counselling-based therapies (for which there are known patient preferences). Also, in the same study, the authors believed that the effectiveness of the stepped collaborative care model was limited because it did not tackle common co-morbidities of depression (such as pain, anxiety and substance abuse) (Pyne et al., 2010: 819).

In some studies there was some data on the measures of variance (e.g. standard error/deviation) for numbers of visits or other units of service use. Wider variances might provide indirect support that shared care is leading to more tailoring – that is, perhaps under shared care the same patient group shows wider variation in their service usage rates (implying that either some are getting more or some are getting less than under usual alternative care). Other, more direct, evidence of tailoring would come from documenting the frequency of treatment changes, or changes in the pattern of follow-up monitoring. Whether driven by clinical considerations or by patient preferences, better tailoring to need seems to be a well-recognised mechanism of many models of health care improvement. However, better tailoring of care to need can only, by definition, be as cost-effective as the specific treatments and monitoring strategies that people get at each 'level' of care provided.

CONCLUSION

Our experience from conducting our systematic review of the cost-effectiveness of shared care suggests two complementary approaches for using the logic of realist enquiry to explain differences in costs and cost-effectiveness between different models of care, programmes or other complex interventions. First, we have shown that for some types of programme or service change, it is possible to specify cost-effectiveness-specific programme theories. In fact, some of these programme theories of cost-effectiveness – for example, better tailoring of care to need – are so closely linked to notions of efficiency that it could be argued they are more like Pawson's notion of transferrable 'conceptual platforms', and so they might be applicable to explaining the cost-effectiveness of a wide range of programmes or service changes (Pawson, 2013).

As well as being able to specify such cost-effectiveness-specific theories for shared care, we have shown that it is possible to express some of them in terms of mechanisms, relevant contexts and particular outcomes (i.e. the basic components of realist explanation-building). A possible exception to this might be when care (e.g. follow-up appointments) is directly shifted to less costly settings or practitioners, or when some component of an intervention (e.g. access to a specialised drug) is both very costly and unique to the new intervention. Arguably, to explain the resulting cost-difference due to 'shifted care' or similar situations requires not so much theory as basic arithmetic. However, we believe such deterministic, linear 'hard-wiring' of cost-differences will not be a feature of all complex interventions, and many other determinants of resource use will be more multi-level, variable, behaviour-dependent and context-sensitive. They will therefore require a more realist logic of enquiry to elucidate them. As well as our example, others have begun to use cost-effectiveness-specific programme theories within realist reviews (Charles et al., 2013; Charles, 2014) or to use realist evaluation to explain 'economic interventions', such as policies regarding fees to access care (Marchal et al., 2013a).

The second approach, which could complement the development and refinement of cost-effectiveness-specific programme theories, involves raising the recognition that all three of the main components of realist explanations – contexts, mechanisms and outcomes – can either *require* additional resources in order to exist or *impact* on resource use. This endorses and extends Dalkin et al.'s recent argument that the realist notion of mechanism should more clearly disaggregate the mechanism reasoning and mechanism resources (Dalkin et al., 2015). It also underlines the importance of economic evaluators not just becoming more aware of the importance of context in a general sense, but in the more specific ways in which particular contexts influence different mechanisms within programmes and may influence either cost-differences or effectiveness differences (or both together). Where realist evaluators may need to learn more is how resources consumed in different decision contexts or at different overall volume affect whether and how much there is actually an opportunity cost for those resources.

Considering these suggested approaches together, we do not suggest a new sub-genre of 'realist economic evaluation'. This would, we believe, unhelpfully and artificially separate evaluations and explanations of effectiveness from cost-effectiveness (including explanations of changing patterns of resource use). Our main conclusion is that these goals will always be inextricably linked and are therefore best evaluated together (cost-effectiveness after all includes effectiveness). In a way, the common realist expression of what a programme theory is (reasoning *and resources* – as captured by the Pawson quotation at the beginning of this chapter) already firmly acknowledges this. Instead, we think that evaluations could more explicitly theorise and capture the resource requirements and consequences of hypothesised programme mechanisms, outcomes and contexts. Such process evaluations are now increasingly encouraged and funded alongside effectiveness evaluations of complex interventions, including greater endorsement that they should be theory-driven, at least in the UK (Moore et al., 2015).

Another conclusion from our review and analysis, is that the cost-effectiveness of generic models of care like shared care can only be as cost-effective as the underlying treatments and disease-monitoring strategies around which their protocols are built. If 'stepping up' a patient with depression to a stronger and more expensive drug and more frequent monitoring by psychiatric specialists does not reflect additional effectiveness of that new treatment and better management of side effects through closer monitoring, then in this case the cost-effectiveness of sharing care will be undermined. Unfortunately, in different chronic disease areas even knowledge about the relative cost-effectiveness of existing treatments is often poor.

For existing realist evaluators, this is neither rocket science nor hard-core economics; for example, the hypothetical 'mechanism' of more experienced practitioners making quicker yet more effective treatment decisions will have the expected resource consequence of shorter clinical encounters, but at the expense of higher pay rates per minute as the additional (or marginal) 'cost' of applying this greater clinical experience. These things can often be measured, or at least observed at some level. Investigating the contexts in which experienced practitioners really do add value in this way might entail an exploration of, for example, the types of patients that benefit most and why, practitioner personality traits or team cultures supportive of less risk-averse practice. Encouragingly for realist researchers, insights about resources and what drives the cost of a particular programme do not reside solely in 'economic studies'; so reviews that aim to explain cost-effectiveness may gain highly relevant insights about resource use from effectiveness studies or process evaluations (Anderson, 2010; Anderson and Shemilt, 2010). The apparent belief that valid evidence about costs and cost-effectiveness only comes from one class of study design (that is primarily economic evaluations) is an unfortunate side effect of the close alignment of systematic review methodology with clinical epidemiology, where a rigid, almost unidimensional hierarchy of study design validity still reigns.

Other aspects of complex health and social interventions do raise additional quite specific challenges for understanding resource use and economic evaluation. Issues of scale affect both effectiveness and costs. Varying decision contexts (including different budget constraints) also mean that the same services or programmes can have quite different opportunity costs in different places and populations. Furthermore, people in different countries and cultures may value health, non-health and equity outcomes differently (especially where the primary outcome may be information rather than health or other, more measurable outcomes).

Progress in this area of evaluation more fundamentally needs a larger community of economic evaluators and economists willing to learn about and try out realist approaches in their evaluative studies. Equally, progress also needs more realist evaluators who are both undaunted by the jargon of economic evaluation methods and keen to fully theorise the role resources play in intervention mechanisms, contexts and outcomes. Just as realist evaluators come to grasp the bold assertion from Ray Pawson that all programmes 'are theories incarnate', perhaps they also need to recognise more fully that all programmes are *resources*, intentionally reconfigured in order to foster and catalyse mechanisms that 'infiltrate the subjects' reasoning' (Pawson, 2013: 128).

While our insights in this chapter have drawn upon our own experiences of trying to understand complex health interventions, the imperative of cost-effectiveness and efficiency as goals is also central to other areas of policy evaluation and organisational management. In these other policy areas, the methodological habits, home disciplines and epistemological starting points of economic evaluators may make them more amenable to using realist and theory-driven evaluation approaches than seems to be the case in health and medical research (where, arguably, the experimental imperatives of clinical epidemiology have been the dominant methodological influence on economic evaluation methods). And of course, as well as extending knowledge and skills into perhaps unfamiliar territory, evaluators will also simply need more time or access to additional data sources in order to broaden their focus to resources and costs; only then will they be able to evidence the underlying mechanisms and contexts that seem to explain the patterns in them. Research funders too will need to recognise this. This way we might increase confidence that full exploration of programme theories of effectiveness should produce explanations of cost-differences and cost-effectiveness as an inevitable and valuable by-product.

This chapter is a revised and expanded version of a journal article on 'realism and resources' published by two of us in the Sage journal *Evaluation*: R. Anderson and R. Hardwick (2016) 'Realism and resources: towards more explanatory economic evaluation', 22 (3): 323–41.

ACKNOWLEDGEMENTS

The contribution of RH, MP and RB to this research was supported by the National Institute for Health Research (NIHR) Collaboration for Leadership in Applied Health Research and Care South West Peninsula. The views expressed are those of the author(s) and not necessarily those of the NHS, the NIHR or the Department of Health. RA would like to thank several people for the valuable conversations and generous contributions to two earlier (sadly unsuccessful) grant applications, the crafting of which probably formed an early basis of the ideas presented in this chapter; they are: Steve Birch, Jo Coast, Ian Shemilt, Geoff Wong and, of course, Ray Pawson. We are also very grateful to Jo Greenhalgh for her very useful comments on an earlier version of the chapter.

8

DATA GATHERING IN REALIST REVIEWS

Looking for needles in haystacks

Geoff Wong

WHAT THIS CHAPTER IS ABOUT

In realist reviews, finding documents that contain enough relevant data of sufficient rigour is a key process. This chapter aims to describe and explain what the challenges are in identifying relevant literature and to suggest how they might be overcome. The specific challenge of how to understand and deal with the issue of rigour of the data in realist review is discussed in detail. Six challenges are identified, illustrated with one or more examples, and then one or more solutions are provided. Examples used include a realist review on the implementation of legislation for public health, the IMPACT review on antimicrobial prescribing practice of doctors in training and a realist review of Internet-based medical education. The chapter concludes that there are many ways to overcome some of the issues encountered in realist reviews and that there is often more available evidence than first meets the eye.

How this chapter will help you to do realist research

This chapter provides tricks of the trade in realist review, enabling you to better understand and so overcome or avoid the most common challenges. The chapter not only describes these challenges in full but provides academic examples to enhance your understanding.

A practical tip: a take-home message from the chapter

Six practical solutions to the common challenges faced by realist reviewers are provided to help you find the needles of relevant information in the literature haystack – for example, relevant data does not only exist in research studies but can be found in other sources such as newspapers and radio programmes.

INTRODUCTION

In realist reviews (or syntheses – the terms are synonymous) the data needed to develop, corroborate, refute and/or refine context-mechanism-outcome configurations (CMOCs) and programme theory or theories (PT) comes mainly from documents. Therefore, it goes without saying that finding documents that contain relevant data of sufficient rigour is a key process in realist reviews.

In this chapter, my aim is not so much to describe and explain the process of searching databases (this is something I will leave to those better qualified than me, such as information scientists and librarians), but more to describe and explain what the challenges are and to suggest how they might be overcome. I have identified each challenge, illustrated it with one or more examples and then suggested one or more solutions. In addition, where relevant, I have provided a realist perspective on the issues raised.

I make no claim that I have identified all the challenges someone doing a realist review would face, or that any suggested solutions I propose are the correct and only ways. Those challenges that I do identify and propose solutions for are drawn from my experience of either doing or helping others to do realist reviews, along with what I have learnt from working on the RAMESES I project in developing quality and publications standards for realist reviews and training materials (www.ramesesproject.org) (Wong et al., 2014b). Furthermore, with the increasing use of realist reviews, my hope is that methodological development will take place and better solutions emerge. My final 'disclaimer' is that I am a health services researcher. As such, the examples I have used in this chapter come mostly from health services research. This does not, however, in any way imply that I think the issues raised in this chapter are specific to health services research only. On the contrary, my goal has been to frame the challenges and potential solutions in such a way that they have relevance for realist reviews done in any field.

GATHERING DATA

One of the most commonly used ways to search for documents that might contain data relevant for realist reviews is by searching electronic databases. You will note that all of the examples I have used in this chapter have done this to varying degrees. There are many databases, each of varying completeness and indexed and updated to differing degrees. To complicate matters, different software is available to search one or more databases, some free and others requiring a subscription, some easy to use and others requiring more expertise. And to make matters worse, different research disciplines will have specific databases that are more likely to index research in that field. In essence, knowing which database to search, how and with what software is a specialist area of expertise. This is not to say that the 'average' realist reviewer cannot do so, but more that to do this well and efficiently requires great knowledge and skill. We thus come to my first suggested solution.

Suggested solution 1: Go and seek help from your friendly local librarian or information specialist. For a funded research realist review project, I would strongly suggest asking for funding for dedicated time and input from a librarian or information specialist. There is, however, one caveat to this suggestion which relates to the type and amount of data needed in a realist review – an issue that I come to next.

RELEVANT DATA

Data are relevant in a realist review when they are able to help us develop, corroborate, refute or refine aspects of a realist programme theory (or theories). Such data may come from many types of sources, not all of which are documents. For example, in our realist review which developed a programme theory on the implementation of legislation for public health (Pawson and Wong, 2013; Pawson, Owen and Wong, 2010a; Pawson, Wong and Owen, 2011a, 2011b; Wong, Pawson and Owen, 2011), an interview on the radio (the *Today* programme) provided us with ideas for a middle-range programme theory (Pawson, Owen and Wong, 2010b). Listening to the exchange we were able to develop five questions that formed the backbone of our programme theory (not initially realist in nature), which we then refined against data included in the realist review.

Another commonly used non-documentary source of data is the 'stakeholder' group. These groups may be called different things, but it is not their name but the composition of such groups and the ways they contribute to a review that is important. Group composition and contribution does vary across reviews, but they appear to share a number of common features. They tend to include individuals who have some content expertise about the topic area. So, for a healthcare intervention, it might be professionals who deliver the intervention, patients with exposure to or who have the condition in question and researchers who have studied the topic. These 'content' experts are then asked to help with one or more of the following: advice on what might be in a programme theory; feedback of their views about the credibility and/or completeness of a programme theory; and/or where to find additional data (e.g. in the form of additional documents). In two reviews I have been involved in, the stakeholder group was asked to assist with all three of these issues (Nyssen et al., 2016; Wong et al., 2015). In the IMPACT review on the antimicrobial prescribing practice of doctors-in-training (Wong et al., 2015), we asked the stakeholder group to take on an additional task – that of helping us to identify and develop recommendations. We had asked them to assist with these tasks as we had anticipated that executing the realist review itself would not be as challenging as identifying what could practically be changed in a health care system that was renowned for being resistant to change (Allcock et al., 2015). So, in this case, what we wanted to draw on was the 'insider' knowledge of those who worked in the system for their insights and advice. To this end we deliberately sought out individuals whom we thought would have more relevant 'insider' knowledge to consult.

A final point to note relates to the documents that are included in a realist review. In the same spirit as hinted at above, data are data and, as already outlined in quality standards for realist review, searches should not be 'driven by a methodological hierarchy of evidence (e.g. privileging RCTs) rather than the need to identify data to develop, refine or test program theory/ies' (http://ramesesproject.org/media/RS_qual_standards_researchers.pdf). Thus, it should be expected that nuggets of information can come from any documentary sources – such as books, policy documents, theses (Pawson, 2006a). Only then would it be possible to get around the issue of not being able to find enough data to corroborate, refute or refine programme theory. To illustrate, two realist reviews relied exclusively on trying to make sense of complex interventions using only randomised controlled trials (Brown et al., 2016; Kane et al., 2010). In both cases, the authors concluded that while purely relying on the data included in such trials can be useful, important details are missing. As Kane et al. explain: 'The RCTs under review offered a fair amount of information about the interventions and only some information about context – allowing us to formulate only generic hypotheses. Disentangling context from intervention elements was a daunting task, particularly when doing this across RCTs (Kane et al., 2010). It should also not be forgotten that within any included document, especially studies, relevant information may be found just about anywhere within the document. As a general rule of thumb, within published studies, the 'background' or 'introductory' sections are often a good source of information about how the authors think the intervention they are reporting on is thought to work. This section may even go so far as to contain a summary of the substantive theories that have been used to design the intervention. Another potentially fruitful source of information is the 'discussion' section of published studies. When the trial of a complex intervention has failed to meet up to its expectations, the authors will often provide possible explanations for why. With a bit of imagination these explanations can often be turned into middle-range theories (ideally realist) that can be empirically 'tested' against data found within documents and other sources included in a realist review.

Suggested solution 2: Be imaginative and inclusive about where relevant data might come from. Sources of data come in all forms – not just research studies. Within research studies, read the whole document – you are not just interested in the results or findings section.

PROGRAMME THEORY

The role of programme theory in relation to data gathering is often overlooked. The hint is its name: *programme* theory – 'the theory about what a programme or intervention is expected to do and in some cases, the theory about how it is expected to work. Realist programme theory goes a little further and includes descriptions of contexts, mechanisms and outcomes' (http://ramesesproject.org/media/Realist_reviews_training_materials.pdf).

Programme theories contain abstract ideas or concepts. These concepts can help to direct searching. For example, in our realist review on interventions to improve the antimicrobial prescribing practice of doctors in training, we deliberately developed a programme theory early on. We did this by drawing on the project team's content expertise and through some informal searching with the aim of identifying theories that explained how antimicrobial prescribing interventions worked for doctors in training and why, when such interventions worked as expected and when not (and for whom), and why the intended outcomes were often not achieved in practice. Early iterations of our programme theory indicated that the concept of hierarchies was an important influence on the antimicrobial prescribing practice of doctors in training. While we had some data to enable us to infer that hierarchies were important, we needed more data in order to fully unpack the influence of hierarchies on prescribing behaviour. We had only been able to find some documents from our initial search that contained relevant data on hierarchies. We therefore conducted another search but this time focused on doctors in training and the contextual dynamics of hierarchies, teamworking and decision-making. We went on to use the additional documents we retrieved to further refine our understanding of the influence of hierarchies on prescribing within programme theory.

In explaining what a programme or intervention is expected to do and/or how it works, realist programme theory uses a realist logic of analysis, as captured in context + mechanism = outcome (C + M = O). This simple analytic heuristic provides us with another avenue for gathering data – by turning our attention to mechanisms. The trick here is to identify what the causal mechanisms are in a programme or intervention and then search for sources that provide relevant data on the behaviour of these mechanisms but under different contexts (see Williams and Westhorp in this volume).

This focus on mechanisms can help to get around the issue of not finding enough relevant data in your specific topic area; for example, it may be that searching has found either (a) none or (b) only a small number of closely related studies of a similar programme or intervention.

To illustrate the value of focusing on mechanisms, consider our review 'Policy Guidance on Threats to Legislative Interventions in Public Health: A Realist Synthesis' (Wong, Pawson and Owen, 2011). In this review we developed a programme theory to assist policy and decision-makers to assess the feasibility of implementing public health legislation. We then illustrated the application of programme theory on legislation to ban smoking in private vehicles carrying children. When we undertook this review in 2010, very few jurisdictions had implemented such legislation, no evaluations had been undertaken and so we found few to no data to corroborate, refute or refine some aspects of our programme theory. One aspect that we found no specific data on was on the enforcement of legislation banning smoking in private vehicles carrying children (see Figure 1 or Table 1 in Wong et al., 2010). The problem was that no one had undertaken such research when we conducted our review. To address this issue, we undertook additional searching that focused on the mechanism that we had good reason to believe was in operation in this part of our programme theory – namely the wish to protect children. Our searches were designed to pick up studies that might contain data of this mechanism in closely related contexts. To this end we searched on two fronts in this review – the enforcement of legislation on vehicle behaviours alone and when such legislation was aimed at protecting children. For the former we searched for evaluations of the enforcement of legislation prohibiting mobile (or cell) phone usage in vehicles and for the latter legislation mandating the use of child car restraints (e.g. baby or child seats). These searches provided relevant data that indicated that not only was legislation banning smoking in private vehicles carrying children likely to be enforceable but also self-enforcing (see Tables 3 and 4 respectively in Wong et al., 2010).

In both examples above, the programme theory helped us by providing direction on what additional relevant data were needed. In the first example, the 'clue' from the programme theory was at the conceptual level (hierarchies) and from the second example at the level of mechanisms.

Suggested solution 3: Develop a programme theory early on in your realist review – the more realist the better. Any is better than none. The programme theory can help you to identify what kind of data you need at the conceptual or context, mechanism or outcome level.

RIGOUR, DATA 'QUALITY' AND MORE ...

A recurrent issue that vexes realist reviewers is the concept of rigour of relevant data used in realist reviews. Rigour may be defined as whether the methods used to generate the relevant data are credible (or plausible) and trustworthy (http://ramesesproject.org/media/Realist_reviews_training_materials.pdf). In effect, rigour is about the 'quality' of data. But there is more than meets the eye on the issue of 'quality' or rigour and this is addressed in this section.

Sadly, there is not a short answer to this issue, but an understanding of the nature of the 'product' of a realist review may help. Realist reviews are much more about explaining phenomena than calculating the size of their effects. To do so realist reviews have to develop and refine theories that are based on data found within included documents. Some data will be empirically derived, such as responses to a questionnaire or interviews; others might be opinion or speculation, for example as might be found in an editorial. Regardless of how the data has come about, it may still be relevant, i.e. the data can help us corroborate, refute or refine an aspect of programme theory.

Underlying any theory will be its argument(s) – the reasons given in support of a theory. Ideally, we would want our arguments to be based on 'good' reasons – by this I mean the reasons underpinning any theory to be reasons which are both trustworthy and plausible. Things are trustworthy when they can be relied on as being honest and truthful. To have trustworthy reasons we need trustworthy data. To have trustworthy data we need to know where the data has come from so we can judge their trustworthiness. Things are plausible if they can be believed or are credible.

The point I am making here is that 'quality' considerations in realist reviews need to be made at more than just the level of the data from the included documents and other sources. This is because a theory is more than just data. Considerations of quality at the level of data are important but too narrow. Put very simplistically, to (for example) develop a theory, data need to be identified as being relevant, analysed, inferences made and arguments and theory constructed. Hence, judgements about 'quality' need to be made, for all of these processes and at the very least at the levels of data, argument and theory (Figure 8.1). Such an approach might seem to be fiendishly complicated, but in the following section I will discuss and illustrate possible ways of dealing with the vexed question of 'quality' in realist reviews through the consideration of trustworthiness and plausibility.

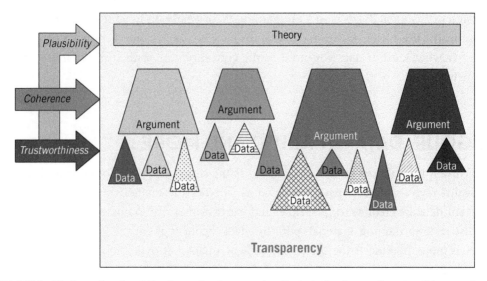

NB: Within this figure the size of the shapes has been used to illustrate the degree of trustworthiness and coherence of data and arguments respectively. The colours simply illustrate that data or arguments are different and varied.

FIGURE 8.1   The relationships between theory, arguments, data, trustworthiness, coherence, plausibility and transparency

Trustworthiness

In many review approaches, judgements about the trustworthiness of data are carried out using rating scales that assess the rigour of the processes that have been used to produce the data. This works well and is simpler to apply when the data needed to support an argument are based on aggregating a singular type of data – e.g. numerical (as in a Cochrane systematic review), and the product of the review is not theory. However, it is much more practically challenging to efficiently use rating scales when data needed to support an argument are of multiple types, e.g. numbers, quotes, opinions, policy statements, concepts – and the product is theory. On top of all this, a theory is likely to be based on multiple arguments and, as I have pointed out above, a focus on data quality is simply too narrow a way of assessing 'quality'. Because a theory is built up from many arguments based on the analysis and interpretation of much data, it becomes a monumental and possibly impossible task to have to individually rate the 'quality' of all the data that have been used. In addition, this assumes that rating scales exist for each type of data and that those that do exist are considered to be acceptable.

In any realist review, the norm is that a programme theory is underpinned by multiple arguments (reasons given in support of a theory) based on analyses and interpretations made on 'nuggets' of data almost always spread across multiple documents and other sources. To make any realist review manageable, the reviewers have to take a more pragmatic and global approach when it comes to judging data 'quality'. The following considerations may help when considering the trustworthiness of data:

- assume that data which has been obtained empirically have used some sort of method(s) and so are unlikely to be simply fabricated;
- where it is unclear if any methods have been used to obtain data, treat them with scepticism; and
- always try to find more than one source of data that is relevant to an aspect of programme theory.

These strategies are suggested so as to encourage the review team to remain sceptical and continue to seek out more data (hopefully of greater trustworthiness).

To illustrate the points above, in our realist review 'Internet-based Medical Education: A Realist Review of What Works, for Whom and in What Circumstances' (Wong, Greenhalgh and Pawson, 2010), about a third of the way through the review, we noted in a study by Sargeant et al. the following section of text which was located in the Introduction:

Considering interactive on-line CME [Continuing Medical Education] an innovation, Rogers' Diffusion of Innovations suggests that individuals' perceptions of an innovation determine its rate of adoption and that these perceptions are shaped by several factors. Two that are important to CME are relative advantage (the degree to which a new idea is perceived as superior to the existing practice that it replaces) and compatibility (the degree to which an innovation is perceived as similar to previous experience or to beliefs and values). (Sargeant et al., 2004: 227)

These data were not empirically generated, but were the opinion of the authors about how best to conceptualise online CME; however, it was based on substantive theory – i.e. Rogers' diffusion of innovation theory (Rogers, 1995). What we did not do was to attempt to rate the quality of these data: if we had (assuming there was a rating scale we could have used to rate the 'quality of a conceptualisation'), it would probably have fallen into the category of 'mere opinion', thus calling into question its trustworthiness. How trustworthy these data were does not, however, necessarily have any relation to how relevant they might be and we thought at that time that they might be relevant. This led us to deliberately seek out more data to try to understand if this 'mere opinion' about how best to conceptualise online CME might have data to support its relevance and usefulness. On re-analysis of the included documents we had already analysed, and later all other included documents we were going to analyse, we found clear indications that this was a highly relevant and useful conceptualisation – and in fact this became the turning point of our review. Conceptualising Internet-based medical education as (more specifically) a technological innovation enabled us to develop a section of the programme theory that was able to explain initial and continuing usage.

Plausibility and coherence

However, the trustworthiness of data is just one narrow but important dimension of the judgements needed regarding 'quality'. In an ideal world, any realist programme theory is underpinned by arguments that are based on the most trustworthy data. However, this is often not achievable and data of varying trustworthiness are all that we can find for use in a realist review. In such a situation, even data of limited trustworthiness can make some contribution to building arguments underpinning a realist programme theory which are plausible. To judge plausibility we need to introduce another concept here – *coherence* (how logical and consistent an argument is). When making judgements about the coherence of programme theory (or any theory), one approach is to apply the reasoning set out in 'Inference to the best explanation'. This reasoning is based on the belief that a theory is more likely to have coherence because it offers a good explanation (Haig and Evers, 2016). Using this reasoning, coherence may be judged by the following criteria:

- consilience (or explanatory breadth) – the ability of the theory to explain as much as possible of the data;
- simplicity – the theory is simple and does not have to have special (or 'ad hoc') assumptions made to it to explain data;
- analogy – the theory fits in with what we currently know and/or substantive theory.

So, when it comes to judging 'quality' in a realist review, we need to consider the trustworthiness of the data, but also the coherence of the programme theory or theories that have been developed and refined based on these data. Judgements of coherence can be carried out using the criteria set out in 'Inference to the best explanation'. The highest 'quality' theory is plausible because it has coherence and is based on trustworthy data.

Another illustration is needed here regarding the levels of at which 'quality' judgements are needed and on this occasion we return to our review 'Policy Guidance on Threats to Legislative Interventions in Public Health: A Realist Synthesis' (Wong, Pawson and Owen, 2011). In this review, one aspect of our programme theory (see Wong et al., 2011: Figure 1 or Table 1) was to ask policy- and decision-makers to consider if they might expect opposition to public health legislation they were planning to implement. In our review we 'road tested' our programme theory using the example of legislation to ban smoking in private vehicles carrying children. We found a single study from Australia (where such legislation had been enacted in the state of South Australia) by Freeman and Chapman that provided data that the legislation was not opposed by the tobacco industry. This study was a search of media databases looking for newspaper articles reporting on this legislation (Freeman, Chapman and Storey, 2008). This was not a systematic review but had been undertaken using transparently described methods. Going back to my earlier points about the trustworthiness of data – these data on the lack of opposition to the legislation was not of the highest 'quality' but was relevant. On its own, it would have been hard for us to develop much of an argument for this section of the programme theory. We could not find further data on the issue of opposition from the tobacco industry to this legislation that origi-nated from Australia. We needed more data and so, as an alternative strategy in 2010, we emailed British American Tobacco Australia to ask them about their position regarding the legislation and received this reply:

Thanks for your email. In its submission to the Preventative Health Taskforce consultation, British American Tobacco Australia (BATA) stated their position on smoking in cars containing children. I have attached the relevant section below.

SMOKING IN CARS CARRYING CHILDREN: BATA POSITION SUMMARY

BATA supports the sensible regulation of tobacco products, while ensuring that adult smokers can make informed choices about the use of such products. We accept that environmental tobacco smoke is an issue of public importance and believe that smokers should be mindful of others' comfort and should not smoke around young children.

We do not support attempts to ban or regulate against smoking in private dwellings or private vehicles that are not containing children. We believe that people should not smoke around young children. However, we think this is more effectively achieved through education and encouraging greater personal responsibility amongst smokers. Governments at all levels need to be very careful in balancing the civil rights of the smokers with those of non-smokers.

While the only way to avoid the risks of smoking is not to smoke, a real world view suggests that a large number of people will continue to choose to smoke despite knowledge of the risks. To this end we are committed to working with government and relevant stakeholders to discuss the steps that existing smokers might take to potentially reduce the risks of smoking. Instead, BATA believes that education is an extremely important and effective measure in addressing such issues, without unfairly restricting the rights of adults to smoke.

At the level of the trustworthiness of the data, these represent a position statement from a tobacco company and if they were to be rated for 'quality' with an instrument would again likely fall into the category of 'mere opinion'. As the public proclamations of a tobacco com-pany, questions could also be raised about the plausibility of such data.

In our initial searching we had found documents that contained data that in the United States, the major tobacco companies (BATA included) had signed the US Master Settlement Agreement of 1998 which prohibits any activity targeting tobacco products at youths. Drawing on these data, the email from BATA and other aspects of our programme theory, we were able to develop a plausible theory for this aspect of our overall programme theory. While some of the data had questionable trustworthiness (e.g. the email from BATA), our theory had coherence with other data (e.g. the US Master Settlement Agreement of 1998). Thus we argued that:

Put together, we can infer that specifically for a smoking ban in vehicles carrying children, lobbying and opposition may be muted. Three important contextual constraints are apparent that (if present) limit and may be used to counter opposition and lobbying, namely – the importance a society places on enacting Millian principles; the extent to which the US Master Settlement Agreement of 1998 is legally enforced; and the extent to which tobacco companies enforce (or are forced to enforce) their own public statements on smoking and children. (Wong, Pawson and Owen, 2011: 222)

The example above has hopefully illustrated how even what might be perceived as 'low-quality' data can be used to build a credible argument. It also shows that in a realist review additional searching is often needed and should be driven by the need to find data to corroborate, refute or refine aspects of the programme theory. In other words, additional searching should be purposeful. These additional searches are also a strategy to overcome a problem that evidence synthesis researchers face – that of the 'empty' reviews. These are reviews where there are no or not enough documents to undertake a review. As an aside to this example, before and after the implementation of legislation banning smoking in private vehicles carrying children in England on 1 October 2015, opposition was muted (http://blogs.springer.com/ijph/current-debate/tobacco-control).

The analogy that might be useful here to consolidate my point might be that of what happens in a United Kingdom court of law when a case is heard. Put very simply the steps are as follows: the police gather evidence on a suspect and the lawyers for the prosecution and defence then analyse the evidence to build arguments, that the suspect is innocent or guilty respectively. A judge and jury then make judgements about which arguments they find most plausible and come to a verdict.

The evidence used to support a case is never all of the highest 'quality' – i.e. the most trustworthy data. In addition, it is expected that the evidence comes from multiple sources. For example, to illustrate my point in terms of the 'quality' of evidence, the police may gather evidence on a suspect and find that the witnesses may be less than reliable – some keep changing their stories and there may be discrepancies between them. Only one out of three eyewitnesses may have identified the suspect in an identity parade. There are CCTV images, but not of where the crime took place and as it was at night they are rather unclear.

The suspect has no alibi, but then the police have no indication of what the motive might be. They and the prosecution lawyers do, however, agree they have enough evidence (albeit of variable trustworthiness) to build arguments of sufficient coherence that a judge and jury will find plausible enough to find the accused guilty.

When it comes to the need for multiple sources of evidence, my illustration above highlights that just one source of data is not enough. If the only evidence the police had to go on was that one eyewitness picked out the suspect in an identity parade, then their argument that he is guilty would be rather implausible. There might be a host of reasons the suspect was present at the crime scene – e.g. he could just as likely have been an innocent bystander!

Mapping the above analogy onto data 'quality' judgements in realist reviews, we can see many similarities. The data that realist review teams gather (from included documents and other sources) are not all of the highest 'quality' – i.e. they will be of variable trustworthiness. These imperfect data can still, however, be assembled into coherent arguments that underpin one or more programme theories. Any claims that the reviewers make on the plausibility of their programme theory or theories will be based on both the trustworthiness of their data and the coherence of their arguments. However, reviewers should also bear in mind that while they may make claims that their programme theory is plausible, others (e.g. fellow researchers, policy- and decision-makers or examiners) may disagree. Also, the review team should be wary of making proclamations that they have arrived at the final truth regarding a topic. The realism that realist review is based on assumes that we can only ever get close to a complete understanding of the realm of the real, thus our knowledge claims will always be incomplete.

The law court analogy serves to provide two final points of importance – namely transparency and fallibility. In a court of law, both the prosecution and defence lawyers have access to all the evidence gathered. Their respective arguments are thus based on the same evidence. The implication for realist reviews is that it is important to provide, as much as is practically possible, all the data used to build the arguments that underpin a programme theory. By doing so it enables those that disagree to be specific about what they disagree about. This should go some way to avoiding the accusation that a realist review team has been 'subjective' and 'made things up'. Any such accusation should be directed at specific data, analyses, interpretations and/or arguments upon which there is disagreement. The response to any such accusation of 'subjectivity' or 'making things up' by a realist review team should be a request for clarification, for example by asking: 'So why do you think we have been subjective?', 'What exactly is it that you disagree with?' and/or 'What data are you drawing on to underpin your arguments?' Science moves forward through disputation (Campbell, 1988), but this disputation has to be specifically informed by data.

The other important point is the fallibility of arguments. Judgements by a judge and jury are fallible because they are judgements about plausibility based on the coherence of arguments and the trustworthiness of the evidence. New and more trustworthy evidence may emerge and the defence lawyers may use such new evidence to build arguments that the convicted is innocent and a case is re-tried. We should thus expect that this is also the situation for any programme theory from a realist review. Relevant new data can be used to further corroborate, refute or refine the arguments underpinning a programme theory. As such, realist review findings should always be considered to be the 'best that we know at this point in time with what data we have' and so be open to refinement as new relevant data emerges.

Suggested solution 4: Realist reviews often have to rely on data from multiple sources that are likely to be of varying trustworthiness. Rather than spend time rating the 'quality' of these data, focus instead on finding sufficient relevant data to build plausible programme theory (or theories) underpinned by arguments that have coherence.

Suggested solution 5: Assume that you will be challenged on your findings – be transparent. Provide (as much as is practically possible) all relevant data that has been used to build the arguments that underpin your programme theory (or theories).

Suggested solution 6: The findings from any realist review are fallible and best thought of as the 'best that we know at this point in time with what data we have'. Hence, as more data emerges, programme theories are likely to need to be further refined.

CONCLUSION

In a realist review, gathering relevant data needed to develop and then to corroborate, refute or refine aspects of one or more programme theories is challenging. However, there are tricks of the trade that can help. Firstly, you are not alone. If at all possible, recruit the help of a librarian or an information scientist to help you in your searching. Secondly, relevant data do not just exist in research studies. A broad range of sources may be useful, from the obvious (e.g. published studies) to the less obvious (e.g. newspapers and radio programmes). In addition, in all data sources (published studies included) remember that relevant data might be found in any part of the source. Thirdly, develop a programme theory early on in your review – it will help you to identify what data you need. Fourthly, realist reviews often have to rely on data from multiple sources and they are likely to be of variable 'quality' – i.e. trustworthiness. Even data of variable 'quality' can be used to build arguments that have coherence to underpin one or more programme theories. In judging the plausibility of a programme theory (or theories), consideration should be given to the coherence of the underpinning arguments and trustworthiness of the data used to construct the arguments. Fifthly, and related to the previous point, transparency is important and as much data as possible should be provided. That way, when disagreements occur, it is possible for the disputation to be focused on specifics. Sixthly and finally, all findings from realist reviews are fallible. With time, new data are bound to emerge and further programme theory refinement may then be needed.

To conclude, in a realist review the challenges of finding sufficient relevant data to develop, corroborate, refute or refine programme theory are not insurmountable. The six suggested solutions I have provided in this chapter may help. You may be surprised to find that there are more needles in the haystack than you might think!

ACKNOWLEDGEMENTS

We would like to thank Sonia Dalkin for her invaluable feedback on the contents of this chapter.

FUNDING

No funding was received for writing this chapter. However, when writing this chapter I received funding from two projects funded by the United Kingdom's National Institute for Health Research (NIHR) Health Services and Delivery Research (HS&DR) Programme and one from the Programme Grant for Applied Research (PGfAR) Programme. The views and opinions expressed therein are those of the author and do not necessarily reflect those of the HS&DR or PGfAR Programme, the NIHR, the NHS or the Department of Health.

9

SCOPING AND SEARCHING TO SUPPORT REALIST APPROACHES

Andrew Booth, Judy Wright and
Simon Briscoe

WHAT THIS CHAPTER IS ABOUT

Realist approaches have witnessed vigorous debate on the appropriate role of systematic literature searching in generating and testing theory. This tension between realist creativity and the systematic, defensible searching process underpins this chapter. Literature searching in support of realist review requires an exacting blend of sampling and search techniques, which are explained throughout the chapter using the six elements of a 'realist search': formulating search questions; background search/scoping the literature; search to track programme theories; searching for empirical evidence; final search to refine programme theories; and documenting and reporting the realist search. By mapping the realist search on to Pawson's realist review stages, the authors provide a 'how to' for realist literature searching. The chapter concludes by discussing future directions for the realist search which the authors suggest will mirror those for other theory-based reviews, utilising emerging information-retrieval technologies such as text-mining and full-text retrieval.

How this chapter will help you to do realist research

The debate in this chapter focuses on realist reviews but is also relevant when literature searching for realist evaluation. It will help the reader to understand the process of searching for literature within a realist research framework and to avoid realist review pitfalls, such as only conducting one literature search at the beginning of the research process.

A practical tip: a take-home message from the chapter

Regardless of whether you are conducting an evaluation or a synthesis, harnessing complementary perspectives by juxtaposing primary data from stakeholders alongside published literature strengthens your realist approach.

INTRODUCTION

Realist approaches have witnessed vigorous debate on the appropriate role of systematic literature searching in generating and testing theory. Conventional systematic reviewers find realist review overly dependent on the theoretical resources mobilised within the review team; not every realist review can access experts with multiple candidate theories at their fingertips. Systematic reviewers resist 'magicking' programme theories from thin air before legitimising the process through the quasi-systematic, codified and quasi-explicit process of the realist review. Advocates of the realist approach demonstrate a comparable resistance to technical elicitation of programme theories, claiming that it cannot be done. Occupying the middle ground, Ray Pawson, when posting to the RAMESES discussion list, contends:

The mystery of theory generation lands on our table. Personally ... I like a bit of magic in conjuring them up. Alas, I suspect we can't include hocus-pocus in the RAMESES declarations. (Pawson, 2012: online)

This tension between realist creativity and the systematic, defensible search process under-pins this chapter. On the one hand, literature searching techniques must demonstrate the transparency required by those commissioning, funding and using realist projects. On the other hand, search techniques must remain sensitive to the needs of the realist explorer and, in some cases, be adapted and tailored specifically to advance realist methodology. This debate focuses on realist reviews but is also relevant when searching literature for real-ist evaluation.

So how do scoping and searching acknowledge the requirements of a realist approach? Four realist principles seem particularly important (Emmel, 2013):

1. *Acknowledging that all we have are fragments* – a realist search seeks to identify related research reports in order to tease out an understanding of programme theory and context.
2. *Recognising that realist enquiries require large amounts of data for theory testing* – systematic search approaches should ensure that the sampling frame from within which data is explored includes as many relevant studies as the team can realistically process.
3. *Agreeing that theory testing is unpredictable, unstable and uncertain* – a realist search is flexi-ble and agile, supporting opportunistic forays into the literature with suitably robust search methodology.
4. *Accepting that data collection is iterative* – having assembled a core of literature, the team progressively identifies further 'lines of enquiry' requiring collateral searches of related literature from multiple disciplines.

Juxtaposing primary data from stakeholders alongside published literature offers a power-ful interpretive lens for exploring real-world problems and solutions (Carey et al., 2015). Stakeholder experiences of programmes or interventions offer authentic data for realist research. The quest for common mechanisms that underpin policy or practice places a pre-mium on accumulated knowledge.

Regardless of whether you are conducting an evaluation or a synthesis, harnessing comple-mentary perspectives strengthens your realist approach. This chapter describes search processes and techniques that contribute to a realist review (or evaluation). We present elements of the realist search in a linear format, but in fact the proposed methods for each element can be used at any stage of an evaluation or review; there are no prescriptive rules about when to use a particular approach, only that you explain the logic of your approach. As Pawson says, 'realist review is not a review technique but a review logic' (2004: 19). Similarly, given examples illustrate how the 'realist search' is not a single search technique but rather a search logic.

The 'Realist Search' and Synthesis

Many search techniques have been developed to support systematic reviews. In contrast to systematic reviews, which are typically topic based, realist reviews represent a theory-based approach to synthesis. Search methods to support realist exploration require a modified approach (Table 9.1). Realist reviews develop and test programme theories to explain how, why and in what settings complex interventions work (Pawson et al., 2004) by searching for theories *and* contextually situated evidence, not simply empirical studies. Systematic reviews, by contrast, are criticised for 'stripping away' external context (Wieringa and Greenhalgh, 2015). The three authors of this chapter have drawn upon their experience of supporting systematic reviews when contributing to realist review projects, selecting judiciously from the systematic review toolbox to respond to challenges posed by their review teams. In doing this we have sought to preserve the transparent and explicit reporting of methods required for all systematic approaches to reviewing the literature.

TABLE 9.1 Differences between the systematic review search and the realist search

	Searching to support systematic reviews	Searching to support realist reviews
Structure of search	Structured within clearly bounded and pre-specified inclusion criteria	Structured according to emergent criteria that develop as theories are proposed, tested and refined
Timing and frequency of search	Typically, conducted at the beginning of the review	Conducted iteratively throughout the review
Functions of search	Identifies empirical evidence using topically relevant terms from titles/abstracts/keywords of bibliographic database records	• *Theory elicitation*: identifies theories, 'buried' at outset of the search (and not specified as keywords) or, if known, not occurring in titles, abstracts or index terms of database records • *Theory testing and refinement*: identifies empirical evidence using topically relevant terms from database records
Sampling approach	Requires comprehensive, exhaustive search for relevant literature	Seeks to sample literature and attain modest forms of theoretical generalisability from evidence

Literature searching in support of realist review requires an exacting blend of sampling and search techniques (Pawson, 2006a). Realist searches are not necessarily comprehensive. You may use comprehensive sampling to construct an initial sampling frame of empirical papers. This sample could be used as a source of initial programme theory (alongside more conceptual papers) but, more importantly, will be used in the subsequent testing of programme theories. For example, a review of appointment reminder systems mapped literature by clinical area, population, intervention type and study type (McLean et al., 2014). Purposive sampling techniques were used to explore different mechanisms associated with the diverse scenarios identified from the mapping. Another realist review required an initial exhaustive search for UK examples of community engagement (Harris et al., 2015) and then mapped search results by condition, population and context, using maximum variation sampling. Specific projects were selected from each context (e.g. school-based, volunteer-based, etc.) for complementary searching (Booth et al., 2013).

Complementary searches (for example, citation searches) and canvassing theory from stakeholders and the project team are at least as important as conventional literature searching. Realist searches are typically iterative:

Searching is likely to be iterative because, as the synthesis progresses, new or refined elements of theory may be required to explain particular findings, or to examine specific aspects of particular processes. (Wong et al., 2014)

Iterative searching is useful when key terminology or the full scope of a literature search is unknown at the outset of the search. A realist search may be modified to seek theories which were unknown at the start of the search but have emerged as new lines of enquiry are investigated. Figure 9.1 contrasts the sequential systematic review search with iterative realist review searches.

COMPLEMENTARY SEARCHING TECHNIQUES

The iterative nature of realist searches means that complementary search techniques such as snowball searching, citation searching, the CLUSTER method and contacting authors (see below) assume prominence, particularly during theory identification. Just as realist evaluation may require purposive, snowball sampling of informants, so realist reviews may require snowball sampling of the literature (Pawson et al., 2004; Wohlin, 2014) – from a small set of key references you gradually build up, as the analogy implies, to a larger set of references (Greenhalgh and Peacock, 2005).

Systematic review searches and realist searches also share similarities. Search methods for realist reviews adapt and enhance methods used for systematic reviews. Skills developed from working on systematic reviews are transferable to realist reviews.

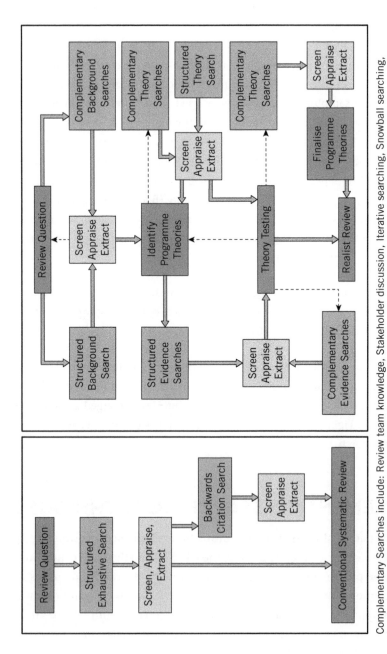

FIGURE 9.1 Iterative nature of the realist search compared to the sequential systematic review process

Complementary Searches include: Review team knowledge, Stakeholder discussion, Iterative searching, Snowball searching, Contacting Authors, Citation Searches, Berry picking (CLUSTER)

THE ROLE OF THE INFORMATION SPECIALIST IN SUPPORTING REALIST APPROACHES

Realist reviews identify and manage literature in different formats from diverse sources. Information specialists possess valuable expertise in search tools and techniques, documenting searches and reference management software (Table 9.2):

It is a good idea to get an information professional involved in order to pick the brains of someone who has knowledge of the spread of potentially useful databases and experience of the nuances of search terms and search techniques. (Pawson, 2006b)

TABLE 9.2 Tips for effective working with information specialists

Play to strengths	Allocate tasks between information specialist search expertise and reviewer subject knowledge
Use close working	Communicate regularly, anticipating further searches as the review evolves
Manage expectations	Agree time frames and a manageable volume of search results
Be flexible	Jointly plan pragmatic searching using techniques that mirror the needs of the review
Keep an open mind	Describe the data you would like to find before suggesting where and how to search (the information specialist may have different ideas)
Tap into expertise beyond 'searching'	Utilise information specialist procedures for tracking search activities, managing references and documenting search methods

ELEMENTS OF A 'REALIST SEARCH'

In reinterpreting Pawson (2006b) we identified six principal elements to a 'realist search:

1. To formulate specific questions as lines of enquiry (Denyer and Tranfield, 2009).
2. To explore a proposed area of research to ascertain previously published research and, if necessary, refine the research question (*the Background Search*) (Pawson, 2006b).
3. To identify theories as hypothetical explanatory accounts of how an intervention works in order to identify programme theories (*the Search for Programme Theories*) (Pawson, 2006b).
4. To identify empirical evidence for context-mechanism-outcome configurations to test and refine the programme theories (*the Search for Empirical Evidence*) (Pawson, 2006b).
5. To respond to new information needs as they emerge during testing and refining of the initial programme theory (*the Final Search to Refine Programme Theories*) (Pawson, 2006b).
6. To document the search process in an explicit and transparent manner (Wong et al., 2013; Wong et al., 2014b).

These elements and associated search techniques are summarised in Table 9.3. Although presented sequentially, useful techniques from an early stage of the realist review may be applied, or even extended, later in the review.

TABLE 9.3 Principal stages and associated search techniques for a realist search

Search Stage	Purpose	Options	Tools and Resources
Element 1 – Formulating Search Questions	To formulate specific lines of enquiry to be pursued by literature searching	**P**opulation, **I**ntervention, **C**omparison, **O**utcomes (PICO) **P**henomenon of Interest, **C**ontext (PiCo) **S**etting, **P**erspective, phenomenon of **I**nterest, **C**omparison, **E**valuation (SPICE) **C**ontext, **I**ntervention, **M**echanisms, **O**utcomes (CIMO)	PICO, PiCo, SPICE, CIMO (Davies, 2011) Search procedures for theory (Booth and Carroll, 2015)

Search Stage	Purpose	Types of Evidence	Search Techniques and Complementary Strategies
Element 2 – Background Search	To get a 'feel' for literature; to explore quantity and quality of literature and to define boundaries to scope; 'sizing up' subsequent review	Theorising; reviews; blogs; social media; grey literature; professional and/or trade journals	Search procedures for theory (Booth and Carroll, 2015) PubMed PubReMiner text analysis; PubVenn text analysis; citation mapping; citation tracking; team discussions; stakeholder consultation
Element 3 – Search for Programme Theories	To construct an explanatory hypothesis for how an intervention works within specific contexts	Logic models; introduction, discussion and conclusion sections; discursive articles; qualitative research; professional journals and media	Purposive sampling for related papers CLUSTER methodology (Booth et al., 2013) Full-text searching using logic model string (Kneale et al., 2015)
Element 4 – Search for Empirical Evidence	To identify research literature to test initial programme theory	Systematic reviews, RCTs, qualitative research; 'sibling studies'; grey literature	CLUSTER methodology (sibling studies) (Booth et al., 2013) Citation tracking; authors' web pages
Element 5 – Final Search to Refine Programme Theories	To link programme theories across disciplines and to relevant mid-range theories	Mid-range theories; 'kinship studies'	CLUSTER methodology (kinship studies) (Booth et al., 2013) Named theory searches Compendia of mid-range theories, models, etc.; citation tracking
Element 6 – Documenting and Reporting the Realist Search	To ensure that users are provided with necessary information to assess quality and rigour	RAMESES reporting standards (Wong et al., 2013)	RAMESES training materials Quality standards for realist syntheses and meta-narrative reviews (Wong et al., 2013)

Element 1 – Formulating Search Questions

Most structured literature reviews require that you formulate a focused question. Population Intervention Comparison Outcome (PICO) or Setting Perspective Interest (phenomenon of) Comparison Evaluation (SPICE) (Davies, 2011) are question formulation tools commonly used in traditional systematic reviews but have more limited application to realist syntheses. A CIMO structure (context (C), interventions (I) and outcomes (O) alongside mechanisms (M)) resonates with Pawson's realist interpretation of evidence-based practice (Pawson, 2006b; Denyer and Tranfield, 2009; Briner and Denyer, 2012). CIMO offers a structure for the over-arching review question and a starting point for programme theory searches. Realist reviews frequently refer to context-mechanism-outcome (CMO) configurations when developing programme theories. Protocols have used a CMO/CIMO structure during the question for-mulation stage (Maidment et al., 2016; Turner et al., 2016). Completed reviews have utilised the CIMO structure during the search (Booth et al., 2013) and at subsequent stages of data analysis (Ellwood et al., 2016). You can recognise the CMO structure from such descriptions as: 'in these circumstances (context) the programme works in this way (mechanism) and produces these outcomes'. Jagosh and colleagues (2012) provide an example:

A community experiences a high level of unemployment to which an employment training program is offered (context). But the program has low enrolment and attrition (outcome). The reason is that people have difficulty getting to the venue, owing to a lack of public transportation (mechanism).

Element 2 – Background Search/Scoping the Literature

For most types of literature review, preparation includes sensitisation to (getting a 'feel' for) the literature (Pawson, 2006b). A background (scoping) search helps to explore the quan-tity and quality of the literature and to define preliminary boundaries to the scope; 'sizing up' the forthcoming review (Pawson, 2006b). Pawson (2006b) likens this to 'a preliminary range-finding exercise', recognising that the final scope for your synthesis may move over time or that your efforts may focus on a particularly fruitful target. Topic-based searches combine words, phrases and index terms (subject headings) and are used to retrieve a set of records of potential relevance to the search question (described in Element 4). You can use your scoping searches both to identify more immediate programme theories and to explore the range of programme theories and literature.

In a realist context it is challenging to define scope; shared mechanisms broaden beyond an intervention and emergent mid-range theories may extend across multiple disciplines.

Scoping is prefaced by conceptual 'mapping the territory' (Pawson, 2006b). Mapping and searching are iterative and extend throughout the review. You want to explore as diverse a relevant literature as is feasible without seeking comprehensive coverage. It is more productive to select a 'spread' of databases from different disciplines (Pawson, 2006b) rather than identifying high-yield databases for a particular topic. Subsequently, you might purposively select samples from your results focusing on particular countries (such as low- and middle-income countries) or service settings (such as general practices).

Scoping approaches can be illustrated from a 'systematic realist synthesis' of the Plan-Do-Study-Act (PDSA) approach to quality improvement (Curnock et al., 2012). The team first conducted a background search, following up references from an opportunistic subset of recent papers to identify diverse perspectives and theories. They then engaged with known experts in the field before making definitive decisions on searching and extraction. According to Pawson (2006b: 86), 'the measure of the success of such a scoping search is to enable the reviewer to make an initial judgement on whether the right volume of materials of the right substance is out there to answer the questions the review is likely to pose.'

Tools to Support Scoping

Pawson (2006b) contends that 'no specific technical tricks or procedural rules' are required for scoping. Nevertheless, several tools can help to assess the quantity or diversity of the literature – to fulfil expectations that searches use systematic and auditable methods:

- *PubMed PubReMiner* (http://hgserver2.amc.nl/cgi-bin/miner/miner2.cgi) analyses a pre-specified set of PubMed MEDLINE records for frequent terms, authors, journals and countries of publication, etc. Similar facilities are available via Scopus and Web of Knowledge.
- *PubVenn* (https://pubvenn.appspot.com) demonstrates a graphical display of scope. Entering two search terms linked by AND (e.g. 'Plan Do Study Act' AND 'quality improvement') visually displays the number of records within each set and the overlap between the two sets.

Element 3 – Search for Programme Theories

Realist reviews identify, develop and test programme theories to explain how an intervention works in specific contexts. A programme theory search aims to identify a 'long list' of candidate theories and mechanisms before refining them into a prioritised set for theory testing. Programme theory searching is iterative; as theories emerge you explore related literature, with complementary searches becoming ever more important. Searching for programme theories is challenging; studies of programme theories rarely include 'theory' in their titles or abstracts, few reports focus on programme theories but may refer to them in the Introduction, Discussion or Conclusion sections of an article (Booth and Carroll, 2015). No single method exists with which to identify programme theories, although the authors are aware of several diverse approaches. Experimentation with search methods such as berry picking (Bates, 1989: 409), citation searching and other elements of 'CLUSTER' searching (Booth et al., 2013) is the norm. Pawson and colleagues (2004) advocate such targeted search approaches to purposively sample-related papers that explore the programme theory. These search techniques may also be useful, alongside database searches, for identifying empirical studies. Information science literature offers guidance when using these approaches.

Berry picking involves an 'evolving search', in which a 'query is satisfied not by a single final retrieved set, but by a series of selections of individual references and bits of information at each stage of the ever-modifying search' (Bates, 1989). Instead of conducting a pre-specified topic-based search, the searcher 'forages' using six search techniques: checking cited references; citation searching; searching relevant journals; browsing information that is physically or virtually proximate to items of interest; using subject-indexed databases; and author searching (Bates, 1989). Berry picking allows the searcher to move quickly – haphazardly but successfully – into new territory which appears to be fruitful, much like foraging for berries. The advantages of berry picking are clear: you do not know your full information need at the outset of a realist search, particularly when identifying theories or before you have fixed inclusion criteria (Pearson et al., 2011).

The rationale for *citation searching* is that references which cite or are cited by an index paper share an affinity (whether topical, methodological or some other link) with that paper. Starting with these index papers, you follow cited and citing references, screening each result for relevance to the review question. You document each iteration of citation searching with the number of search results and references selected for further citation searching. You can identify *cited* papers manually by consulting reference lists. To identify *citing* papers, you need access to a citation index: Web of Science and Scopus index citations from pre-specified lists of journals while Google Scholar uses automated web-crawlers to identify scholarly literature and indexes grey literature, books and book chapters (Haddaway et al., 2015). Numbers of citations vary by the citation index being used (Kulkarni et al., 2009). You may export sets of Web of Science and Scopus results to reference management software. Citation searching on Google Scholar using the freely available *Publish or Perish* software (www.harzing.com/resources/publish-or-perish) offers a more systematic and auditable method of harnessing this freely available source of citations. Although evidence on the added value of citation searching is equivocal (Wright et al., 2014; Linder et al., 2015) it can be useful when it is difficult to define search terms for a topic-based search (Greenhalgh and Peacock, 2005; Papaioannou et al., 2010).

Studies identified by citation searching can include 'clusters' of reports from the same project as the index paper ('sibling studies') or reports with conceptual similarities to the index paper ('kinship studies') (Booth et al., 2013). A UK Health Technology Assessment report on interventions to prevent postnatal depression (Morrell et al., 2016) used search filters to identify 22 trial reports. The team then used Google Scholar to conduct citation searches to identify directly related or associated qualitative evidence. The realist analysis used sibling studies to supplement the trial reports with valuable contextual detail and programme theory. Kinship studies were assessed for relevance on a case-by-case basis. Sibling reports may be plentiful; one analysis found that almost half of identified trials yielded an average of five published study reports per trial (Ebrahim et al., 2016).

CLUSTER searching harnesses citation searching, berry picking and author searching (Booth et al., 2013) and uses a systematised approach tailored to the specific requirements of realist syntheses (Booth et al., 2013). CLUSTER searching includes:

1. a search to identify a 'cluster' of documents with a shared context within which interventions are delivered;
2. a search for theories;
3. a search for antecedent and contemporary projects.

CASE STUDY 9. 1: CLUSTER SEARCHING

A review on community-based peer support for health literacy faced challenges in operationalising 'community engagement', 'peer support' and 'health literacy' within topic-based searches (Harris et al., 2015). From a database search, 39 UK references were prioritised. Citation searches of these 39 references yielded relevant papers not retrieved by the topic-based searches. Eight UK-based projects were selected for an extended CLUSTER search. The Glasgow Gay Men's Task Force project offers a published exemplar for the CLUSTER method (Booth et al., 2013).

The search for context begins with key *citations*, i.e. references of particular relevance to the review question. The searcher then checks publication lists of *lead authors*, contacting them to unearth relevant *unpublished material*. Citation searches of key citations use a *citation index*. Next comes a search for *theories* (e.g. searches for 'diffusion of innovations theory' within the reference management library and using Google Scholar produced 49 references including a shared conceptual link to a UK-based project on school-based peer support). Further citation searching can be used to identify antecedent (*early examples of*) and *related* contemporary projects.

Components for these three stages are represented by the CLUSTER mnemonic (Citations; Lead authors; Unpublished material; Scholar searches; Theories; Early examples; Related projects) (see Case Study 9.1).

Contact with authors may unearth published material not retrieved by topic-based searches and unpublished relevant material. Evidence on the usefulness of contacting authors is equivocal (Hawker et al., 2002; Ogilvie et al., 2005).

Stakeholders may offer leads to relevant literature, especially in conjunction with a literature search for theories, ideas and opinions on why the intervention might work (Pawson et al., 2004). Searches for theories can identify large volumes of literature that are prohibitive to screen; you will identify multiple programme theories and your subsequent evidence search (Element 4) may unearth further programme theories. At some point, reviewers and stakeholders may prioritise programme theories, selecting those to be tested with evidence (Pawson et al., 2004). A realist review of patient-reported outcome measures (Greenhalgh et al., 2017) identified nine CMO configurations and from these developed three overarching programme theories.

Sources of Programme Theories

Programme theories appear wherever stakeholders (for example, policy-makers, commissioners, professionals and the general public) discuss assumptions about a programme. Documents reporting theories and opinions (formative theories) are similarly wide-ranging and include consensus papers, policy reports, legislative documents, business plans, editorials and research articles (Pawson et al., 2004; Wong et al., 2013; Otte-Trojel and Wong, 2016). Radio broadcasts (Pawson, 2008), blogs and social media discussions may highlight the ideas and assumptions of stakeholders.

The selection of sources evolves as your review progresses, targeting promising sources of evidence and adapting them for forays into other disciplines. For example, when developing programme theories for a realist review of demand management (Pawson et al., 2016), literature searches revealed a GP trade journal, *Pulse*, as a rich source of theories. The sources chosen were modified to include databases that abstract *Pulse* and other health service trade journals.

As with other forms of systematic review (Lefebvre et al., 2011), you are advised to search multiple sources. For realist reviews the use of multiple sources helps in unearthing the diversity of programme theories required to address the review question. It is tempting to select a large number of sources 'just in case' they offer a unique contribution but, if your realist search is to remain pragmatic, you must select a manageable and parsimonious set of resources.

An assessment of current realist review practice found substantial variation in the number of databases searched (Berg and Nanavati, 2016). Realist reviewers tend to mirror recommendations for systematic review searching (Lefebvre et al., 2011). Grey literature sources, Internet search engines and stakeholder consultations are correspondingly more important for realist reviews and helpful parallels exist with qualitative syntheses (Booth, 2016). Database selection varies by topic and field of research. However, a feasible multi-strand approach will include multi-disciplinary or single-discipline research databases, citation databases, grey literature databases and websites or web-based repositories with the exact choices determined by the review topic (see Case Study 9.2).

CASE STUDY 9.2: SOURCES OF THEORY AND EMPIRICAL EVIDENCE SEARCHES

The Patient Reported Outcome Measures (PROMs) realist synthesis (Greenhalgh et al., 2017) sought literature discussing if, when and how the feedback from PROMs improves health services and individual patient care.

The review team compiled a library of relevant studies supplemented with a broad search for 'buried theories'. Sources included major health databases (e.g. MEDLINE), specialist subject databases and citation databases. Health Business Elite and HMIC provided coverage of government reports, policy documents and trade journals with opinion articles on health service management. PsycINFO and the NHS Economic Evaluations Database were chosen to reflect the inclusion of PROMs in mental health research and economic evaluations. Citation searches were conducted through the Web of Science, supplemented by Google Scholar and Scopus. The reviewers used Google to refine their theories with literature beyond the health domain (e.g. benchmarking theory in management literature).

Literature for theory development and testing came from health policy documents, PROMs manuals, systematic reviews and journal articles. The team sought 'buried theory' within the discussion sections of systematic reviews and within letters, editorials and commentaries. The information specialist designed search strategies to identify opinion pieces (Box 9.1) using publication type search terms.

BOX 9.1 SEARCH STRATEGY TO RETRIEVE COMMENTARIES AND OPINION PIECES

1. Comment/
2. Letter/
3. Editorial/
4. news/ or newspaper article/

5. "Comment on".ti.
6. (letter* adj3 editor*).ti.
7. opinion*.ti.
8. (view or views).ti.
9. comment.cm.
10. or/1–9 [Commentary and Opinion Pieces]

Database record fields:

.ti denotes the title field; .cm denotes the comments field; / denotes a subject heading

Element 4 – Searching for Empirical Evidence

The search for empirical evidence seeks to identify research with which to test the initial programme theory. Use your initial programme theory to identify search terms that represent key concepts, categorised into sets in a structured topic search using Boolean operators. You need two or three sets of search terms to avoid missing relevant references while minimising irrelevant references. The most appropriate sets of terms will depend on the review topic, but tested search structures, such as PICO, SPICE and CIMO, may be useful in constructing search queries. Search terms which describe two or more of the following are useful when combined using the AND Boolean operator:

1. a context or population group in the initial programme theory;
2. a mechanism (e.g. incentives) in the initial programme theory;
3. a phenomenon of interest in the initial programme theory.

For example, the initial topic search for the IMPACT review combined the population group (junior doctors) AND the phenomenon of interest (antimicrobial prescribing) (Wong et al., 2015). A follow-up search focused on the influence of a mechanism (hierarchies) on a phenomenon of interest (decision-making among junior doctors). This example illustrates the usefulness of an initial broad search for empirical evidence on the initial programme theory as a whole before focusing on a particular mechanism.

To find evidence of the programme theory at work in other situations, you can expand your initial list to include search terms for other contexts, population groups and/or phenomena of interest. For example, a search for empirical evidence on hospital league tables might also include search terms for school league tables which share a similar performance-based theory of motivation (Pawson et al., 2004). In addition to expanding your search terms, you should broaden to appropriate additional sources for these topics;

for example, following up your search for hospital league tables in a health database with a search for school league tables in an education database.

You should augment your initial list of search terms for concepts with terms 'objectively derived' from the titles, abstracts and indexing terms of literature identified early in your review (Hausner et al., 2012). This ensures that the search strategy reflects the published literature, particularly for complex interventions where terminology is poorly defined. You can refine your search strategies using search filters or database limits (e.g. publication dates or language). Search filters are ready-made lists of terms applied to a search strategy to narrow down or refine topic search concepts. Filters are often designed to retrieve particular study designs, for example to limit search results to potential RCTs (Lefebvre et al., 2011). RAMESES guidance cautions against use of *study design* filters (Wong et al., 2013), given that traditional evidence hierarchies do not apply to realist syntheses (Pawson et al., 2004). However, it is useful to limit specific realist searches to particular *types of evidence*. For example, searches for theory (see Table 9.2) can target systematic reviews, logic models or opinion pieces (letters, editorials) (see Box 9.1). Search filters can be identified via the InterTASC Information Specialists Subgroup Search Filters Resource website (ISSG, 2017).

As Brad Astbury contends in Chapter 4 of this collection, your search for empirical evidence should aim for the point at which additional evidence does not add to, or contradict, evidence already identified, a modest form of theoretical generalisability. You will need to sample the literature rather than identify an exhaustive body of literature, and this requires that you privilege the specific over the comprehensive. This differs from searching to support systematic reviews, which aims to retrieve an exhaustive body of literature, i.e. to identify every item of literature that addresses the review question. For example, in the IMPACT review an initial broad search for evidence on antimicrobial prescribing in junior doctors was immediately followed by a second narrow search for a specific mechanism. Your appropriate approach is determined by the review's aims and, practically, by the time and resources available (Pawson et al., 2004).

Element 5 – Final Search to Refine Programme Theories

During your search for evidence, you may uncover arguments that refine the programme theory more by chance than intent. As you uncover 'new' theories, you will need to decide whether to include each new theory in the review. For example, in the PROMs Feedback Realist Synthesis (Greenhalgh et al., 2017), background searches, programme theory searches and evidence searches all contributed literature to the development of programme theories. Iterative identification and refinement of theories throughout a realist review contrast with the linear progression of a systematic review. Final searches then explore chosen theories and include searches for specific, named theories, e.g. the theory of planned behaviour or the diffusion of innovations theory (Booth and Carroll, 2015).

Element 6 – Documenting and Reporting the Realist Search

RAMESES standards exist for the conduct (Wong et al., 2014a) and reporting (Wong et al., 2013) of a realist review. Realist searches can only be assessed if their methods are clearly conducted and reported to these standards. Table 9.4 contrasts 'inadequate' and 'excellent' realist searches (Wong et al., 2014a).

TABLE 9.4 Contrasting inadequate and excellent realist searches

'Inadequate' Realist Search	'Excellent' Realist Search
Driven by hierarchy of evidence (e.g. privileging RCTs) rather than by need for data to develop, refine or test programme theory/ies	Driven by objectives and focus of the review
Not informed by objectives and focus of the review	Search strategy piloted, refined and checked for 'fitness for purpose'
Database(s) contain narrow subject matter (e.g. limited to specific topics)	Documents harvested from diverse sources for theory development, refinement and testing No restrictions on study/documentation types
Searching only at outset of review with no iterations	Further searches undertaken for theory development, refinement or testing as understanding of the topic area increases
Database(s) contain narrow subject matter (e.g. limited to specific topics)	Searching beyond the programme; inferring that the same mechanism(s) is in operation

Source: Adapted from Wong et al. (2014a).

The RAMESES standards acknowledge the centrality of the search within *Scoping the Literature* and *Search Processes* (Standards 7 and 8) (Wong et al., 2013). Items specified in *Search Processes* correspond to the STARLITE mnemonic for reporting literature searches (Sampling strategy, Type of study, Approaches, Range of years, Limits, Inclusion and exclusions, Terms used, Electronic sources) (Booth, 2006). A scoping review of published realist reviews found excellent overall compliance with *Search Processes* but poor compliance with *Scoping the Literature*. Conformance with *Comparison with the Existing Literature* was similarly poor (Berg and Nanavati, 2016).

Iterative searching makes it difficult to demonstrate the 'explicitness, comprehensiveness and reproducibility of search strategies' (Dixon-Woods et al., 2006). Realist syntheses typically involve multiple iterations that unravel in a complex messy fashion (Wong et al., 2011). Approaches such as berry picking are criticised for lack of transparency and reproducibility; more problematically, your iterative searches may defy documentation completely (Finfgeld-Connett and Johnson, 2013)!

In contrast to iterative approaches, structured topic searches are easy to record and replicate. Systems used to document topic searches can be modified to include complementary searches in realist reviews. For example, the PROMs feedback realist review team (Greenhalgh et al., 2017) set out to record search activities throughout an 18-month period using:

- a 'search results table' to record the database name, platform, coverage dates, search date, type of search, limits and number of hits from complementary search approaches;
- a 'search timeline' recording search activity by the information specialist and by individual reviewers plus changes in direction of searching.

Reference management software is critical to managing search results. Removal of duplicates minimises repeat screening of the same studies. Managing references within folders helps to track ongoing searches and screening decisions. Use of tracking documents, a shared reference library and regular communication within the team ensure an auditable record of formal searches and search decisions. However, informal opportunistic searching (e.g. to pursue programme theory) subverts documentary control. Study flow diagrams summarise the search and selection of studies for theory development and testing from database subject searches, from personal libraries and from purposive searches and reference checking.

A NOTE ABOUT THE 'REALIST SEARCH' AND EVALUATION

This chapter focuses on how techniques of literature searching contribute to realist reviews. However, literature searches also enhance the interpretive power of a realist evaluation. Published accounts of similar programmes, from similar or different contexts, may help you to unearth programme theories to compare with local perspectives. The RAMESES standards for realist evaluation stress that you should 'compare and contrast the evaluation's findings with the existing literature on similar programmes, policies or initiatives' (Wong et al., 2016). You may use published evaluations to identify evaluation methods, outcome measures and measurement tools. Reference to the external literature may help you to connect locally generated programme theory to wider mid-range theory (Punton, 2016). Differences in literature searching between realist evaluation and realist review are of degree, not kind.

FUTURE DIRECTIONS FOR THE 'REALIST SEARCH'

Developments in literature searching for realist reviews mirror those for other theory-based reviews. Emerging information-retrieval technologies such as text-mining and full-text retrieval are likely to prove influential within the next decade (Lefebvre et al., 2013).

Text-mining involves deriving 'knowledge and structure from unstructured data (i.e. text)' (O'Mara-Eves et al., 2015) and can be used to identify potentially relevant studies more efficiently than manual screening. Text-mining ranks retrieved studies from a conventional search by relevance, enabling the searcher to retrieve a wider range of literature than is feasible to screen manually. For a realist search this would facilitate importing mechanisms from beyond the main focus of the research without having to screen the inevitably larger set of search results retrieved by searching a range of subject areas. Full-text retrieval facilities (Lefebvre et al., 2013) may play an extended role within realist reviews in making it possible to search for mechanisms and theories within the publication itself, rather than in biblio-graphic records (Booth and Carroll, 2015).

The tendency for funded studies to comprise multiple study elements offers further opportunity to enhance literature search procedures. A randomised controlled trial may be accompanied by one or more qualitative studies, an economic evaluation and survey activity. The trial may comprise pilot or feasibility studies, a process evaluation and interim reports of findings to help in understanding the interplay of context and mechanisms (Booth et al., 2013).

Methodological developments will likely involve greater use of diverse sampling methods (Booth, 2016). Domain analysis offers one way to gain a richer understanding of context (Briscoe, 2016). Domain analysis examines how information is described and organised within different fields of study (Hjørland, 2002). The approach may be particularly useful in realist reviews given that context shapes the search terminology and selection of sources.

CONCLUSION

Techniques for the realist search position themselves between the prescriptive systematic review paradigm and a 'free spirit' of qualitative enquiry, blending the fingertip search of the systematic reviewer with the intuitive leads of the fictional detective. For this reason, analogies with systematic reviews only take the reader so far – the realist search is of its own kind. In this chapter we have mapped both established search procedures and innovative methods against six key stages of the realist search process, adapted from Pawson (2006b). With progressive refinement of established search procedures and innovative generation of intuitive methods, the realist community can benefit from ongoing developments in retrieval, particularly within interpretive theory-led approaches to evidence synthesis.

10

EVIDENCE FROM REALIST RESEARCH, ITS INFLUENCE AND IMPACT

Mark Monaghan and Annette Boaz

WHAT THIS CHAPTER IS ABOUT

This chapter discusses how 'impact' has been conceptualised and argues that the reason why traditional systematic reviews have limited impact on policy is because they are not equipped to tackle complexity or variations in context. Realist reviews are proposed to examine how contexts shape the mechanisms through which interventions work and thus, it is argued, have the potential to inform policy-makers about how and why an intervention is likely to thrive or wither on their patch. This chapter charts the interactions between a team of realist reviewers and policy-makers to interrogate the idea that realist reviews have more relevance to policy-makers. Realist reviews are not a panacea for the 'implementation gap'. However, because they actively involve policy-makers in eliciting and testing the ideas and assumptions underlying how interventions are intended to work, realist reviews help policy-makers 'think through' how and why interventions may prosper or falter. They also create relationships between the research team and policy-makers which are conducive to reshaping how policy-makers think about an intervention, if not the immediate uptake of findings. Thus, the chapter argues for a revised programme theory of the impact of realist reviews.

How this chapter will help you to do realist research

This chapter will challenge researchers to consider how they define impact and help them to articulate why realist reviews are expected to have greater relevance to policy-makers. It provides practical lessons on the key mechanisms researchers need to foster throughout the process of conducting a realist review to create a context in which policy-makers have the space to consider how an intervention is intended to work and why it may or may not flourish locally. It reminds researchers that the benefits of this process may not be visible immediately in the shape of policy changes, but rather reassures them that changing the way policy-makers understand an intervention can have a longer-term impact on their thinking which may only become evident in the future.

A practical tip: a take-home message from the chapter

The findings from realist reviews that pay due respect to complexity and context may have greater relevance to policy-makers. Policy-maker involvement is an important causal mechanism. The *process* of conducting a realist review has a causal link to the policy relevance, not just the products of this labour.

INTRODUCTION

Towards the end of the twentieth century it became accepted wisdom, in advanced industrialised societies at least, that plausible social and public policy formulation would be buttressed in some way by credible research in the search for 'what works' (Nutley et al., 2007). In the UK, the term evidence-based policy-making became synonymous with the New Labour government elected in 1997. Although an elusive term, the concept of evidence-based policy-making described a process whereby policies would be based more on evidence and data than ideology and where they would also be kept under continuous review in the form of rigorous evaluation. Such reviews, as per the UK National Audit Office (NAO) (2001: 12), would 'determine when the time was right to modify a policy in response to changing circumstances' so that they 'remain relevant and cost-effective'. If policies fall short of these minimal expectations, the NAO concluded, then they should be terminated.

This was the policy side of the bargain. Arguably the most cited example of this call to arms was from David Blunkett, then Secretary of State for Education, who in a speech to the UK Economic and Social Research Council (ESRC) stated that 'the Government expects more of policy makers', including a better use of 'evidence and research in policy making' (Cabinet Office, 1999). For the evidence community, there was a clear imperative to provide robust evidence for policy. Over time this has mutated into a broader agenda around the impact of research not only in policy-making but in and on society. That said, we are now in a period where public-funded research is under increased scrutiny and where a climate of hostility towards research is visible. Its use in policy is uncertain and possibly unwanted, but researchers nonetheless must engage in impact activity.

In this chapter, we consider the issue of impact. In doing so, we use a narrower definition looking mainly at the relationship between evidence and policy. A considerable amount has been written on this topic over recent years. Much of it has been dominated by methodological disputes over the most effective way to go beyond a reliance on individual studies by gathering and synthesising evidence to inform policy.

Pawson (2006b) suggested that a new form of review – namely realist synthesis – could be more useful to policy-makers than traditional forms of review because of its broader scope and the consideration not only of what works, but also of what works for whom in what circumstances and why. In this way, realist reviews, as they became known, were better able to deal with the complexities of the policy process and could enable policy-makers to target interventions to local circumstances, but, perhaps most importantly, could begin to cumulate evidence about policy successes and policy failures. In this chapter we attempt to take stock and look forward. In doing so we address some of the claims made on behalf of realist review. We discuss the contributions made by realism to debates around evidence-based policy-making and, by association, research impact. We consider how the process of realist review differs from other forms of review and whether it equates to any privileged position in influencing policy. We pay attention to how realism has impacted on the most recent incarnation of policy-oriented learning – implementation science – and whether it achieved its goal of cumulating evidence from policy evaluation.

We do this by charting the fortunes of one programme of realist work. One of this chapter's authors, Annette Boaz, along with Ray Pawson (Boaz and Pawson, 2005), examined the potential of systematic reviews to influence policy. The policy in question was that of 'mentoring',[1] a widely used but poorly understood intervention. In many ways mentoring stands as an example par excellence for the necessity of developing systematic reviews as a way of influencing policy. The chapter is organised in the following way. The following section offers a broad overview of the emergence of the impact agenda, or more accurately agendas as there are more than one. We then move on to discuss the primacy of systematic review as the so-called gold standard of evidence and moving on from this consider the significance of the development of realist review. We then consider some lessons from realist reviews before looking at the status of realism in the broader field of impact analysis. Finally, we offer some concluding remarks documenting how realist approaches not only offer specific guidelines and strategies on how to influence policy via evaluation and systematic review, there are signs that they might also be conceptualised in the future as being able to provide a framework for how impact can and should be considered.

IMPACT DEBATES

During the 2016 referendum campaign on whether Britain should remain within or leave the European Union, Michael Gove, a then government minister and leading campaigner for 'Leave', declared with some irony that British people no longer trusted, and have 'had enough' of, experts (Menon and Portes, 2016). There are two parts to the irony. Firstly, as Tieberghien and Monaghan (forthcoming) note, Gove had spent the prior months specifically seeking out the views of experts on penal reform. Secondly, the government of which Gove was a senior part had just overseen a research assessment exercise which, among other things, had sought to scrutinise and quantify the utility of expertise under the aegis of the impact agenda.

The impact agenda has given impetus to calls for researchers to demonstrate the impact of their research beyond the academy, often measured in terms of changes to society, culture and the economy. Broadly speaking, the notion of an impact agenda is misleading. There are two discernible agendas here. On the one hand, there is the government-led version. We might call this the administrative impact agenda. The recent Research Excellence Framework (REF) exercise carried out by the Higher Education Funding Council for England (HEFCE) is indicative. REF 2014 analysed the quality of the research carried out in UK higher education institutions from 2008 to 2013. Research impact provided one of the key criteria on which the final judgements were made. According to HEFCE (2014), impact related to benefits beyond the academic community to:

one or more areas of the economy, society, culture, public policy and services, health, production, environment, international development or quality of life, whether locally, regionally, nationally or internationally. (HEFCE, 2014, cited in Greenhalgh et al., 2016: 15)

Research funders, particularly those from central governments, have become ever more keen to demonstrate that government-funded research is having an impact. This impact may be on policy, but it can be, and frequently is, broader than this. This impact can include, but is not limited to:

the many types of beneficiary (individuals, organisations, communities, regions and other entities); impacts on products, processes, behaviours, policies, practices; and avoidance of harm or the waste of resources. (Greenhalgh et al., 2016: 15)

The second impact agenda can, for convenience, be called the critical version. This has a longer lineage and a narrower, more critical focus. It mainly concentrates on the barriers and facilitators of the research and policy relationship where the former impacts on the latter. Whereas the administrative impact programme is government-led, the critical programme is more a product of the academy, particularly academics studying the use of research evidence across a wide range of policy domains. It has its own journals – for instance, *Evidence and Policy*[2] – and has given rise to specific research centres such as the Research Unit for Research Utilisation currently located at the University of St Andrews and the Evidence for Policy and Practice Information (EPPI) Centre at the Institute for Education, University College London.

The impact agenda is at the forefront of debates around evidence-based policy-making in society. The rules of engagement, in terms of demonstrating impact on behalf of research-ers, is decided by the governmental administrative approaches. This is in spite of the fact that the linear logic on which this is based has been called into question. Indeed, scholars of research utilisation have put forward various models to explain the possible ways evidence can influence policy. Nutley and colleagues (2003) refer to three main kinds of connection. First, the instrumental model assumes that scientific knowledge can be directly relevant to policy decisions if the research can be found or created. This model, sometimes referred to as the linear or engineering model (see Young et al., 2002), has been largely discredited. Instead, it is widely thought that evidence has a more indirect influence on policy, namely by altering the way policy-makers conceptualise and frame certain issues and problems. This is referred to as the enlightenment model. Thirdly, it is also acknowledged that knowledge utilisation may involve issues of political power (such as political/selective use of scientific knowledge) whereby aspects of scientific knowledge that suit the interest of powerful groups are directly harnessed at the expense of others that reveal uncomfortable 'truths'.

Of course, scientific knowledge is just one type of information competing with other types of knowledge to influence policy decision-making. Weiss (1995) summarises this as 'the 4 I's' model where interests, ideology, institutions and information all impact on decision-making. More recently, Best and Holmes (2010) have moved the debate on, discussing three generations of thinking on knowledge transfer. They argue that the first generation was concerned with dissemination and the second with building relationships between research producers and users. The third generation focuses on taking a systems approach to tackling barriers to research use.

In recent years, then, researchers have focused on the potential of individuals and organisations working in the 'space' between research, policy and practice. So-called knowledge brokers and boundary spanners have been deployed to facilitate research use, including building relationships between stakeholders (Ward et al., 2009, 2012). In the most basic terms, knowledge brokers are intermediaries. They act as go-betweens for the evidence and policy communities. They can be academics taking secondments in policy departments or policy analysts working in academic settings. They could also be representatives from bespoke knowledge-brokering organisations who are equally comfortable in the world of evidence production and policy formulation. The task of the knowledge broker is best thought of as being one of translation, providing both sides of the evidence and policy communities with detailed knowledge of how the other works and what the other needs. It is not an easy task and there are, to date, very few evaluations of whether this strategy works. In a recent article, Kislov and colleagues reflect on the 'dark side' of knowledge brokering (Kislov et al., 2017) stemming from the status of the broker as an intermediary in need of an advanced skill set that can only be developed in time, a luxury not always in ready supply in policy circles. Other promising developments include the emergence of implementation science, which focuses specifically on the activities and competencies required to transfer research into policy and practice (Eccles and Mittman, 2006).

The utility of knowledge brokering is currently unknown. For realist researchers, as we shall see, brokering represents less a link in the chain between research and policy than it is part of the overall enterprise of research production. Here it sits alongside other strategies that have been employed to try and bridge the evidence to policy gap. One of the key developments in later manifestations of evidence-based policy-making, taking a lead from evidence-based medicine, has been the shift from using individual studies to inform policy to the primacy of systematic review. Realism has permeated this modus operandi in the form of realist reviews or syntheses (e.g. Pawson, 2006b). The remainder of this chapter considers the development of systematic review in its mainstream form and how the realist version departs from this. It also looks at the implications for the emergence of realist review and how this is now feeding into broader debates about impact and how to measure it.

THE EMERGENCE OF SYSTEMATIC REVIEW

The gap between evidence production and policy formulation is well known, but despite recent attempts to fuse what Caplan (1979) described as the two communities of research and policy, they often coexist rather than combine. Fox (2017) highlights how systematic reviews have become part of the policy landscape during the last three decades. They have been particularly prominent in health sciences. Fox notes how systematic reviews have pro-liferated in recent years, suggesting that in the late-1980s, health-sector journals published on average between 80 and 90 systematic reviews a year. Two decades later this figure had risen to approximately 2,500 and by 2015 'more than 8,000 systematic reviews that meet international standards are now published annually in the literature of the health sector' (Fox, 2017: 88).

Reflecting on the emergence of systematic review, Pawson (2006b: 8–9) observes that in their early manifestations they were developed to try and overcome the sense of disappoint-ment surrounding evaluation and its failure 'to feed significantly and successfully into the policy process'. The benefit of systematic review, at least in theory, rests on its application in the process of policy formulation. It this sense, it is prognostic. Evaluation research, meanwhile, is more diagnostic. Its stock is at its highest once the policy or programme is embedded. Furthermore, for Pawson (2006b: 9) the benefits of reviews revolved around the 'stunningly obvious point about the timing of research vis-à-vis policy – namely, that to inform policy, the research must come before the policy'. In addition to timing and location within policy, the accumulation of evidence and its consolidation in a review have advan-tages over relying on the single study, not least in the way that biases can be ironed out via multiplication. Systematic reviews aim to 'capture and pool the burgeoning mass of primary research activity', in effect undertaking a scientific stock-taking exercise on any given topic, and so, in theory, stand arguably the best chance of providing the evidence- base of what works for policy decisions.

Despite their apparent abundance, there is, according to Fox, an increasing ambiva-lence or diminished interest associated with the use of reviews and their overall utility. Fox (2017: 89) describes how in the third edition of *Systematic Reviews on Health Care: Meta-Analysis in Context*, the editors had decided to replace the chapter detailing the use of systematic review for evidence-based policy-making with a short summary. Despite the protestations of Fox himself and his submission of an extended, several thousand-word piece, it did not make the final cut. Similarly, Fox notes, the first nine issues of the journal *Public Health Reviews* include 'no articles linking systematic reviews to policy for public health, and, likewise, the book *A Systematic Review of Key Issues in Public Health* (Boccia et al., 2015), does not, according to Fox, 'describe actual and potential uses of systematic reviews to inform policy'.

Although some of the evidence presented by Fox for this ambivalence can be described as 'anecdotal', he goes on to explain a number of impediments to the increasing influence of systematic reviews on policy (in health). These include: (a) vested interests – where those with 'financial interests in particular interventions and care processes' cast doubt on the findings of systematic reviews, doing so by criticising evidence-based medicine or policy as offering nothing more than 'cook-book medicine' and 'interfering with professional autonomy' or 'disregarding clinical judgement' (Fox, 2017: 89); (b) political expediency – the favoured programmes of policy-makers may get sidelined if they have not been the subject of a review because of their 'inadequate evidence-base; (c) co-production – policy-makers frequently find themselves in the more passive role of consuming published research rather than taking a more active role in setting its agenda or priorities'; and (d) methodological flaws – according to Fox (2017: 90) the absence from most reviews of findings from 'research in disciplines of the policy sciences' hinders their utility. Allied to this point, Fox points to the work of Ioannidis (2016) on the lack of international standards for methodology which means that there is a 'mass production of redundant, misleading and conflicted systematic reviews and meta-analyses' which has 'reached epidemic proportions' (Fox, 2017: 91).

Although promising, systematic reviews do, however, still need to deal with the perennial challenge when trying to exert influence over policy. Policy makers and politicians can't be expected to and, in fact, don't read anything like a large proportion of published research (Weiss and Bucuvalas, 1980), but the review synthesis was supposedly a step towards making this more of a possibility. Systematic reviews initially presented new challenges in terms of how best to summarise the evidence in a form that is digestible to policy makers. For Fox, the solution to these problems requires that policy makers and research professionals and their associates address two clusters of issues. The first includes more policy funding for research and the second is addressing urgently the lack of scientific integrity and, therefore, credibility of systematic reviews. This is linked to the challenge of 'expanding the methodology for conducting systematic reviews'. (Fox, 2017: 91)

The interesting aspect, for current purposes, is what is not said in the article. The lack of stakeholder engagement is seen as the problem. There is then a clarion call for more reviews to incorporate findings from the 'political sciences and sociology'. The work of Greenhalgh and colleagues (Best et al., 2012) is singled out as an exception due to the diversity of types of evidence included in the review. The basic methodology of the review is, however, treated as unproblematic. It seems that Fox is here calling for more realist reviews without uttering the words. Realist reviews are about much more than allowing in a wide range of types of knowledge. By seeking to identify the generative mechanisms that exist between cause and effect and locating this in specific contexts, realist reviews do trade plural forms of evidence to understand policy. Furthermore, they directly implicate the contexts seen as contingent in these causal accounts. In terms of outputs, they generate insights into the mechanisms at work within programmes and the interplay between mechanisms and different contexts. This begs the question, then, of how evidence can speak more directly to policy and how it can encapsulate a broad church of evidence, while retaining its scientific integrity. For realist researchers, including Ray Pawson, there was and is potential in the emergence of realist synthesis.

CONSIDERING THE EMERGENCE AND REACH OF REALIST REVIEW

The dominant paradigm – often referred to as meta-analysis – is the review methodology based on a successionist model of causation and underpinned by the logic of aggregation. This model adopts an external view of causation and seeks to ascertain whether a programme or intervention works to deliver a desired outcome. For those working in this tradition, the randomised controlled trial (RCT) is seen as the gold-standard method for determining this kind of causality. By randomly assigning participants to a group within a study, one of which will receive an intervention and one that will not, researchers working within this paradigm seek to establish what they argue to be causation. For reviews, this process is scaled up. The multiplied findings of RCTs are seen to be the gold standard of systematic review.

This understanding of review has received a certain amount of criticism. Fox (2017) has already pointed out the limited kinds of evidence that can be included in such studies. In addition, due to the restrictive nature of inclusion criteria in studies and the heterogeneity of evidence, verdicts are delivered that read either 'not enough evidence' or 'no overall winner', a problem magnified by the fact that interventions frequently work in one context but do not travel well. In short, meta-analysis based on successionist logic is poor at dealing with complexity and with different contexts (Greenhalgh, 2014). Or to rephrase, evidence of complexity and context is purposefully excluded from such studies. Sampling procedures based on principles of randomisation and control are championed as being capable of eliminating confounding causal explanations so that a single cause can be isolated and seen to lead to certain effects. Another way this happens is to achieve control by statistical techniques. Here correlations are observed and cause is established post hoc through techniques measuring statistical significance. In both scenarios, however, the aim is to reveal a pure relationship uncluttered by extraneous and confounding factors through the elimination of bias. All the mess and background of the social world is placed firmly inside the black box.

It was with this in mind that Pawson (2006b) suggested a new form of review – namely realist synthesis – stemming from a generative view of causation (Bhaskar, 1997) which has at its core the need to explain why social regularities occur, not merely that they do occur, as in the successionist version of causation. As Sayer (2000: 14) explains,

causation is not understood on the model of the regular success of events ... the conventional impulse to prove causation by gathering data on regularities, repeated occurrences is, therefore, misguided: at best these might suggest where to look for causal mechanisms. What causes something to happen has nothing to do with the number of times we observe it happening (Sayer, 2000: 14)

Translated into policy, this encourages researchers to think beyond whether a programme works and to consider 'what works for whom in what circumstances and why'. In effect, this is about embracing the complexity of the social world and the role of context.

Interventions and programmes are highly contingent on context – they are not universally successful and estimates of net effect are not useful when attempts are made to implement policy in the real world where context varies significantly.

Since the publication of *Realist Evaluation* in 1997 (Pawson and Tilley, 1997), *Evidence-Based Policy: A Realist Perspective* in 2006 (Pawson, 2006b) and various others besides, much ink has been depleted on defining and designing the way to complete realist evaluations and realist reviews. Here we consider their utility and usability in policy (see Box 10.1).

The first point to note is that realist research is not a panacea. Indeed, the sense of frustration that has been documented by many thinkers who have tried to use research to shape policy is shared by realist researchers. Pawson (2006b: 175) reflects on the process:

My own impression of my own efforts to get my own reviews noticed is that much of the recent governmental head-nodding to evidence-based policy is mere lip service. As one moves up the policy-making ladder through 'analytic divisions' to 'policy divisions' the appetite for evidence dwindles. As one ascends the intervention hierarchy from practitioners to managers to bureaucrats to the political classes, the capacity to absorb complex information dwindles by the bullet point. (Pawson, 2006b: 175)

Despite this sense of despondency, we consider some of the lessons afforded from realist review for the broader impact agenda and for the future of systematic review as a means of realising evidence-based policy-making.

BOX 10.1 THE MENTORING REVIEW: AN AUTOBIOGRAPHICAL ACCOUNT

In 2003 Ray Pawson and Annette Boaz obtained funding to both conduct and promote the use of a realist review on youth mentoring. There are many ways to think about improving research use, but in this case Pawson and Boaz focused on building relationships with potential stakeholders. This approach has been described in the literature as the 'second generation' of thinking on knowledge transfer (Best and Holmes, 2010). They sought to work with potential users, arranging to meet and discuss the review with key stakeholders within government and in partner organisations throughout the review process. At an early stage, they met with government analysts with an interest in youth mentoring to identify potential topics for the review. Given the fast-moving policy environment, government analysts were reticent about predicting what might be a 'hot topic' once the review was finished so left the researchers to decide where to focus for the review. To support engagement, Pawson prepared briefings and other stimulus materials in discussions about the review right from the outset. Later meetings and events were arranged to share the findings with policy-makers. Pawson and Boaz even pitched the idea of co-production, or at the very least close working, throughout the review process, but analysts within government were more content to leave them to 'get on with it'.

Boaz has written elsewhere about how the attempt to promote the use of the review felt like following many paths through a policy maze, the majority of which seem to go nowhere (Boaz et al., 2008). The most successful journey towards promoting the use of the mentoring review straddled two major government departments, involved many individuals, took a considerable period of time (35 additional days over ten months) and faced a number of potential dead ends. Initial contact was established through an existing relationship between Pawson and the analytical team in the department. The first meeting with analysts provided useful insights into the policy agenda and identified an opportunity or policy window (Kingdon, 1984), in the form of an imminent Green Paper on youth offending. The government analysts invited the researchers to get back in touch once the review was more fully developed. However, the first two attempts to give a presentation on the research in this government department ended with meetings cancelled at short notice. The research contact in one government department reflected later in an interview that the review was almost too timely: 'It was a struggle to organize not because policy people aren't interested ... but because it's fitting it in, in the context of frantic Green Paper deliberations.' Seven months after the review was completed Pawson finally had a chance to present the research to policy-makers. The seminar was attended by seven policy-makers from several relevant government departments.

The seminar was just one part of a wider programme of utilisation-focused activity. However, this description of the process of organising one seminar indicates the time and energy required to promote research use. This effort is not associated with direct use but with securing an opportunity to share the findings with potential users. Thus the outcome of interest (utilisation) remained at least one step beyond the efforts to present the research. Although a government researcher contrasted the review (favourably) with traditional systematic reviews that 'stripped out all the context', the only evidence of getting close to a visible impact on policy came from a conversation in a lift with a junior member of the policy team working on the Green Paper. The researchers were expressing their disappointment that the review didn't get a mention in the paper. The junior policy analyst explained how the review had been included in the text of the Green Paper, but was lost in one of the final edits.

SOME PROVISIONAL LESSONS FROM AND FOR REALIST REVIEW

The mentoring case also reveals that promoting research use is a full-time job, whatever the research. The constellation of features required to promote use in this instance (a partnership, an accessible location for a seminar and existing networks) echoes themes in the academic literature (Walter et al., 2003). However, there are hidden elements of chance (in establishing positive partnerships) and resource requirements (organising events, hiring rooms, the time of those attending) that have to be supported by a considerable amount of drive and enthusiasm for the business of promoting the use of research, once the intensive period of research production has passed. Funding for promoting research was and remains highly unusual (despite the dominant research impact discourse).

The relational approach adopted by Boaz and Pawson allowed the researchers to exploit opportunities as and when they arose. In a sense, what is being advocated here is a limited form of co-production. Pawson notes that the most effective review in terms of impact may well be the one with the least surprises and this 'requires shrewdness, experience and the ability to converse with policy-makers in refining the precise questions to be put in the review' (Pawson, 2006b: 178). This process is one whereby reviewers will work with policy personnel to set the terms of engagement – terms that are realistic for all stakeholders (including the researchers). In particular, creating space for policy-makers and government analysts to share and discuss their own programme theories at the outset of the review process is crucial to a realist approach. However, while this initial gathering of local knowledge was possible within the mentoring review, a more ambitious goal of co-producing the review proved harder to achieve. In this case, policy-makers were less interested in working closely to co-produce the review, preferring to send the reviewers away to get on with producing the synthesis. That said, impact from research will very much be contingent on the skill and aptitude of the researcher to visit, revisit and be familiar with the world of policy. This returns us full circle. Cooperation is a process that remains continuous throughout the evaluation/synthesis lifespan and beyond. Researchers need to remain open to windows of opportunity for engagement when they arise and, of course, there are no guarantees.

Engagement with government analysts and other stakeholders during the research process also had unintended positive effects in terms of shaping both the content and the presentation of the review. It also built ownership of the review and pre-knowledge of what the review would say. A final benefit came in the form of an education for the research team in vital elements of the political and policy landscape of youth mentoring (Cairney, 2016). However, contra to Fox, the process of early stakeholder engagement is not a panacea and policy-makers are frequently too busy or disinterested to be engaged at an early stage. While many of these observations would be common to research engagement activity around any piece of research, there seemed to be a more comfortable fit between realist philosophy, realist synthesis and the policy process. Where conventional systematic reviews are often considered to be excessively technical, time-consuming to produce and narrow in their focus, realist reviews can engage more closely with the messy world of policy. Furthermore, there are many different types of use, ranging from the tactical to the enlightened (Weiss, 1979).

The fact that realist reviews are not in the business of delivering definitive judgements (it works!) means that they are likely to align better with more enlightened use of evidence in which new knowledge helps to shape thinking, debates and agendas. Arguably, a policy-maker is less likely to pull a realist review off a shelf to back up a decision that has already been made. So how can we gauge the impact of the review? There are at least two ways to answer this question. The first is to consider where the review is now. From our searches, it would seem that the review continues to slowly percolate into the literature, in line with Carol Weiss's vision of enlightened evidence use (Weiss, 1979). At the time of writing, there are 58 citations for the review on Google Scholar.[3] Here, we see evidence percolation in action. Direct impact on policy is a rarity, but evidence can change the way issues are framed through the familiarity fostered via citation. We also found references to Pawson's 'mentoring mechanisms' in a textbook on mentoring, facilitation and supervision, where the mechanisms identified by Pawson are listed in a text box (Scott and Spouse, 2013). The Pathways of Youth Mentoring model from the original review is reproduced in a subsequent review of the literature, and Pawson is thanked for his contribution to knowledge on mentoring in the acknowledgements section (Philip and Spratt, 2007). These examples of 'knowledge creep' (Weiss, 1980) don't add up to a shift in mentoring policy and practice, but the initial process of engaging with stakeholders documented above should serve as a warning, or at least lead to more realistic expectations for researchers that this is a likely outcome of review work. The above also provide examples of impact in terms of influencing academic literature and debates rather than shifts in policy and practice in youth mentoring.

There are, however, other lessons and advice that can be taken from this account that focus more on process than outcome. Here, we see an overlap with other (non-realist) attempts to influence policy. We can condense these into various themes. The first theme, it can be argued, is not realist at all, but is now established wisdom and, even more than that, it is an expectation that researchers will collaborate widely in the research process, but especially with policy-makers and commissioners, from design through to dissemination. As part of a discussion on prioritising questions for a systematic review, Pawson (2006b: 81) states that because time is the most precious but scarce commodity in research, pragmatic decisions need to be taken on the *specifics* of the review (our italics), so 'a particularly characteristic trait, a feature of palpable novelty, a point of potential fragility or an area of dispute within a programme may be singled out as the burning issue for review'.

It is one of the most widely known drawbacks of evidence-based policy-making that researchers frequently decry that policy-makers have a poor grasp of research in terms of methodological prowess and the capacity to nurture nuance. One frequently cited solution is that researchers must provide policy-makers with easily digestible findings.

Pawson (2006b: 168) notes that realist reviews are able to walk the corridors of power and 'talk the talk', and what is more they can do so in the mother tongue of the policy-maker:

> Policy-makers are likely to struggle with data that reveal, for instance, the respective statistical significance of an array of mediators and moderators in a meta-analysis. They are more likely to be able to interpret and to utilize a full-blown realist explanation of why a programme theory works better in one context than another. Although these two investigatory thrusts serve to answer rather similar questions, the one that focuses on sense-making has the advantage. This is especially so if the investigation focuses on adjudicating between rival explanations, thus providing justification for taking one. (Pawson, 2006b: 168)

Although co-production is not solely associated with realism, it is a key opportunity afforded by a realist approach to review. As realism embraces the complexity of the social world, the issue of research bias is less a central benchmark of quality to this approach as it is for traditional forms of review. As the mentoring example shows for realist reviews, such co-production is seen as an important part of surfacing programme theories through the initial collection of possible explanatory theories but also in checking out at later stages in the review process whether the emerging synthesis has face validity for policy-makers.

ANALYSING IMPACT

In an era of increasing scepticism around the use of research and expertise, attention has turned towards how impact can be measured and monitored. In their narrative review of research impact in the field, Greenhalgh and colleagues (2016) note that numerous different impact typologies have been developed over the past few years, each with their own philosophical underpinning. These typologies are ways of measuring the impact of research rather than the process of ensuring the impact of research. Table 10.1 provides an overview of the different philosophical starting points of thinking about research impact. As can be seen, the realist philosophical approach is listed as one such tool of measurement.

Firstly, the realist approach to measuring impact is heavily influenced by the Pawsonian CMO configuration. This is, for Greenhalgh and colleagues (2016), at the heart of the realist assumption about what constitutes realist research knowledge. The purpose of this configuration is to develop theoretical generalisations that provide the impetus for (constrained) action. Other assumptions of realist inquiry include naturalistic research employing 'an open house' approach to methods, which in turn are mobilised with the express intention of contributing to theory development and testing. At the heart of the realist review, however, is the notion that no two interventions are configured in the same way. This is one of the foundation stones of what makes a realist review realist and how realism can provide an overall strategy for thinking through impact.

TABLE 10.1 Philosophical assumptions underpinning approaches to research impact

Perspective	Positivist	Constructivist	Realist	Critical	Performative
Assumptions about what [research] knowledge is	Facts (especially statements on relationships between variables), independent of researchers and transferable to new contexts	Explanations/interpretations of a situation or phenomenon, considering the historical, cultural and social context	Studies of how people interpret external reality, producing statements on 'what works for whom in what circumstances'	Studies that reveal society's inherent conflicts and injustices and give people the tools to challenge their oppression	Knowledge is brought into being and enacted in practice by actor-networks of people and technologies
Assumed purpose of research	Predictive generalisations ('law')	Meaning: perhaps in a single, unique case	Theoretical generalisation (what tends to work and why)	Learning, emancipation, challenge	To map the changing dynamics of actor-networks
Preferred research methods	Hypothesis-testing; experiments; modelling and measurement	Naturalistic inquiry (i.e. in real-world conditions)	Predominantly naturalistic, may combine quantitative and qualitative data	Participatory [action] research	Naturalistic, with a focus on change over time and network [in]stability
Assumed way to achieve quality in research	Hierarchy of preferred study designs; standardised instruments to help eliminate bias	Reflexive theorising; consideration of multiple interpretations; dialogue and debate	Abduction (what kind of reasoning by human actors could explain these findings in this context?)	Measures to address power imbalances (ethos of democracy, conflict management); research capacity building in community partner(s)	Richness of description; plausible account of the network and how it changes over time
Assumed relationship between science and values	Science is inherently value-neutral (though research can be used for benign or malevolent motives)	Science can never be value-neutral; the researcher's perspective must be made explicit	Facts are interpreted and used by people who bring particular values and views	Science must be understood in terms of what gave rise to it and the interests it serves	Controversial; arguably, actor-network theory is consistent with a value-laden view of science
Assumed mechanism through which impact is achieved	Direct (new knowledge will influence practice and policy if the principles and methods of implementation science are followed)	Mainly indirect (e.g. via interaction/enlightenment of policy-makers and influencing the 'mind lines' of clinicians)	Interaction between reasoning (of policy-makers, practitioners, etc.) and resources available for implementing findings	Development of critical consciousness; partnership-building; lobbying; advocacy	'Translations' (stable changes in the actor-network), achieved by actors who mobilise other actors into new configurations
Implications for the study of research impact	'Logic models' will track how research findings (transferable facts about what works) are disseminated, taken up and used for societal benefit	Outcomes of social interventions are unpredictable; impact studies should focus on 'activities and interactions' to build relations with policy-makers	Impact studies should address variability in uptake and use of research by exploring context-mechanism-outcome-impact configurations	Impact has a political dimension; research may challenge the status quo; some stakeholders stand to lose power, whereas others may gain	For research to have impact, a re-alignment of actors (human/technological) is needed; focus on the changing 'actor-scenario' and how this gets stabilised in the network

Source: Greenhalgh et al. (2016).

Greenhalgh and colleagues (2016) also suggest that there are a number of frameworks that have been developed to demonstrate research impact. These are mapped on to the philosophical accounts above, although the frameworks are not necessarily limited to one philosophical approach. The established models include the Payback Framework, the Canadian Academy of Health Sciences Framework, Monetisation Models, while a grouping of approaches listed as Societal Impact Assessment and Related Approaches are much more widespread.

The Payback Framework (Buxton and Hanney, 1996), for Greenhalgh and colleagues, is the most widely used. It consists of two elements. Firstly, it is based on a logic model covering seven stages of research from design through implementation to outcomes. Secondly, it highlights five main categories to classify the payback. It should be noted that these are not simply monetary. They include knowledge in the form of academic publications and benefits to future research in the form of advanced training for new researchers, for instance. Other paybacks include benefits to policy, systemic benefits, which in this case related to benefits for the health system, and broader economic benefits (Greenhalgh et al., 2016: 4). Fundamentally, however, the Payback Framework depicts a rather linear account of the relationship between evidence and policy impact. In doing so, it is consistent with the governmental approach to impact we have already critiqued. According to Greenhalgh et al., the established models are not the only strategies being used to measure impact where some newer and promising additions to the literature are becoming visible. It is here that we can once again witness the influence of realist thinking. In terms of measuring impact, realist approaches are still relatively unknown when it comes to providing a framework for research impact. They suggest that only one study (Rycroft-Malone et al., 2015) has attempted to assess impact in a designated realist manner and it was 'resource intensive' to apply (Greenhalgh et al., 2016: 11). The very fact that realist thought is being considered useful not only as a way of providing policy with evidence but also as a way of thinking about the entire endeavour – that is, strategy for achieving impact which recognises specifically that impacts are partial and contextual – is, we think, a significant course for optimism. In essence, not only has realism had some success in influencing small areas of policy (e.g. mentoring) and larger programmes of work (see Kelly's chapter in this volume), its impact is also being seen as a useful philosophical approach for considering what the very nature of impact could and should be.

CONCLUSION

There are elements of the realist approach to systematic review that are consistent with approaches and attempts to use evidence to influence policy. This involves taking ownership of the research, spotting opportunities for impact, but being realistic about the policy landscape. In a similar vein, as pointed out by thinkers such as Caplan and Weiss many years ago, it is incumbent on researchers to transform weighty reports and detailed analysis into accessible formats that speak to the context in which the findings will be used. Where realism departs from other forms of review is that realist advice eschews proclamations that declare programmes to work, precisely because programmes themselves have no causal powers. Instead they offer recipients a range of resources on which to act or not. As Pawson notes, an intervention or a programme is 'a complex system thrust amidst complex systems' (2006b: 168). In this sense, the key realist conclusion is one that shows certain programmes work for certain people in some circumstances and in some respects at the level of theory.

There seems to be something in the form and content of the realist account that has the potential to shift thinking and stimulate new ideas and solutions. This is akin to what Weiss has termed the enlightenment model of research utilisation. The case of mentoring demonstrates that policy-makers appreciated the creative ways in which the realist reviewer moved beyond text and communicated emerging theories using models, diagrams and stories, in essence bringing to the fore the expression of theories of how interventions work, for whom and in what circumstances and why. It also showed that policy-makers do respond well to more contextualised accounts. The case of mentoring also shows how researchers and policy-makers must work together to define and refine the precise questions of the review. Interaction between reasoning (of policy-makers, practitioners, etc.) and resources available for implementing findings is and should be a continuous process. In an ideal world, policy would be involved in establishing contextualised findings as part of a 'no surprises' review, but this is not always achievable in the cut-and-thrust world of policy. In an ideal world also, policy-makers would respond to detailed accounts about the nature of programmes and interventions and the subtler evaluative findings they produce, but this does not always happen and, in many cases, the evidence is siphoned out as programmes shape Bills which become Acts.

Looking forward, the potential of realist synthesis seems to lie in its capability to be useful even if it is not necessarily used. In the world of systematic review, realist approaches have gained some currency. Yet in many ways they also sit at the periphery. We can remind ourselves that Fox (2017) called for more diverse evidence to find its way into review, without acknowledging that this is a forte of the realist approach. The virtues of realist approaches are extolled without acknowledging the approach itself. In studies of research impact, realism stands at the precipice. It is not yet part of mainstream approaches, but its potential has been cited (Greenhalgh et al., 2016).

With its emphasis on the production of circumstantial and conditional 'truths', realism aims to provide the policy and practice communities with a dossier of material that offers them hope in understanding 'complex social interventions' and their likely operation in particular contexts. Realist approaches do not provide a definitive answer as to whether 'something works or not' (Pawson et al., 2005); instead they offer theories on the likelihood of events occurring at particular times in particular fashions. It is the point of the realist review to stockpile lessons from policy. These can be considered a kind of library of mechanisms which then form the starting point for subsequent reviews, with each contribution adding to the encyclopaedia of whether or not a programme works, in what circumstances and in what respects. This, we argue, is precisely the kind of impact that realism can have and it is the kind of impact that impact itself should be – modest, ongoing and realistic.

NOTES

1 Mentoring has been tried across various policy domains as a way of improving outcomes, whether that be the reduction of youth offending, improved performance in school or developing further capacity in the workplace.
2 Both authors have at one time been associated with this journal.
3 These are citations for R. Pawson (2004) 'Mentoring relationships: an explanatory review', http://79.125.112.176/sspp/departments/politicaleconomy/research/cep/pubs/papers/assets/wp21.pdf.

11

REALIST RESEARCH, GUIDELINES AND THE POLITICS OF EVIDENCE

Mike Kelly

WHAT THIS CHAPTER IS ABOUT

This chapter outlines a practical application of realist thinking in the development of guidelines for public health in the UK under the aegis of NICE (the National Institute for Health and Care Excellence). Evidence-based medicine brought to the fore the RCT experimental design on the premise that the method reduces bias so that the relationship between potential interventions or treatments (such as the administration of a new drug or eradication of a risky behaviour) can be said to lead to specific outcomes (hopefully health improvements). This chapter demonstrates how in the complex world of public health the RCT falls short. Why? Because public health improvement often requires fundamental behavioural change. Knowing cigarette smoking causes lung cancer, for instance, does not tell us how to make people quit smoking, nor does it tell you why there remain steadfast differences between social class and ethnic sub-groups in efforts to reduce tobacco consumption. Instead, mechanistic thinking is required.

How this chapter will help you to do realist research

NICE sought to move the evidence-based medicine paradigm into the world of public health by getting as close as possible to understanding the mechanisms of action both of interventions and outcomes and by ascertaining the organisational, social, dynamic context within which interventions occur. As NICE publishes its guidance on its website, readers can access examples of public health guidance developed from realist principles.

A practical tip: a take-home message from the chapter

The realist approach refuses to be drawn into simple linear models and frames questions in ways that are often much more illuminating than simple hypothesis testing, meaning that practical but contingent advice can be generated. Contingency is the enemy of certainty, meaning that (realist) evidence and politics often clash.

INTRODUCTION

In 2005 the then National Institute for Health and Clinical Excellence (NICE – since 2013 known as the National Institute for Health and Care Excellence) was given responsibility by government for the development of evidence-based public health guidelines for the English health service. From the moment that NICE took on this role, the intention was to bring realist principles into the work of developing evidence-based public health guidelines. Members of the public health team at NICE had worked previously with Ray Pawson and were particularly influenced by his thinking about the limitations of evidence-based medicine and of randomised trials and also what possibilities undertaking realist reviews might offer.

The decision to give NICE the task of developing evidence-based public health guidelines was taken during a major reorganisation of government arm's length bodies in 2004. Prior to 2005 NICE had had a strictly clinical role, hence its original name – the National Institute for *Clinical* Excellence. But from 1 April 2005 it acquired the staff and the resources of one of the arm's length bodies which was to be abolished – the Health Development Agency (HDA). The HDA was itself the successor body to the Health Education Authority which in turn had succeeded the Health Education Council. These two older organisations had been responsible for the provision of educational materials, mass media campaigns, advertising and information about many aspects of disease prevention and health protection in England. Perhaps the most well-remembered of all their activities was the 'Don't die of ignorance' campaign at the time of the appearance of HIV and AIDS in the 1980s.

The idea of evidence-based guidelines and the underpinning principles of evidence-based medicine (EBM) share with critical realism the assumption that acting on the world has direct consequences but that our ability to know and understand precisely the reasons why actions have consequences is limited (Bhaskar, 2008). They differ, however, on the nature of what those limitations are. Evidence-based medicine has been built on the premise that it is possible to develop methods of scientific enquiry in which limitations in knowledge can be reduced by eliminating biases. By reducing bias, it is assumed that the relationship between the independent variable (the intervention, say a new drug) and the dependent variable (the outcome of treatment) is as accurate as possible (Egger et al., 2001; Kelly and Moore, 2012). In contrast, the realist position, as advanced by Pawson and others, has focused on the nature of the linkages and the pathways of action between intervention and outcome (Pawson, 2002). EBM, they suggest, is weak on these linkages because of its reliance on correlational trial data and a failure to take in the broader picture because of its very success in controlling confounders! Since public health is concerned with very broad biological, social, organisational and psychological interacting complexities (Kelly et al., 2014), rather than simple linear relationships between single variables (a single drug and its effect on a single aspect of a single disease), the appeal of realism seemed obvious. The approach taken at NICE in public health was to harness the undoubted power of EBM with the focus on real-world complexities provided by realism (Kelly et al., 2009; NICE, 2009, 2012).

The public health programme embraced and tried to bring to its method of developing guidelines Pawson's axiom that Context (C) + Mechanism (M) = Outcome (O). As the evidence was interrogated the review process sought to identify what contexts enable or act as barriers to stop the interventions achieving the intended outcomes (Pawson and Tilley, 1997: 59) and evaluating CMO configurations relating to the successes and failures of the programmes. So many appraisals of evidence included reviews of barriers and facilitators, for example.

The focus in the appraisal of the evidence was on what really happens rather than what ought to happen. The idea was to articulate the reasons why things work (or didn't work) in practice (NICE, 2012).

EBM, CLINICAL MEDICINE AND PUBLIC HEALTH

The origins of EBM are to be found in a number of disparate developments which were themselves responses to several problems in medical practice that had become gradually apparent by the 1970s. First, growth in the numbers of published papers worldwide in clinical medicine was exponential. Even within single specialities it was increasingly difficult, not to say impossible, for even the most assiduous and conscientious reader of the journals to keep pace with scientific developments and, more importantly, to be able to identify the best science and the most effective therapies derived from that science from within the mass of information. Second, it was noted that much medical practice wasn't based on peer- reviewed science in any event! It was based on the power and dominance of influential professors and consultants, royal colleges, specialist medical societies, textbooks, networks of influence emanating from medical schools and clinicians' habits and traditions. New and up-to-date peer-reviewed science came well down on the list of potential drivers of practice. Third, it was claimed that medical science had at best a scattergun approach to determining clinical effectiveness and at worse no scientific approach at all. There was no gold standard and reporting of findings (clinical or research-based) was often haphazard (see Cochrane (1972) for an early and highly influential exposition of these criticisms). So, for example, the means of determining the clinical effectiveness of one pharmacological agent compared with another was rudimentary. It was not based on systematic processes of comparative appraisal (Chalmers, 1998). Clinical judgement was paramount and although the vast majority of doctors sought to work in their patients' best interest it was far from a unified and scientific business. Drug companies brought products to market and then sought to influence prescribers in all sorts of ways, only one of which would be by the power of the scientific data, and of course the dangers of this approach became all too clear as the thalidomide scandal unfolded (Yllner, 2008). In the wider literature, writers like Illich were arguing that medicine was the cause of more ills than it cured (Illich, 1977).

Out of all this there emerged what might accurately be called a social movement whose different activities came to be known as evidence-based medicine. As far as this author is aware, the advocates of EBM never used the term realism to describe what they were doing; indeed their approach was decidedly atheoretical and methodologically narrow, almost to the point sometimes of crude positivism. However, the underlying epistemology, ontology, methods and processes were oriented to the understanding of observable effects of medical interventions. The whole effort was designed to be a sharp break from social processes of influence and power as the basis for medical decision-making. The founders of the evidence-based medicine movement sought to move treatments away from a theoretical and constructivist basis to a solidly empirical one (Greenhalgh, 2001).

The McMaster University Group in Canada was particularly influential and its definition of EBM has been widely cited down the years: 'the conscientious, explicit and judicious use of current best evidence in making decisions about the care of individual patients' (Sackett et al., 1996: 71). In the UK figures like Sir Iain Chalmers and Sir Muir Gray were instrumental in seeking to put the practice of medicine firmly on an evidence-based footing. Very importantly the EBM approach was about reducing risk to patients. The advocates argued that if mechanisms were uncertain, and more importantly still, if outcomes were uncertain and might possibly therefore cause harm, then there was no good reason to proceed with that particular intervention.

A number of ideas followed from these precepts. The starting point should be the evidence and that there should be transparent and reproducible methods for distinguishing good evidence from poor evidence. Mere association, or the assumption that medicine already knew and understood how things worked and which evidence was good or poor, were deemed to be simply not good enough. The criteria for determining the quality of the evidence were derived from the methods used to produce the evidence. Methods that were the least likely to produce biased findings (especially the randomised controlled trial) were defined as more trustworthy than other methods. The next founding principle was that every effort should be made to capture all the relevant scientific literature pertaining to a particular intervention (in other words, to be comprehensive rather than selective in reviewing evidence and literature). The traditional methods of literature reviewing were regarded as inadequate for the purpose, being too haphazard and open to bias. These were to be superseded by systematic and transparent methods of literature searching, of transparent explication of reasons for including or excluding literature in final reports and clear processes for synthesising literature from diverse studies – collectively what came to be called the systematic review. So the techniques of systematic reviewing, meta-analysis and the elaboration of optimal principles of trial design all emerged as tools to provide the basis for EBM (Egger et al., 2001; Greenhalgh, 2001). The target of all of this effort was to eliminate opinion-based medicine which, in the language of realism, we might term practice based on doctors' untested beliefs and theories as to why their treatments, and the ones that they had learned long ago in medical school, worked (without any formal or systematic way of testing that assumption) and why these beliefs were superior to the beliefs of others.

Unsurprisingly, EBM was not of course an approach that immediately found favour with the medical profession and a war of attrition has gone on ever since between the proponents of EBM, especially the methodological purists, and medical practice. However, it is not wrong to say that EBM was one of the most important developments in the medical sciences in the late twentieth century and the idea that peer-reviewed science should at least be a primary, if not the only, driver in intelligent medical decision-making is no longer seriously challenged – although the details and the implications for practice continue to be widely debated and argued over (McCartney, 2012; Greenhalgh et al., 2014).

Now, if clinical medicine had something of an unsystematic approach to evidence in the 1970s, the situation in public health was even worse. There were very few interventions which were based on *evidence of effectiveness* of any kind. Knowledge of whether interventions worked or how they worked was rudimentary and at best anecdotal, at worst pure guesswork. There were very many untested theories and assumptions, but little by way of evaluation of effectiveness. The things which practitioners did in the name of preventing disease and promoting health were based not on evidence of effectiveness but on epidemiological evidence about harms and risk and then for the most part common-sense understandings about how to get people to change their behaviour to reduce risk (Marteau et al., 2015; Kelly and Barker, 2016).

The underlying epidemiology which identified the risks though was of enormous scientific significance. In 1950 and 1952 Richard Doll and Austen Bradford Hill published their first papers (Doll and Hill, 1950, 1952) indicating a very strong link between exposure to cigarette smoke and the development of lung cancer. Following further work by Doll and Hill and the publication of reports by the Royal College of Physicians in the UK (1962) and by the Surgeon General in the USA (US Department of Health Education and Welfare Public Health Service, 1964), there was little room to doubt that there was a causal relationship between exposure to cigarette smoke and not only lung cancer but also heart disease, stroke and a range of other fatal conditions. The famous Framingham study (Dawber and Kannel, 1966; Sytkowski and D'Agostino, 1996) then broke new ground by establishing that there were a whole lot of other risk factors for heart disease in particular which resided not only in our smoking habits but also in our diet and lack of physical activity.

So the solution seemed commonsensically obvious – get people to stop smoking, to eat less fat, salt and sugar, to take more exercise and (more recently) to reduce their alcohol consumption. But what no one seemed to notice, at least initially, was that smoking, drinking alcohol, not doing much physical activity and eating too much constitute *behaviours as well as being risks*. In mechanistic terms, a behaviour, a risk and a cause are not the same thing. Moreover, these behaviours are deeply embedded in the way that people live their lives. Further, the interventions which are likely to bring about successful health-related behaviour change cannot be inferred from knowledge about risk – knowing that smoking causes lung cancer does not tell you *how* to help people to stop smoking. A realist lens helps to disentangle risks from causes, and causes from the kinds of things that are likely to bring about health-related behaviour change. But that lens had yet to be invented at that time and preventive efforts proceeded on the basis of unwarranted faith in beliefs about behaviour change which were not grounded in the then available social scientific knowledge. So, for example, although the risks of cigarette smoking were crystal clear by the mid-1960s, aside from the medical profession, the rest of the population only slowly changed their habits and behaviours in spite of extensive health educational campaigning. A great deal of public health effort over the decades since has continued to be aimed at behaviour change and by the time that EBM came on the scene it was still the case that efforts to moderate diet, obesity and alcohol consumption for the most part bore only the most tangential relationship to evidence derived from psychology and sociology about behaviour and behaviour change (Marteau et al., 2015; Kelly and Barker, 2016).

The move towards a more evidence-oriented approach in public health in England began at the start of the new century. The Health Development Agency had been established in 2000 with the closure of the Health Education Authority. It had from the outset been deeply involved in assessing evidence about public health. It did this, among its other roles, as a consequence of an important change in emphasis in public health policy research. In 2001 the English Department of Health published *A Research and Development Strategy for Public Health* (Department of Health, 2001). This was influenced by the emerging successes with EBM in clinical medicine and it recommended the application of the same principles to public health. This was a significant departure for public health in England. It signalled the importance of putting public health on an evidence-based footing and gave the Health Development Agency some of the responsibility for coordinating and synthesising the evidence.

The Health Development Agency then produced a number of what were called Evidence Briefings (see Killoran et al. (2006) for a discussion of this body of work) and spent a good deal of time reflecting on the appropriate methods of evidence synthesis. This was necessary because, while evidence synthesis was by now well developed in clinical evidence-based medicine, especially in the form of systematic reviews and meta-analysis of randomised controlled trials, this was not the case in public health. The task for the HDA team was to think about how to integrate descriptive epidemiology and such trials as there were with the social scientific understanding of human behaviour (Kelly et al., 2010). These diverse sources did not lend themselves easily to the methods developed in EBM. So a good deal of thought had to go into working out how to combine different types of data generated by different methods by disciplines with widely differing epistemological and ontological assumptions. One approach used was to synthesise review-level data and, although there were some doubts about whether this really did get to grips with the methodological problems and instead simply pushed the review results too far away from the primary studies, this type of early synthesis was well received in the public health community (see, for example, Millward et al., 2003; Mulvihill and Quigley, 2003).

In 2005 the HDA was abolished and some of its functions were merged with NICE which found itself with the responsibility for producing public health guidelines. This was new – the HDA had produced evidence summaries and briefings not guidance, and NICE was to go a step further and produce guidelines for practice. Until then only a few organisations around the world, other than the HDA, had been involved in the synthesis of public health evidence – notably the Centers for Disease Control (CDC) in Atlanta, GA, USA and their Task Force on Community Preventive Services (Briss, 2005). There were few national public health guidelines produced anywhere. So, when NICE acquired the role, this was the first time in any jurisdiction, worldwide, where a single organisation was to have responsibility for public health evidence synthesis and review and for the production of national recommendations about disease prevention, health improvement and health promotion.

EPISTEMIC SHIFTS

The extension of EBM to public health was important because it moved the epistemic grounds in public health and health promotion from a plurality of positions, which included forms of social constructionism and relativism mixed with correlational studies, to one where causes with clear outcomes could be discussed openly. This was a major shift in thinking. Throughout the 1980s and 1990s there had been, in the UK anyway, considerable resistance in some public health and health promotion circles to ideas of really investigating the relationship between interventions and outcomes. Indeed, outcomes, such as improved rates of mortality and morbidity, were sometimes downplayed in favour of a very strong emphasis on processes and engagement. This was perhaps most noticeable in methods and interventions designed to bolster community cohesion and strength by community development (Jones, 1986; Watt and Rodmell, 1988) and in arguments about the importance of building social capital (Campbell et al., 1999). In 1986 the Ottawa Charter for Health Promotion had been published (WHO, 1986) and had majored on empowering communities. The strategy was driven by an increasing recognition that the health of the population is neither the sole product of, nor can it be improved by, individual behaviour change. An approach which foregrounds the relations between classes, genders, ethnicities and the dynamic processes of social change is fundamental to bringing about long-term health improvement. However, in practice the Charter and its spin-offs were interpreted in some quarters as a good reason to retreat from hard numbers and quantitative measurement.

In a similar vein, the emergence of the so-called wider or social determinants approach to public health and especially to explaining the health inequalities in populations seemed to many to offer a message at odds with the principles of EBM (Raphael et al., 2010). If, as the social determinants approach contends, patterns of health and health differences between different groups in the population are the product of economic and political forces like employment, housing, environment and family life (Marmot and Wilkinson, 1999), then attention should focus on the political action designed to change those wider determinants rather than thinking about and trialling interventions on smoking cessation, alcohol consumption reduction, obesity and so on. Not surprisingly therefore, there was considerable resistance and scepticism from some sectors of the public health community about the moral, political, epistemological and practical possibilities of applying an evidence-based approach.

Most of the overt scepticism became much less vocal once the first NICE public health guidelines were produced and pressed into service in smoking cessation, behaviour change and obesity reduction. But this was as much because the zeitgeist was changing. In the aftermath of the publication of the Ottawa Charter, WHO had altered its course in the early 2000s towards an evidence-based approach. A Commission on the Social Determinants of Health was appointed, to be chaired and led by Sir Michael Marmot, one of Britain's most eminent epidemiologists and a long-time advocate for tackling health inequalities. The public health team at NICE was appointed as one of the Evidence and Knowledge networks supporting the Commission. As the work of the Commission got underway it was determined to take an evidence-based approach. When its work was completed in 2009 the evidence base which had been assembled was at that time the most comprehensive and thorough attempt to accumulate and synthesise the evidence about the social determinants of health and how they impact on populations. In addition, they raised a series of questions about mechanisms and causation (Bonnefoy et al., 2007). For example, it is important to understand the mechanisms of effect in different segments of the population and between different populations. So, although it is clear that efforts to reduce tobacco consumption have been very effective in the population of the UK as a whole, there remain widespread differences between different social class and ethnic sub-groups. Why this should be so may be guessed at (there are many competing theories), but a detailed understanding of mechanisms was and is for the most part absent in the evidence. The evidence is likewise missing in understandings of variations across the population in alcohol and food consumption, although common-sense theories abound (Kelly and Barker, 2016).

The final report of the Commission was a political document aimed at policy-makers worldwide and pays scant attention to the evidential or philosophical issues underpinning its recommendations (Commission on the Social Determinants of Health, 2008). But the evidence is available and in the public domain and points to the importance of taking an evidence-based and relational rather than an individual approach to public health and the health of the public (Bonnefoy et al., 2007).

DEVELOPING THE EVIDENCE BASE AND GUIDELINES IN PUBLIC HEALTH IN PRACTICE

With all of this going on, the public health team at NICE got on with the business of producing guidelines. The team at NICE sought to move the evidence-based medicine paradigm into the world of public health, and influenced to a significant degree, as noted above, by Ray Pawson's work, they sought to combine EBM with realism. This had two elements to it. The first was a desire to get as close as possible to understanding mechanisms of action for both interventions and outcomes, but also for the organisational, social and dynamic context within which interventions occur. The public health team at NICE began by trying to develop and explore logic models to understand and to take into account as far as possible the dynamics at work (Baxter et al., 2010; Kelly et al., 2009). The second element was to develop ways of synthesising evidence which was pluralistic and methodologically and epistemologically diverse, and which took account of mechanisms (Kelly et al., 2010). Using Pawson's insight about programme theory, contexts and mechanisms, it was possible to construct detailed models of the interconnections between aetiology and prediction. It is possible to understand the real as against the assumed behaviours and linkages, to peel away the rhetorical statements of the actors involved to see the real linkages or mechanisms in the system. The approach permits forensic detection about why things are the way they are (Baxter et al., 2010).

As the public health programme continued at NICE, successive editions of the methods manuals developed and refined processes which were designed to acknowledge method and disciplinary diversity and evidential pluralism in public health and beyond (NICE, 2016). One of the epistemological issues which became apparent was that in discussions in the guideline committees whose task it was to assess the synthesised evidence, there was invariably a tension. On the one hand, there was a very strong narrative which sought to prioritise the empirical evidence and wherever possible to use evidence drawn from RCTs. On the other hand, in order to interpret the evidence, committee members made use of a range of a priori knowledge, some derived from clinical or public health practice, some from clinical judgement and some from common-sense ideas about the way the world is or ought to be. Clearly, interpretation is grist to the mill of doing science and one of the tasks of the NICE technical team was to remind the committees that evidence never speaks for itself and that it always requires interpretation. In other words, the process wasn't a black box into which evidence was inputted and out came ready-made answers or recommendations. But getting to grips with that interpretive process was tricky (Kelly and Moore, 2012). It was as if the closer the committees got to hard evidence, the harder the answer was to find and other judgements had to be played in.

Interpreting the evidence in evidence-based clinical medicine is relatively straightforward. The evidence deals with specific biomedical and operational analytic levels, relatively well-defined medical problems and the parameters of the decisions which need to be made are delimited by clear clinical questions. In other words, if the problem is one of determining the clinical cost-effectiveness of compound A over compound B, even if the calculations are difficult and the evidence limited, there is an agreed assumption that it will be possible to develop an answer. However, where the evidence is mixed and operating at several epistemological levels, as it does in public health, care has to be taken with what kinds of interpretive and inferential mechanisms are appropriate to use for doing this. In effect, because the evidence is broad and the parameters of the decision relate to several operational levels, multiple potential interpretations may come into play.

Empirical evidence developed by multiple research methods had to be combined with accurate understandings of mechanisms and knowledge derived from practice. This is a combination of Hume's two forms of knowledge – rationalist and empiricist, i.e. that which we know on the basis of our existing ideas, our a priori knowledge; and experience, that which we may observe directly (Hume, 2007). The task centred on working out how best to combine these two forms of knowledge to develop both an understanding of the phenomenon and to make recommendations for the good of the health of the public (Kelly and Moore, 2012).

Prefiguring realism in the *Critique of Pure Reason*, Kant distinguished between phenomena – the world as it appears to be – and noumena – the world as it really is (Kant, 2007). Contemporarily Bhaskar (2008) has observed that we acknowledge that there is a world as it really is, but our science forever falls short of allowing us to understand and observe it fully. The tenets of EBM don't really allow for this, preferring instead an apparently simple and straightforward relationship between science and reality. They assume that evidence can be, if the method is right, unambiguous and unequivocal. But it is not unequivocal. To make sense of phenomena requires the use of both empirical data and disciplined theoretical knowledge (not just surmise and common sense) or, in Humean terms, a mix of empiricism and rationalism to get at the problem adequately. NICE's attempts to synthesise evidence, to develop logic models, to describe human and organisational behaviour was a recognition of this explicitly. It also became clear that it was necessary to try to articulate the values underpinning the whole process not just in terms of exploring and being open about conflicts of interest, but also the deeper values which inform choices about methods and about the inferential reasoning being used to understand empirical information (Kelly et al., 2015).

GUIDELINE DEVELOPMENT

The first guidelines were developed using methods which were highly skewed toward the EBM paradigm. This was deliberate. The topics were smoking and physical activity. These were areas where the evidence was extensive and there were teams of researchers around the UK who were both generating evidence and had experience of working with the old HDA. The need for methodological diversity was not great and the mechanisms of action were downstream, i.e. about one-to-one interventions, and these are pretty well described in the psychological literature. It was felt that if in these two relatively uncontroversial areas the first guidelines could be produced as a proof of concept, the trickier problems could then be addressed subsequently.

So the first two guidelines were brief interventions in primary care for smoking cessation and interventions for increasing physical activity (NICE, 2006a, 2006b). The two guidelines appeared in April 2006, exactly a year after the amalgamation of the HDA and NICE. The appearance of these first two guidelines was important because it demonstrated that the idea of applying the methods of EBM to public health was realisable and did not distort the phenomena in such a way as to make it useless from the perspective of the end user. The whole thing turned out to be extremely good value for money.

In this regard the most vivid, and to all involved actually the most surprising, finding in these first two pieces of work was that these interventions were, when compared to clinical interventions, astonishingly cost-effective. NICE had had from its foundation as a clinical organisation the central remit to determine the cost-effectiveness of what it recommended. This principle of applying health economics to ascertain cost-effectiveness had not been applied to public health interventions in any way systematically across different fields until NICE began its public health work in 2005. This allowed for the comparison of the cost-effectiveness of different public health interventions and clinical interventions to be made. NICE used cost utility analysis to estimate the cost-effectiveness of new drugs and so cost utility analysis was applied to public health interventions.

NICE's public health remit, as it had been established in 2005, was, however, much broader than these one-to-one interventions in primary care. The first opportunity to work on the broader canvas came with the development of guidelines on behaviour change and on community engagement. Both presented considerable, though different, methodological difficulties.

In public health and health promotion, behaviour change is used to describe a range of possible ways of getting individuals and populations to change their smoking, diet, physical activity, alcohol consumption, sexual activity and drug use (Marteau et al., 2015). There is an enormous literature emanating from psychology which describes many different techniques and especially models of the way this happens or is supposed to happen – some of which NICE had considered in its first guidelines on smoking and physical activity. There was also a considerable literature critiquing this downstream approach on the grounds that the focus on the individual inevitably missed the point that these behaviours are located in upstream social and economic contexts which for the most part people individually are unable to do very much about.

The literature pertaining to behaviour change was epistemologically diverse, had some very different ontological assumptions embedded in it, was riven with interdisciplinary hostility, was both highly theoretical and empirical, and even within mainstream health psychology extraordinarily diverse. Obviously systematic reviewing would provide only a partial account of the evidence. So the approach taken was pluralistic and sought to develop a set of general principles which drew upon the diversity of the social sciences (NICE, 2007).

The guidance on Community Engagement had to get to grips with an activity which is about a process or a way of working with communities rather than about necessarily changing them or the individuals in them. The process was conceived as mini complex systems thrust amid larger complex systems (NICE, 2008). It was also an arena where at least some of the advocates for the community engagement approach were committed politically and ideologically to that way of doing things and saw community development not so much as an intervention, but as a social movement standing in opposition to the status quo, especially the status quo as represented by the biomedical thinking dominant in epidemiology and indeed the whole process of doing EBM.

The debates that went on in the two committees developing the guidance were hard work but at the end of the process NICE was able to publish two guidelines which summarised the extant literatures, described the debates and laid out principles which, if a local health authority or local council wanted to pursue either of these approaches, provided a point of reference from which to start. They provided solid platforms for making decisions at the local level. The guidelines did not provide unequivocal 'must dos' but they did outline some of the pitfalls and things to be avoided as well as a comprehensive summation of the literature.

REALISM AND EBM MEET REALPOLITIK

With both the behaviour change and the community development guidance, the issues which arose were intellectually difficult but were confined to either academic and scientific argument about evidence and theory or practical arguments about putting things into practice. There was of course a sense that there were underlying political differences but they weren't in any sense partisan party-political issues, nor did they disturb ministers and senior officials in the Department of Health in so far as they engaged at all with the arguments.

However, it was a very different proposition with two of the guidelines produced in 2010 on the prevention of alcohol misuse (NICE, 2010a) and the prevention of cardiovascular disease (CVD) (NICE, 2010b). In the former, one of the principal recommendations was that minimum unit pricing (MUP) of alcohol was a cost-effective intervention to reduce alcohol consumption, especially among heavy drinkers and young and underage drinkers, very many of whom migrate to the cheapest forms of alcohol – especially cheap sprits and cider. In the CVD guidance there were recommendations about reducing levels of salt, trans-fatty acid consumption and sugar and national policy interventions to reduce the consumption of all three.

In the case of the recommendations regarding MUP, the evidence was garnered from modelling work initially undertaken at the University of Sheffield. There were no RCTs on MUP but in so far as the logic models elaborated in the modelling allowed, the evidence strongly pointed to the fact that the purchase of alcohol increases as it becomes relatively cheaper compared to average earnings (and that condition had prevailed in the UK for at least two decades) (Booth et al., 2008; Marteau et al., 2015). This is the case in the total population and among heavy drinkers and young people who buy the cheapest forms of alcohol they can. With respect to the data about sugar, salt and trans-fatty acids, the data were empirically grounded in numerous studies which would lead one with confidence to argue that government action to bring about gradual change in the availability of salt, sugar and trans-fatty acids in the nation's diet would have population health benefits. In both the alcohol and the CVD guidelines, the evidence was a mixture of empirical information of a variety of kinds assessed for its quality combined with the best theoretical understanding of the dynamics of human conduct and the social and biological mechanisms involved. While the evidence was not absolute, the overwhelming weight of it pointed to the need for national jurisdictions to act.

These two guidelines were published just after the June 2010 general election and the return of the new Coalition government to office. The incoming Secretary of State for Health was distinctly underwhelmed. On the day of the launch of the alcohol guidance, the Department of Health put out a press statement suggesting that NICE did not fully understand the evidence. The suggestion was that MUP would de facto be a regressive tax on the poor and would unnecessarily penalise sensible drinkers. The alcohol industry and its acolytes went into overdrive to get the same or a similar message out. The statements from the Department of Health missed the point. MUP was not about targeting relatively disadvantaged people nor did the guideline assume that poor people are the heaviest drinkers – in fact they are not (Chief Medical Officers, 2016). Nor was MUP about attacking pubs and restaurants, the vast majority of which sell beer and wine well above the kind of minimum price which was the focus of the modelling on which the NICE recommendation was based. The arguments marshalled against the guidelines included the importance of governments not restricting choice, of consumers having the right to drink as much or as little as they please, and that binge drinking among young people was a problem for parents and perhaps the local police, not for the drinks industry or the government. On fats, salt and sugars the same arguments about consumer preferences and choice were advanced with one overarching theme which was that the 'Nanny State' should not interfere in the lives of its citizens.

There are real causes and explanations for why people drink the quantities of alcohol that they do and the amount of food that they eat as well as other health-related behaviours (Blue et al., 2016; Kelly and Barker, 2016). Our scientific understanding of these mechanisms is imperfect. Many different theories may be constructed purporting to explain the mechanisms which of course include the arguments put forward against minimum unit pricing and in favour of consumer choice. The NICE guidelines were based on the best available evidence, not speculation and supposition. They were based on empirical evidence about the way the world is as revealed in scientific investigations as against models of how different interest groups might wish the world to be. Possibility gets reduced to plausibility gets reduced to probability in the process of seeking to find the best and most effective and cost-effective way of dealing with alcohol-related disease or obesity. Interestingly, it became a political argument based on values rather than science, as realism bumped headlong into realpolitik.

Not perhaps surprisingly, the new government did not adopt the recommendations in either the alcohol or the CVD guidance, and promptly revamped NICE's public health programme considerably, continuing to pursue policies about choice and free markets with respect to public health. The evidence, however, is still available and over the years since then has accumulated (Burton et al., 2016; Chief Medical Officers, 2016), with the arguments in favour of MUP, for example, looking rather stronger now than they did in 2010.

One of the casualties of the revamping of NICE's public health programme was the development of realist reviews to underpin guidance development. One of the topics which NICE had been commissioned to consider was about protecting children from second-hand cigarette smoke in cars. As the public health team considered how to appraise and synthesise the evidence, it was recognised that a realist review might be a useful way to proceed. It hadn't been tried before in guideline development and this looked like a methodologically exciting idea. So Ray Pawson and Geoff Wong were commissioned and undertook the work (Pawson et al., 2011a). The resulting reviews were of considerable scientific importance. Unfortunately this programme of work was discontinued following the revamp of the NICE public health programme mentioned above. So the evidence never found its way into guidelines and the guidelines were abandoned. Interestingly, within a couple of years, the idea was back in the minds of parliamentarians and legislation was eventually enacted on the matter, despite the disdain of the then erstwhile Secretary of State. However, the important methodological ideas which were generated by this explicit excursion into realist methodology stands as a testimony to the possibility of integrating realist and EBM approaches.

CONCLUSION

Notwithstanding the political controversies of the day, the response by government to the NICE alcohol guideline demonstrated that democratic politics and an evidence-based approach – or indeed a realist approach – do not always make easy bedfellows. More to the point, perhaps, at least in public policy, there is the requirement for space for disagreements to be aired and articulated within an environment where the evidence is respected but so too is a political decision which rejects that evidence. In this scenario the argument would allow the evidence to be presented and then for it to be rejected, not on spurious scientific grounds but on genuinely political ones such as the argument that voters will find the restrictions on their freedom to drink and eat what they choose unacceptable. It is very important to note that this type of hostile response is likely in many controversial areas of public health. Although NICE never did so, in retrospect the C part of the CMO framework needs to be explicitly expanded to include any likely political or other fallout along with the more prosaic problems of implementation.

This chapter has brought into sharp focus the idea that evidence doesn't begin and end with the production of primary findings or with their synthesis into review-level documents or well-crafted recommendations based on the evidence, or indeed with sophisticated realistic understandings of the data. In public policy, at least, the process continues as the evidence and any resulting recommendations move into the public domain and become the stuff of political argument. In order to fully understand the relationship between interventions and outcomes, we need to be mindful of the processes of implementation, including the power of political resistance, and those processes must form part of any programme theory. Clinical medicine tries to deal with this by distinguishing between efficacy (whether something works in laboratory or controlled clinical conditions) and effectiveness (whether something works in the real world of everyday practice).

Public health at NICE and beyond is still to fully grasp this final part of the pipeline leading to practice and to build into the process of constructing the evidence base these contexts and complexities, including legitimate political opposition.

In a small way the controversy which surrounded the release of the guideline, especially about the prevention of alcohol misuse, was a microcosm of broader issues. The scientific evidence was the best available at the time. It was neither perfect nor was it some fundamental truth about the nature of the human condition. It was as good an account of the phenomena as could be corralled at that time. The process of reviews and synthesis and the deliberation of the guideline committee involved an assessment of the empirical evidence and its strengths and weaknesses combined with an understanding of a range of human conduct derived from psychology, sociology, economics and more broadly. The attacks made on it were drawn from a different but equally legitimate universe of discourse – a political and value-based one. The controversies demonstrate that the difference between the two cannot be resolved by appeal to science. Public health is by definition often highly political. This is true historically: thus the great reforms of the nineteenth century to provide clean water and sanitation, for example, were introduced in the face of tooth-and-nail opposition from all kinds of vested interests that went on for decades. The experience of NICE was similar.

Scientifically the fact that there are differences between EBM and realism should not mean that those differences are irreconcilable. The great strengths of EBM are its transparency, rigour, forensic approach to the evidence and the fact that it is based on peer-reviewed science. The great strength of the realist approach is its acknowledgement of complexity, its refusal to be drawn into simple linear models of the world and its ability to reframe questions in ways that are often much more illuminating than simple hypothesis testing. But these two sets of strengths can be brought together as the efforts of the NICE public health team after 2005 demonstrate. To integrate the approaches requires an open philosophical stance on empirical evidence, on methods and on prior theory. It also requires a recognition of the contingent nature of any evidence-based statement.

The experience of NICE, once it began its public health programme, was one where it was possible to try out new approaches to the development of evidence-based methods, and in particular to draw together the precepts of EBM with the principles of realism. It would be far-fetched to suggest that all the epistemological and methodological issues were solved or reconciled. But pragmatically the guidelines which were developed were stronger as a result and innovative in their way. It was a pity that in the end the politics led to a more narrow approach to the development of public health guidelines being imposed on NICE, but the ideas of pluralism of discipline, method and epistemology have re-emerged in other parts of the evidence-based universe. In health technology assessment – the original part of EBM devoted to the appraisal of new drugs and where randomised controlled trials have been the absolute gold standard – a process called Medicines Adaptive Pathways to Patients (MAPP) is now being advocated (Eichler et al., 2015; Schulthess et al., 2016). This advocacy is on the grounds that health technology assessment's slavish adherence to RCTs means that progress to market is slow, innovation is stifled and important evidence derived from other types of investigation – including observational and qualitative data – is being overlooked. The solution has been – much as public health at NICE had to do – to work out how to embrace other forms of evidence with appropriate rigour and transparency. It remains to be seen whether MAPP is a paradigm shift as some have suggested, it disappears amid the controversies surrounding it (Davis et al., 2016), or it is simply the next logical phase in the development of EBM. Interestingly, developments in genomic medicine and the recognition of the limits of RCTs when dealing with populations that are much more diverse than the trial design traditionally allows, may also impose on EBM a need for realism with its interest in specific and real mechanisms along the causal pathway. In this approach the issue is not about how to integrate social and organisational and behavioural dimensions into the process (which was what public health at NICE was seeking to do), it is about capturing the complexities of the mechanisms of disease causation and treatment at the genomic level. Realism may yet have its day in EBM.

12

REALIST MEMORABILIA

Ray Pawson

WHAT THIS CHAPTER IS ABOUT

The first part of this chapter traces the development of realist philosophy, its associated technical apparatus and empirical examples that together tell a story of the evolution of realist methodologies. This is more than a reading list, it is a guide to support the reader in understanding the scholarship that has refined the ideas of realism. The second part elaborates tħe heuristic device, the acronym that befuddles and enlightens realist researchers in equal measure. It revisits and clarifies the elements of the Context, Mechanism, Outcome (CMO) configuration. The third part draws attention to the enlightenment function of research, drawing on empirical examples from youth mentoring and problem-orientated policing to show how research has the potential to nudge and nurture ways of thinking that eventually find their way into policy and practice.

How this chapter will help you to do realist research

The first part will give you a reading list and the third part a reason to carry on doing realist evaluation, research and synthesis. There is no recipe to follow in the second part, but you will be navigated to the waypoints you must consider in any realist explanation.

A practical tip: a take-home message from the chapter

Rigorous theory-driven realist research is evolving, based on a way of thinking about the world that through practical application has the potential to contribute knowledge in understanding the world.

INTRODUCTION

This chapter has been written approximately 20 years after the publication of *Realistic Evaluation* (1997). It is composed as a thank you note to my friends and colleagues who have contributed the formidable chapters that precede this modest effort. This chapter poses three taxing questions about the realist approach, brutally expressed as follows:

1. Will it last?
2. Why CMO?
3. What's the use?

THE TEST OF TIME

I begin with a reflection on the passage of time and on the questionable stamina of social science paradigms. As Nick Tilley acknowledges in Chapter 1, we took a significant punt in writing *Realistic Evaluation*. Who would take seriously these argumentative urgings of socio-logical outsiders to the world of policies and programmes? As it has turned out and as the citation records now show, realist evaluation (RE) and its equally truculent sibling, realist synthesis (RS), have entered the mainstream. But are they here to stay?

An appropriate yardstick against which to measure the durability of RE/RS is the doom-laden arithmetic of Abbott (2006) in a brutal paper on knowledge accumulation in sociology. The average life of a paradigm, he declares, is only 25 years:

In summary, it seems that sociology is littered with research programs that are exciting for a couple of decades, then peter out into routinism and time serving. The same is probably true of methodologies. There are a number of possible mechanisms predicting this cycle. The most obvious is career structure. Twenty-five years is about the length of time it takes a single group of individuals to make up some new ideas, seize the soap-boxes, train a generation or two of students, and finally settle into late career exhaustion. Their students may keep things going, but their students' students tend to be fairly mechanical appliers of the original insights. The really creative people don't tend to make their careers by hitching themselves to other people's wagons. (2006: 61)

So is the end nigh for RE/RS or are there reasons to believe it has more staying power? I have to admit a sneaking sympathy for Abbot's chronology. My disciplines, sociology and social policy, are unrecognisable from my first acquaintance (though we now go back 50 years!). Novelty has become the watchword – every PhD student learns to justify his/her topic (in Chapter 1) by claiming it has been 'neglected' and so requires (in Chapter 2) a 'rethinking' of methodological fundamentals. Paradigm wars have given way to paradigm proliferation and even the stout, near-sighted endeavour of evaluation likes to promote a self-image of the 'evaluation tree' – a discipline with diverse philosophical roots and endless practical branches (Alkin, 2012).

So why on earth might RE/RS break the 25-year barrier? It is very simple. RE and RS are mere episodes, nothing other than second-cousins, in a long line of established realist think-ing. Realism is transdisciplinary. Realism is here to stay because of its scientific credentials. And here we move onto an altogether braver thesis going by the name of 'evolutionary epistemology', the theory that knowledge itself evolves by natural selection (Popper, 1972). The basic idea is known popularly as the 'survival of the fittest' and, as I see it, realism has survived because it has proved fit for purpose in organising investigation across the full range of scientific and social scientific disciplines.

As remarked – a brave thesis indeed. Much as I would like to prove the point with the definitive historiography of realist ideas and thinkers, my miserable editors have limited me to a handful of words and so I need another way of presenting this formidable intellectual history. Previously, I have attempted to demonstrate a little of this pedigree in a chapter in Pawson (2013) annotating the foundational work of 'seven realist giants' in publications reaching back to the mid-twentieth century. Here, I want to take the opportunity to enlarge upon the width, depth and longevity of the approach but to do so vividly, pithily and parsimoniously. To this end I borrow Alkin's idea and present, from sturdy trunk to flowering canopy, the tree of realist inquiry (Figure 12.1).

The figure presents citations to some of the main contributions to realist thinking. The genesis of all of the main ideas about generative causation, mechanisms of action, contextual constraints, middle-range theory, theory adjudication, permanent social transformation, abstraction, ontological depth, unintended consequences, emergent properties, model building, organised scepticism and so on can be located here. My apologies go to authors whose path-breaking efforts have been squeezed out – most especially to fellow scribes in this volume. To save space, the family tree is largely composed of books though some journal papers get a mention when they best represent a particular outgrowth. The major omission, sadly, is any indication of the nature and detail of each contribution – though I am able here to give a useful indication of the overall structure of the family tree.

To present a picture of realism's transdisciplinary nature I have divided the foliage into four areas labelled 'philosophy', 'sociology', 'evaluation' and, somewhat lamely, 'other disciplines'. This is not always quite so simple – with Campbell, for instance, being both philosopher and evaluator. Realism's longevity, and its victory over the 25-year rule, is indicated quite simply via the dates attached to each citation. The passing years work outwards from trunk to branch, though even this proves tricky. Campbell's work should really lie at the base since he began publishing in 1950, though the most valuable reference is to a 1988 collection of his key papers. Even more out of sync is the dating of the efforts of sociologists Boudon and Goldthorpe whose heydays belong to the twentieth century. On the tree they appear as newcomers because I cite a couple of reflective, 'farewell performances' that emphasise the key role of collective choice mechanisms in social explanation.

As one travels from left to right, the nature of the contributions change in a predictable manner. The philosophers can be consulted on epistemological and ontological first principles, while the other three collectives provide the technical apparatus and the empirical examples. As might be expected, the 'realism' that emerges contains many subtle changes of emphasis. I have no space to plot the similarities and differences but they are easily enough spotted via terminological preferences. A number of tree-dwellers identify themselves as 'critical realists'. Although there are family resemblances galore, I never apply this locution to RE/RS – the essential difference being that the former permits the entry of normative preferences into enquiry while the latter does its level best to avoid them. Just as significantly, there are many, many other artful differences which the historian of ideas may eventually explore.

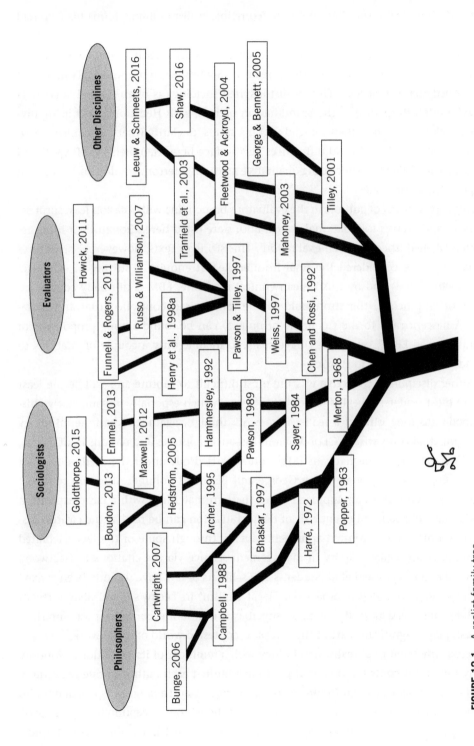

FIGURE 12.1 A realist family tree

For instance, Campbell rather likes the term 'corrigible realism'. Bunge terms his favoured approach 'scientific hylorealism'.

Moving across to the sociologists, Hammersley collects together his formidable array of methodological ideas under the term 'subtle realism'. Sometimes, terminological differences disguise conceptual similarities. Thus realist-inspired sociology is often termed 'analytical sociology'. I often think of it as the Scandinavian branch, with Hedström's text being pivotal. We get closer to home when we read that his aim is 'to clarify what mechanism-based explanation looks like'. Technical differences also surface here. Hammersley, Maxwell and Emmel pursue realist explanation using qualitative methods; Merton, Boudon and Hedström prefer quantitative strategies.

The initial placement of authors in the evaluator's branch line will occasion least surprise; two of Rossi and Weiss's foundational contributions are listed here, though their ideas are more often labelled 'theory-driven evaluation'. This string of texts, however, also ventures into what might be considered the final frontier. Realist enquiry is stirring in evidence-based medicine (EBM) and by this I mean clinical medicine. EBM is normally considered a fortress of empiricism, the stronghold of the randomised controlled trial and meta-analysis. A nascent rival to the Cochrane orthodoxy can be found among proponents of 'mechanism-based EBM', on which I have space to include only a couple of citations to Russo and Williamson and to Howick.

The 'other disciplines' collective was the most difficult to capture and will be the least familiar to most readers. It begins in political science, which especially in comparative historical mode has long utilised a realist framework though, again, the basic terminology differs. Contextual comparison (C) of different historical episodes and nations is, of course, a given. The analysis of mechanisms (M) is often carried out under the methodology of 'process tracing', the key source being George and Bennett's volume. Attention to causal outcomes (O) often utilises an approach called 'pattern matching' with a basic exposition in the Mahoney chapter. Tilly's analysis of democratisation can be read as the clearest justification of a mechanism-centred approach. Moving through some of the less celebrated waters, we discover realist enquiry in management science via the citations to Fleetwood and Ackroyd and to Tranfield et al. Students and scholars of law have recently been coaxed into a more evidence-based approach via 'legal realism' in Leeuw's book. Shaw's recent work, while not badged as 'realist', makes a superb case that subtle, corrigible post-empiricist science can play a significant part in the complex, contested world of social work.

I conclude my attempt at realist dendrology with a reminder of its limitations. Not only are many important contributions omitted, I have limited each author to one text. Many authors here have dedicated entire careers to realist enquiry and a range of personal libraries should be consulted. Eagle-eyed readers will note that there is one exception to the one-book rule. Oh vanity, his name is Pawson! As well as the Pawson and Tilley volume, which is normally considered the birthplace of RE/RS, I have smuggled in an earlier and unloved effort of my own (Pawson, 1989). I insert it to indicate that I have pontificated on the same soap box for considerably more than 25 years, and thus by dint of sheer cussedness I have surpassed Abbot's iron law of paradigm longevity.

The tree in Figure 12.1 is now planted as an item of realist memorabilia. Fellow travellers will be keen to add their own favourite fruits. Readers new to realism, I'm afraid, are presented with what must seem a stonking great, if decorative, reading list.

CMO REVISITED

Battling through the above homework should persuade the reader that RE/RS is no flash in the pan. But what is its signature? What is the defining feature? I scratch my head in coming to an answer here since I've always reached for the magic number seven in describing its essential qualities (Pawson, 2013: 86). It is perfectly possible, however, to see what others have seen. For most citizens the 'CMO configuration' is regarded as the crux of the matter as well, I must confess, as the bone of contention. Before I attempt further clarification another item of realist memorabilia should be tabled. The question posed in this section – namely 'Why CMO?' – has its own signature tune. It should be sung to the melody of Village People's *YMCA* (you might also modify the famous group dance by altering the arm movements signifying each letter). My thanks go to the Sheffield tunesmith Andrew Booth from whom the full lyrics of *Why CMO?* may be obtained (http://singsyn.pbworks.com).

So, why indeed the CMO configuration? These three items make up the fundamental building blocks of *any* causal explanation and I want to use the remainder of this section to support this bold claim. I do so with a series of clarifications to *our* initial formulation of the idea (NB: I'm sharing the blame with Nick Tilley here). We first presented the configuration as a summative equation C + M = O. This makes for poor mathematics, since we didn't really suppose one could *add* C to M. More properly it might be written $O = f(M.C)$, that is, say, outcomes are a function of the relationship between mechanisms and context. Not too many critics have complained on this score – sometimes oversimplification works well.

My second clarification, way too late to put into practice, is to urge flexibility in the ordering of the three items. For the 'intervention sciences' the expression should really have been styled as the 'MCO configuration'. Why? The answer is that theory and research invariably start with mechanisms before moving to investigations of contexts, which then combine to help us understand outcome patterns. For instance, in pharmaceutical enquiry, the starting point lies in basic research understanding the 'mechanism of action' (e.g. the drug may reduce pain by blocking excessive levels of cellular signalling). This mechanism is observed in various contexts (*in vitro*, in animals, in volunteers) before being tested in a tightly defined group of eligible patients in a randomised trial in order to measure effect sizes (i.e. outcomes). Likewise, in social programme evaluation, it is generally better to begin by asking why an intervention might work (i.e. what is the mechanism?) before thinking about the contexts that might support or stifle its action. The O is in the correct place, but only when both M and C have been contemplated can one understand outcome patterns.

This rule of thumb, however, does not apply in other forms of causal analysis. For instance, in comparative historical research the sequence is probably better rendered OCM. Consider Barrington Moore's classic *Social Origins of Dictatorship and Democracy* (1966). He begins by identifying an outcome pattern – agrarian states that have evolved along three routes, namely democracies, fascist dictatorships and communist dictatorships. He then moves to context, identifying the pre-existing characteristics of two or three nations that followed each path. The main analytic works come next – trying to unravel the historical and social process that lead to each outcome. The mechanisms in this scenario are the collective choices and power plays of key state actors. The completed explanation ties together the three components.

The third clarification, already attempted several times (e.g. Pawson and Manzano-Santaella, 2012), concerns the selection of candidates for our three explanatory pivots. Novice researchers really struggle with this one – so once more unto the breach. The difficulty is that in racing to construct a CMO table it is often tricky to assign a programme theory to the three categories. Hence the plaintive cry: 'is "X" a context or a mechanism?' Outcomes, by the way, tend to be less troublesome. I've struggled to provide a succinct solution to this conundrum and so was exceedingly pleased to come across this brilliant little cameo by Gill Westhorp, which she elaborates on in Chapter 3 of this collection but which was first published on the RAMESES discussion list:

In a realist view, things 'aren't' C, M, or O … they *function as* C, M or O in a particular part of the analysis. I use the example of self-esteem. You might have a program which intends to raise students' self-esteem. In that case, self-esteem is an outcome. Or you might have a program which intends to increase the proportion of disadvantaged students who complete high school, and works in part by raising their self-esteem. In that case, self-esteem is a mechanism. Or you might have a program that works best for students who already had high (or low) self-esteem. In that case, self-esteem is a context. And, of course, you can have a program which intends to raise self-esteem (interim outcome and mechanism) in order to increase school retention (higher level outcome) and which works best for students with moderate levels of self-esteem (context).

Complexity grows, moreover, when one appreciates that over time concepts routinely change place within a CMO configuration. For instance, any substantial reform in a welfare regime will, in the course of time, become the background which constrains later innovations. Mechanisms evolve into contexts. Take the example of 'direct payments'. These have been introduced to some welfare recipients in order to let them choose and buy the services they prefer instead of passively receiving them at the behest of the providers. Investigation of this policy at time 1 would delve into the way in which the introduction of self-choice mechanisms generates a different portfolio of services. At time 2, supposing that direct payments become the norm, the increased expectations and the personal control that have been so established become the context, which may then assist or may then hinder the next generation of policy modifications. The moral of the tale is that researchers are the authors of these configurations. CMOs are hypotheses. They become real only when they are tested and when and if they are able to explain the changes generated by an intervention.

A fourth point of clarification also begins with another, related cry for help from tyro researchers. Encouraged to think deeply about why, for whom and in what circumstances an intervention might operate, it soon becomes apparent that Ms and Cs and Os queue up in ever-elongating lists. When and how does the researcher stop? The answer to the puzzle is well enough established, namely to think in configurations and to inspect only those contexts and those outcomes that are 'relevant' to a particular mechanism. Again, I suspect that beginning researchers find this injunction difficult. What is it that tells us context X is relevant and how do we make the judgement that context Y can be jettisoned? It is probably insufficient to issue another high epistemological principle, known as the doubt/trust ratio, which explains that *all* scientific enquiries confront a limited numbers of explanatory factors, while taking others for granted (Campbell, 1988: 319). We need instructive examples of the 'hit list' and the 'trash can' revealing how particular elements may warrant investigation or may be ignored. To this end I introduce another item of realist memorabilia (Figure 12.2).

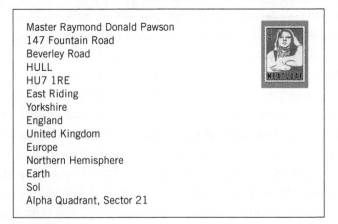

11-year-old gets to grips with 'context'

FIGURE 12.2 Choosing contexts

This is a PowerPoint slide I use to explain the selectivity issue. Its origins go back to school days and a childish competition I recall about compiling the 'world's longest address'. My effort might have looked a little like Figure 12.2. The serious point here is that each line is more or less *relevant* for different explanations and for different tasks. If you wanted to ensure your letter arrives, line 5 is the most 'relevant'. If you want to know which football and cricket clubs I support, lines 4 and 7 are the most 'relevant'. If you wanted to know my parental social class and indeed my father's occupation, line 2 is most 'relevant' (Fountain

Road was an inner-city, working-class community and number 147 a corner shop). If you want to know which queue I join in the airport arrivals hall, lines 9 and 10 provide the 'relevant' information (and also indicate, post-Brexit, that this might change). And if you wanted to know why the little green man from the planet Zog would find my pale skin revolting, the 'relevant' information belongs at lines 12–14. It's as easy as that.

Alas, it is not quite as easy as that. Following the example too closely leads us to another common error in understanding the role of context in programme evaluation. Contexts are most definitely not limited to location. To use the now standard 4I's formulation, context may refer to *any* characteristic of:

- the *individuals* who partake in the programme;
- the *interrelationships* between stakeholders;
- the *institutional* arrangement into which the programme is embedded;
- the *infrastructure* – the wider societal, economic and cultural setting of the programme.

In short and frustratingly, it turns out that context can refer to absobloodylutely anything. The golden rule, the only rule, is to hypothesise and test those contexts of which a strong case can be made for their relevance. So let me extend this clarification with another example, which may help to enlarge the idea of contextual relevance. In some cases it may turn out that apparently 'small' contexts may overcome 'big' policy reforms. An example is the introduction of Referral Management Centres (RMCs) in the UK NHS. These were introduced to manage high and sometimes eccentric levels of referrals from general practitioners (GPs) to hospital consultants. The RMC was tasked with checking, formalising and standardising the cases that should properly be referred. RMCs struggled to find acceptance and were sometimes abandoned because they jarred with some diminutive but particularly sturdy contexts.

The first of these, context 1, might be labelled 'custom and practice'. The business of referrals is tied up in entrenched local knowledge. These are the long-established rules of thumb, hard-won tricks of the trade, which help GPs to find ways *through* and sometimes *around* a byzantine system. GP X just 'knew' that consultant Y would respond to referrals of patient of type Z and they were damned if they were about to relinquish that knowledge. Also relevant is context 2, namely 'professional closure'. The new regime caused considerable resentment with both GPs and consultants on the grounds that RMC 'operatives' could never match the qualifications and experience required to make fine and critical clinical judgements on the lives of individual patients. Readers interested in following how these tensions played out are referred to Pawson et al. (2016).

My fifth clarification turns to realist understanding of outcomes. I begin with the reminder that O stands for outcome patterns (in the plural). There is a remorseless political pressure to draw the outcome question back to one lurking question – 'did it work?' From the start, Nick Tilley and I used two expressions – 'outcome footprints' and 'outcome signatures' – in the attempt to suggest that programme impact is always complex and multi-faceted. I feel that we have only partially succeeded in that mission. To be sure many, many realist evaluations have made great strides in uncovering the most basic outcome pattern, namely that an intervention works differently at the *sub-group* level. According to the level of the intervention, countless studies now demonstrate differential impact across individuals, groups, communities, institutions, regions, etc. Less well studied, but equally important, are longitudinal outcome patterns. Durability and sustainability are prized assets of an intervention but are seldom tracked or well understood. As such, they represent a crucial opportunity for realist thinking.

Interventions based on performance targets provide a simple illustration. One of the current political hot potatoes in the UK is the waiting-time target in Accident and Emergency Units in public National Health Service hospitals. A maximum four-hour target was introduced in 2004 and measures of compliance have fluctuated wildly over the years. Let me tell a hugely abbreviated tale of the mechanisms and contexts that might account for this pattern. In the early years there was a gradual decline in waiting times along with some surprisingly precipitous decreases. The former are probably associated with the improved management and additional resources that hospital trusts devoted to A&E. The sharper drops might well be due to a measure of 'gaming' in the way the target is monitored. If the registration, triage, assessment and treatment process is broken down into a series of discrete steps, it becomes possible to advantageously 'reset the clock' commencing the waiting-time measures. Latterly, the waiting times have again shifted upwards. Here the explanation lies in contexts outside the A&E. It has become increasingly difficult for patients to receive same-day appointments in other NHS services with the result that, in some minds, A&E provision, despite the tedium, remains a reliable way of 'being seen'. To repeat, the simplification in these few lines is breathtaking. The point, however, is that performance management in any domain will see similar *outcome fluctuations* and that CMO configurations provide the apparatus for understanding and anticipating them.

UTILISATION

We move to the third of my taxing questions – what is the use of realist evaluation/realist synthesis (RE/RS)? This issue requires a re-examination of the realist stance on 'research utilisation'. The foundational idea, of course, is that research can and should provide a trustworthy foundation for policy and practice. Writing at the start of 2017, in the maelstrom of hyperbole on 'post-truth', 'fake news', 'alternative facts' and so on, the very idea of evidence-informed policy is under threat. I have attempted to spell out a realist position on research utilisation on several occasions, usually as a tailpiece to my various books, the most indicative chapter being, 'Flying the Tattered Flag of Enlightenment' in Pawson (2006b). Realist research harbours decidedly modest expectations on utilisation, captured in another phrase that I have always been fond of using and which now takes on an entirely new meaning, namely that 'politics will always trump evidence'.

In my book *Evidence Based Policy* (Pawson, 2006b) RE/RS is aligned to Weiss's (1979) 'enlightenment model' of research utilisation. Here is her famous rendition of the idea:

It is not the findings of a single study nor even of a body of related studies that directly affect policy. Rather it is the concepts and theoretical perspectives of social science that permeate the policy process ... The imagery is that of social science generalizations and orientations percolating through informed publics and coming to shape the way people think about social issues.

This formulation has the great advantage of avoiding both the self-delusion of those who believe that policy-makers choose interventions on the basis of meta-analytic forest plots and the gross, post-truth pessimism of those who suppose that policy-makers always pick and choose their favoured 'facts'. However, what worries even proponents of the perspective is that policy enlightenment, as described above, seems capricious. The researcher would seem to play an entirely passive role in an unplanned process. Is it possible to add a little more muscle to the endeavour?

Let me begin with a brief sideswipe. The origins of post-truth thinking have been much debated – growing populism, under-education, relentless political spin, mass-media trivialisation, postmodern culture and so on. One of the more interesting speculations, with more than a grain of truth, is the claim that 'people have had enough of experts'. There is indeed a problem with some elements of the evidence community who, without a care, are willing to make simple extrapolations into the future. The main culprits are the economic forecasters who seem to imagine that present statistical formulations on, say, growth rates can be cast forward. Invariably, within a few months, underlying conditions change and the forecast fails. Quite blithely, these experts then go on to issue 'revised' forecasts, which in turn meet the same wretched fate. Just as culpable in my view are the what works clearinghouses, making over-confident declarations on 'what works' and 'what doesn't'. The problem in both examples is the lack of appreciation of persistent and inevitable contextual change, which will always throw a current regularity out of kilter. No programme will work universally. Every programme will work somewhere. This couplet marks a limiting condition of evaluation research and should be the start of any advice to policy-makers and practitioners.

Returning to the properly cautious enlightenment model, let me attempt to clarify the two major points, namely: (a) what form of evidence is supposed to circulate; and (b) under what conditions does it do so. On the first issue one notes that even within her brief definition above, Weiss manages to describe no less than four potential evidential units that may constitute the medium of policy percolation (namely 'concepts', 'theoretical perspectives', 'generalisations' and 'orientations'). The realist position, I venture, aspires to be rather more precise on this score. Realist enquiry produces explanations and explanations are thus the intended medium of policy learning. In describing this function previously, I have used the terms 'middle-range-theories', 're-usable conceptual platforms' and 'mechanism libraries' to describe the intended knowledge base. Underlying all of these terms is the idea that RE/RS will fetch up with a dynamic, explanatory 'model' of the interacting system of mechanisms, contexts and outcomes associated with a particular family of interventions. Given that the Ms, Cs and Os associated with any intervention are potentially infinite, the construction of such models is decidedly difficult.

There is a demanding trick to this trade. Realist models should be comprehensive enough to reveal the complexities awaiting any programme *and* yet be readily intelligible enough to bring a sense of recognition to any practitioner *and* also offer a practical blueprint to assist in implementing any further such interventions. I reach for another piece of memorabilia to illustrate this formidable task. Figure 12.3 is a PowerPoint slide providing a system model of youth mentoring programmes.

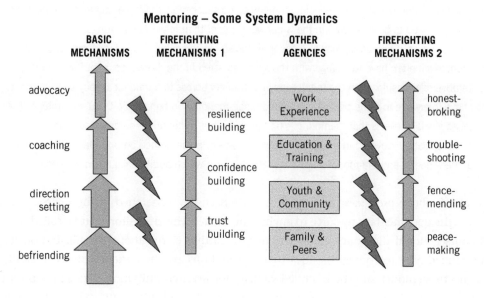

FIGURE 12.3 Youth mentoring programmes: a system model

The slide is a distillation of a small mountain of evidence contained in a realist synthesis of these programmes (Pawson, 2006b). While every picture tells a story, Figure 12.3 is insufficient to carry a full explanation. There is, of course, a need to provide some accompanying narrative describing how particular interventions have progressed or faltered through the model. Here you have to imagine Pawson 'talking through' the slide, a longish soliloquy that goes something like this:

The evidence indicates that 'mentoring' takes on highly diverse forms. On the left we have the various mentoring mechanisms embedded in interventions seeking to deal with the problem of disaffected, excluded youth. Some mentors seek to befriend, some try to encourage mentees to reset their goals, some begin coaching to improve life chances, and some act as advocates for their protégés in the wider world. The width of these mentoring 'arrows' assembles the basic evidence on the frequency with which each path is pursued and on its likelihood of success. The passage through all stages is relatively rare. The lightning strikes in the next column represent a common finding that mentoring relationships fracture frequently. The relatively brief and intermittent meetings between mentor and mentee do not and cannot remove the subjects from those contexts that generate their malaise. Gang fights, family bust-ups, drug binges, school exclusions and so forth frequently break a developing partnership. The review revealed the deployment of another range of 'fire-fighting' mechanism. The initial mechanisms have to be reconstructed – trust has to be recreated to enable befriending, confidence-building and reliance-building are required to encourage the mentee to face adversity and to face it again and again. Once more the evidence suggests that a dwindling number of partnerships are able to cope under such constant strife. The next column is suggestive of another key finding, namely that in the more successful cases the mentor has to liaise with a number of other agencies. If mentees do succeed in shifting attitudes and behaviours, the changes need to be registered in the wider world rather than in weekly meetings. Breakdown (the additional lightning bolts) may also occur at this stage. To enable this broader transformation the mentor will often have to engage with the agencies listed in the 'boxed' column. For instance, cooperative relationships with the mentor may not transfer across to a training agency and the mentor may have to engage in some peace-making and fence-mending on behalf of a truculent protégé. The model as a whole reveals that mentoring is no 'quick fix' but rather an 'endurance race'. Traversing the tortuous path uncovered in the review requires levels of perseverance beyond that of the typical (volunteer) mentor and the model maps the many points at which additional support is needed.

All of the above processes have, of course, been closely researched in the review, which acts as the documentary resource to anchor the model. This depository can be called upon, of course, should the policy audience press for further clarification. The illustration here is intended only to convey the idea that explanations are the currency of realist synthesis and these models are the intended vehicles for research utilisation. The aim is both to satisfy realist science (in its endeavour to capture the multiple contingencies that shape programme outcomes) and to provide policy enlightenment (in the need to offer relatively brief and comprehensible prototypes that can shape future planning).

But did it do so? Did this model provide enlightenment? The answer alas is a resounding NO. I leave the sometimes solemn, sometimes hilarious details of our efforts to propel the review into youth policy to Chapter 10. I say 'our' efforts for Annette Boaz joined me in this misbegotten quest. What this episode tells us, though it is hardly news, is that policy enlightenment only follows with a great deal of forward planning. To illustrate, I turn to a further case study in which the model-building side of realist enquiry is married to a purposeful relationship with the policy community.

My example relates to the field of problem-oriented policing (POP). Readers will notice that it borrows one of Weiss's utilisation terms, this being an 'orientation' that has been supported for many years and thus has had the wherewithal and opportunity to percolate into practice. The elemental idea is that crime is heavily patterned and that instead of 'blue-light' policing (one-off responses as crimes occur) a more systematic approach should be installed, beginning with an understanding of the mechanisms and contexts that encourage crime outcome patterns (Tilley, 2002). A simple example of such a recurring pattern is the phenomenon of repeat victimisation (RV) (Pease, 1998; Farrell, 2005). Our first model

(Figure 12.4) provides a middle-range explanation for the genesis and persistence of RV and thus a rationale for directing police attention to the problem.

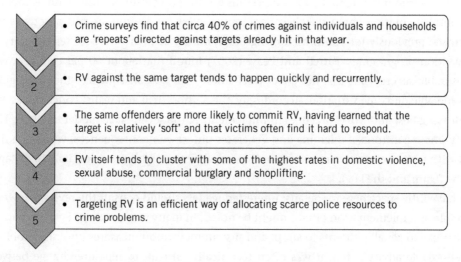

1
- Crime surveys find that circa 40% of crimes against individuals and households are 'repeats' directed against targets already hit in that year.

2
- RV against the same target tends to happen quickly and recurrently.

3
- The same offenders are more likely to commit RV, having learned that the target is relatively 'soft' and that victims often find it hard to respond.

4
- RV itself tends to cluster with some of the highest rates in domestic violence, sexual abuse, commercial burglary and shoplifting.

5
- Targeting RV is an efficient way of allocating scarce police resources to crime problems.

FIGURE 12.4   The relevance of repeat victimisation to crime prevention

This model, both in general orientation (POP) and in this particular embodiment (RV), has found wide acceptance as 'an attractive crime prevention strategy with much potential' (Farrell, 2005: 164). We thus turn to research on how to prevent repeat victimisation. As ever, the implementation of such interventions turns out to be complex with ample scope for glory and for misadventure. Another model, a basic linear logic model of the implementation chain as might be applied in interventions to prevent repeat household burglary, is presented in Figure 12.5.

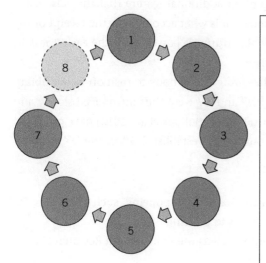

Key:

1. Crime analysis to measure and identify 'hotspots' of RV.
2. Contact potential victim community to raise awareness of the problem.
3. Consider potential 'off-the shelf' deterrent programmes that may attack RV.
4. Adapt selected programme, with community involvement, to meet local needs.
5. Ensure that all residents, including victims, adopt the chosen preventative measures.
6. Maintain prevention efforts (including periods after a funding cycle).
7. Scrutinise shifts in RV rates in order to evaluate the progress of the intervention.
8. Reset intervention to deal with implementation inconsistencies and unintended consequences.

FIGURE 12.5   Preventing repeat household burglaries: a system model

The key to the right summarises the seven initial stages, building the programme through a liaison with crime analysts, community leaders, local residents and area police officers.

It goes without saying that I make no claims for this programme as some kind of panacea. The implementation chain sketched here proves every bit as arduous and porous as that discussed previously for youth mentoring programmes. In their review of ten burglary RV prevention programmes, Farrell and Pease (2007) found that about 60 per cent met with measurable success. But this net effect calculation is of no consequence since it disguises considerable outcome variation. Accordingly, the authors' real and realist concern was with identifying best and worse practices in implementing the seven-stage model in Figure 12.5. Every phase confronts a dilemma and generates unforeseen consequences, which are then met with further corrective measures (as illustrated by the highlighted and italicised Stage 8 in the figure and the key).

I have little space here for details; interested readers should consult the review. However, a couple of implementation pitfalls might be noted. In many cases, at Stage 5, it was particularly tricky to get all residents to adopt and sustain prevention measures ('not my problem', 'unaffordable advice', etc.). It was often technically difficult to measure change between Stage 1 and Stage 7 accurately (problems with under-reporting crime and with address-tracking). Best practice to overcome such dilemmas is then examined in a third phase of the review. These further mechanisms are then built into a dynamic model, which is constantly 'reset' at Stage 8. In short, we see the research building to provide an overall explanatory account of the intervention, which, as one of the authors put it, will 'inform (that is revise and improve) further research and prevention efforts' (Farrell, 2005: 164).

We are back at square one with an affirmation that the transferable lessons of evaluation research are iterative, dynamic system models. And here I reach the point of bringing POP and RV to the table, namely the all-important additional feature that they also carry institutional credibility. As we shall see, this medium is what accounts for the receipt of the message. Speaking complex, contingent, corrigible truths to power is not the easiest task in the world – so how did it work in this example?

The police are no more likely than any other professional body to rush off to the library in search of evidence to bolster their duties. POP and RV were thus introduced slowly and painstakingly using very many carrots and the odd stick. Bullock et al. (2012) have produced a short history of the initiatives used to encourage and establish POP in the UK, which I summarise as follows:

- major strategic reports and overviews on the state of UK policing, such as arguing for more systematic and less piecemeal approaches to policing;
- installation within the Home Office of Units such as the Policing and Research Group, which was sympathetic to POP philosophy;
- seed-corn funding and research support for small-scale POP demonstration projects enabling local police services to experiment with pilot projects;

- a major government-funded programme – The Crime Reduction Programme – encouraging partnerships to implement and evaluate POP;
- an Annual National POP conference, with linkages to international events, proving support for local projects to network and to publicise their activities;
- an annual award for good practice in POP (not sadly Top of the Pops but the Tilley Award – a title that might just suggest certain friendliness to a particular research strategy);
- media coverage for POP provided by many of the above initiatives.

I don't want to give the impression that any of this was plain sailing. POP has had many critics who dismiss it as 'administrative criminology' (Mayhew, 2016). The brickbats come from both sections of the police (who have always preferred more robust and direct methods in dealing with criminals) as well as academics (who regard the approach as 'atheoretical', even though most of them wouldn't recognise a theory if one punched them in the face). My point is simply that the enlightenment function of research is not capricious and toothless. It can be nudged and nurtured. And in so doing some of the complexities, which are the stuff of rigorous research, can find their way into policy and practice. This is the realist way.

CONCLUSION

For a final word I return to Abbott's brilliant little paper (2006). Every social scientist should read it, though a good many of us will want to resist it. We should not take offence, however, at his withering prose of which I have provided a sample above. So, for instance, while I recognise only too well the phrase 'late-career exhaustion', I'm busy resisting dementia and dodging bullets in trying to stretch the realist cause into evidence-based clinical medicine (Pawson, 2018). And while you, dear reader, might feel besmirched by his description of tyro researchers as 'mechanical appliers of the original insights', you should rise above it.

The second half of Abbott's piece consists of a conceptual analysis of the very idea of 'knowledge cumulation' and it is here that his pessimism runs too deep. He considers a number of possible interpretations of the notion, rejecting all 'fundamentalist' models claiming to discover absolute truths, before settling on his preferred notion of cumulation as a mere belief system – we cling onto the *myth of progress* because of our desperate need to feel part of 'something that is going somewhere'. What remains unconsidered in his 'discard pile' is the more modest and more measured notion of cumulation embodied in realist analysis. RE and RS are not fundamentalist; we do not suppose that we uncover the law-governed fate of social programmes. Each evaluation contributes an understanding of some of the contingencies that contribute to programme success and to programme failure. The next evaluation provides a little more learning. Realist synthesis can pull together more comprehensive models of the intended and unintended pathways. Accumulation, however, is always partial – we never posses the totality of knowledge to be certain of the fate of some future version of an intervention implemented in an untried situation.

But partial knowledge represents real progress. I have tried to demonstrate this with the meagre examples here. More significantly, the editors and contributors here have produced a volume in which every page attests to the adaptability of realist analysis. *Doing Realist Research* is a portrait of a rather resolute family – seekers of practical methods for dealing with the complexities of social explanation.

We are indeed contributing to 'something that is really going somewhere'.

REFERENCES

Abbott, A. (2006) 'Reconceptualizing knowledge accumulation in sociology', *American Sociologist*, *37*(2): 55–66.

Alkin, M. (2012) *Evaluation Roots*. Thousand Oaks, CA: Sage.

Allcock, C., Dormon, F., Taunt, R. and Dixon, J. (2015) *Constructive Comfort: Accelerating Change in the NHS*. London: Health Foundation.

Anderson, R. (2003) 'Book Review: Realistic Evaluation', *Applied Health Economics and Health Policy*, 2(1): 65–7.

Anderson, R. (2010) 'Systematic review of economic evaluations: utility or futility?', *Health Economics*, *19*(3): 350–64.

Anderson, R. and Haas, M. (2001) *Cost-effectiveness of Shared Care Compared with Usual Hospital-based Care for People with Hepatitis C*. [Project Report 17]. Sydney, NSW: CHERE (Centre for Health Economics Research and Evaluation), pp. 1–47.

Anderson, R. and Shemilt, I. (2010) 'The role of economic perspectives and evidence in systematic review', in I. Shemilt, M. Mugford, L. Vale, K. Marsh and C. Donaldson (eds), *Evidence-based Decisions and Economics: Health Care, Social Welfare, Education and Criminal Justice*. Oxford: Wiley-Blackwell, pp. 23–42.

Archer, M.S. (1995) *Realist Social Theory: The Morphogenetic Approach*. Cambridge: Cambridge University Press.

Archer, M.S. (2015) *Generative Mechanisms Transforming the Social Order*. New York: Springer International.

Astbury, B. (2013) 'Some reflections on Pawson's *Science of Evaluation: A Realist Manifesto Evaluation*', *19*(4): 383–401.

Astbury, B. and Leeuw, F. (2010) 'Unpacking black boxes: mechanisms and theory building in evaluation', *American Journal of Evaluation*, *31*(3): 363–81.

Bardach, E. (2004) 'The extrapolation problem: how can we learn from the experience of others?', *Journal of Policy Analysis and Management*, *23*(2): 205–20.

Bates, M.J. (1989) 'Design of browsing and berrypicking techniques for the online search interface', *Online Review*, *13*(5): 407–24.

Baxter, S., Killoran, A., Kelly, M.P. and Goyder, E. (2010) 'Synthesising diverse evidence: the use of primary qualitative data analysis methods and logic models in public health reviews', *Public Health*, *124*(2): 99–106.

Beck, U. and Beck-Gernsheim, E. (2002) *Individualization: Institutionalized Individualism and Its Social and Political Consequences*. London: Sage.

Becker, H.S. (1998) *Tricks of the Trade: How to Think About Your Research While You're Doing It*. Chicago: University of Chicago Press.

Befani, B., Lederman, S. and Sagar, F. (2007) 'Realistic evaluation and QCA conceptual parallels and an empirical application', *Evaluation*, *13*(2): 171–92.

Bennett, A. (2013) 'The mother of all isms: causal mechanisms and structured pluralism in International Relations theory', *European Journal of International Relations*, *19*(3): 459–81.

Bennett, S., Agyepong, I.A., Sheikh, K., Hanson, K., Ssengooba, F. and Gilson, L. (2011) 'Building the field of health policy and systems research: an agenda for action' [online], *PLoS Medicine*, *8*(8), available at https://doi.org/10.1371/journal.pmed.1001081 (accessed 24 May 2017).

Berg, R.C. and Nanavati, J. (2016) 'Realist review: current practice and future prospects', *Journal of Research Practice*, *12*(1): Article R1.

Berlin, L.J., Ziv, Y., Amaya-Jackson, L. and Greenberg, T. (2007) *Enhancing Early Attachments – Theory, Research, Intervention and Policy*. New York: Guilford Press.

Best, A., Greenhalgh, T., Lewis, S., Saul, J.E., Carroll, S., Bitz., J. (2012) 'Large-system transformation in health care: a realist review', *Milbank Quarterly*, *90*(3): 421–456.

Best, A. and Holmes, B. (2010) 'Systems thinking, knowledge and action: towards better models and methods', *Evidence Policy*, *6*(2): 145–59.

Bhaskar, R. (1997) *A Realist Theory of Science*. London and New York: Verso Books.

Bhaskar, R. (2008) *A Realist Theory of Science*. London: Routledge.

Bierstedt, R. (1960) 'Sociology and humane learning', *American Sociological Review*, *25*(1): 3–9.

Birch, S. (2002) 'Making the problem fit the solution: evidence-based decision-making and "Dolly" economics', in C. Donaldson, M. Mugford and L. Vale (eds), *Evidence-based Health Economics: From Effectiveness to Efficiency in Systematic Review*. London: BMJ Books.

Birch, S. and Gafni, A. (2003) 'Economics and the evaluation of health care programmes: generalisability of methods and implications for generalisability of results', *Health Policy*, *64*(2): 207–19.

Blackman, T., Wistow, J. and Byrne, D. (2013) 'Using qualitative comparative analysis to understand complex policy problems', *Evaluation*, *19*(2): 126–40.

Blaikie, N. (2007) *Approaches to Social Enquiry: Advancing Knowledge*. Cambridge: Polity.

Blalock, H. (1961) *Causal Inference in Nonexperimental Research*. Chapel Hill, NC: University of North Carolina Press.

Blau, P. and Duncan, O. (1978) *The American Occupational Structure*. New York: Free Press.

Bloor, D. (1978) 'Polyhedra and the abominations of Leviticus', *British Journal for the History of Science*, *11*(3): 245–72.

Blue, S., Shove, E., Carmona, C. and Kelly, M.P. (2016) 'Theories of practice and public health: understanding (un) healthy practices', *Critical Public Health*, *26*(1): 36–50.

Boaz, A. and Pawson, R. (2005) 'The perilous road from evidence to policy: five journeys compared', *Journal of Social Policy*, *34*(2): 175–94.

Boaz, A., Grayson, L., Levitt, R. and Solesbury, W. (2008) 'Does evidence-based policy work? Learning from the UK experience', *Evidence and Policy*, *4*(2): 233–53.

Boccia, S., Villari, P. and Ricciadi, W. (2015) *A Systematic Review of Key Issues in Public Health*. New York: Springer.

Bonnefoy, J., Morgan, A., Kelly, M.P. et al. (2007) *Constructing the Evidence base on the Social Determinants of Health: A Guide* [online]. Concepción and London: Universidad del Desarrollo and the National Institute for Health and Clinical Excellence; available at http://cdrwww.who.int/social_determinants/ knowledge_networks/add_documents/mekn_final_guide_112007.pdf (accessed 24 May 2017).

Booth, A. (2006) '"Brimful of STARLITE": toward standards for reporting literature searches', *Journal of the Medical Library Association, 94*(4): 421–9.

Booth, A. (2016) 'Searching for qualitative research for inclusion in systematic reviews: a structured methodological review', *Systematic Reviews, 5*(74): 1–23.

Booth, A. and Carroll, C. (2015) 'Systematic searching for theory to inform systematic reviews: is it feasible? Is it desirable?', *Health Information and Libraries Journal, 32*(3): 220–35.

Booth, A., Harris, J., Croot, E., Springett, J., Campbell, F. and Wilkins, E. (2013) 'Towards a methodology for cluster searching to provide conceptual and contextual "richness" for systematic reviews of complex interventions: case study (CLUSTER)', *BMC Medical Research Methodology, 13*(118): 1–14.

Booth, A., Meier, P., Stockwell, T. et al. (2008) *Independent Review of the Effects of Alcohol Pricing and Promotion, Part A: Systematic Reviews*. London:Department of Health.

Boudon, R. (1974) *Education, Opportunity and Social Inequality*. New York: Wiley.

Boudon, R. (1981) *The Logic of Social Action*. London: Routledge.

Boudon, R. (1991) 'What middle-range theories are', *Contemporary Sociology, 20*(4): 519–22.

Boudon, R. (2013) *Sociology as Science*. Oxford: Bardwell Press.

Bowlby, J. (1982) *Attachment and Loss, Vol. 1: Attachment*. New York: Basic Books.

Briner, R.B. and Denyer, D. (2012) 'Systematic review and evidence synthesis as a practice and scholarship tool', in D. Rousseau (ed.), *The Oxford Handbook of Evidence-Based Management*. New York: Oxford University Press, pp. 112–29.

Briscoe, S. (2016) *How Theories of Information Can Contribute to the Development of Literature Search Methods for Realist Reviews*. 2nd International Conference on Realist Evaluation and Synthesis (CARES), 2–6 October, London.

Briss, P. (2005) 'Evidence-based: US road and public health side of the street', *Lancet, 365*(9462): 828–30.

Brown, H., Atkin, A., Panter, J., Wong, G., Chinapaw, M. and Van Sluijs, E. (2016) 'Family-based interventions to increase physical activity in children: a systematic review, meta-analysis and realist synthesis', *Obesity Reviews, 17*(4): 345–60.

Bullock, K., Erol, R. and Tilley, N. (2012) *Problem Oriented Policing and Partnerships*. London: Routledge.

Bunge, M. (2006) *Chasing Reality: Strife Over Realism*. Toronto: Toronto University Press.

Burton, R., Henn, C., Lavoie, D. et al. (2016) 'A rapid evidence review of the effectiveness and cost-effectiveness of alcohol control policies: an English perspective', *The Lancet, 389*(10078): 1558–80.

Buunk, A.P. and Gibbons, F.X. (1997) *Health, Coping and Wellbeing: Perspectives from Social Comparison Theory*. Mahwah, NJ: Erlbaum.

Buunk, A.P. and Gibbons, F.X. (2007) 'Social comparison: the end of a theory and the emergence of a field', *Organisational Behavior and Human Decision Processes, 102*(1): 3–21.

Buunk, B.P., Collins, R.L., Taylor, S.E., Van Yperen, N.W. and Dakof, G. (1990) 'The affective consequences of social comparison: either direction has its ups and downs', *Journal of Personality and Social Psychology, 59*(6): 1238–49.

Buxton, M. and Hanney, S. (1996) 'How can payback from health services research be assessed?', *Journal of Health Services Research and Policy*, 1(1): 35–43.

Byford, S. and Sefton, T. (2003) 'Economic evaluation of complex health and social care interventions', *National Institute Economic Review*, 186(1): 98–103.

Byng, R., Norman, I. and Redfern, S. (2005) 'Using realistic evaluation to evaluate a practice-level intervention to improve primary healthcare for patients with long-term mental illness', *Evaluation*, 11(1): 69–93.

Byrne, D. (2002) *Interpreting Quantitative Data*. London: Sage.

Byrne, D. (2005) 'Complexity, configurations and cases', *Theory, Culture and Society*, 22(5): 95–111.

Byrne, D. (2011) 'What is an effect? Coming at causality backwards', in M. Williams and W.P. Vogt (eds), *The Sage Handbook of Innovation in Social Research Methods*. London: Sage, pp. 80–94.

Byrne, D. (2013) 'Evaluating complex social interventions in a complex world', *Evaluation*, 19(3): 217–28.

Byrne, D. (2016) 'Explanation and empirical social research – getting beyond description whilst still making it interesting', in L. McKie and L. Ryan (eds), *An End to the Crisis in Empirical Sociology*. London: Routledge, pp. 101–16.

Byrne, D. and Callaghan, G. (2013) *Complexity Theory and the Social Sciences*. London: Routledge.

Cabinet Office (1999) *Modernising Government*. London: HMSO.

Cairney, P. (2016) *The Politics of Evidence Based Policymaking*. Basingstoke: Palgrave Macmillan.

Cameron, S. (2006) 'From low demand to rising aspirations: housing market renewal within regional and neighbourhood regeneration policy', *Housing Studies*, 21(1): 3–16.

Campbell, C. and Mzaidume, Z. (2001) 'Grassroots participation, peer education, and HIV prevention by sex workers in South Africa', *American Journal of Public Health*, 91(12): 1978–86.

Campbell, C., Wood, R. and Kelly, M. (1999) *Social Capital and Health*. London: Health Education Authority.

Campbell, D.T. (1986) 'Relabeling internal and external validity for applied social scientists', *New Directions for Program Evaluation*, 31: 67–77.

Campbell, D.T. (1988) *Methodology and Epistemology for Social Science: Selected Papers*. Chicago: University of Chicago Press.

Caplan, N. (1979) 'The two communities: theory and knowledge utilization', *American Behavioural Scientist*, 22(3): 459–70.

Carey, G., Malbon, E., Carey, N., Joyce, A., Crammond, B. and Carey, A. (2015) 'Systems science and systems thinking for public health: a systematic review of the field', *BMJ Open*, 5(12): 1–9.

Carmack-Taylor, C.L., Kulik, J., Badr, H. et al. (2007) 'A social comparison theory analysis of group composition and efficacy of cancer support group programs', *Social Science and Medicine*, 65(2): 262–73.

Cartwright, N. (2007) *Hunting Causes and Using Them*. Cambridge: Cambridge University Press.

Chalmers, I. (1998) 'Unbiased, relevant and reliable assessments in healthcare', *British Medical Journal*, 317: 1167–8.

Charles, J. (2014) *Reflections on Using Realist Methodology to Explore and Explain Costs and Cost-effectiveness – The FEMuR Feasibility Trial*. CARES Conference, 28 October, Liverpool.

Charles, J.M., Edwards, R., Williams, N. et al. (2013) 'The application of realist synthesis review methods in public health economics', *The Lancet*, 382: S28.

Chen, H.T. (1990) *Theory-driven Evaluations*. Newbury Park, CA: Sage.

Chen, H.T. and Rossi, P.H. (1987) 'The theory-driven approach to validity', *Evaluation and Program Planning*, 10(1): 95–103.

Chen, H.T. and Rossi, P.H. (1992) *Using Theory to Improve Program and Policy Evaluation*. Westport, CT: Greenwood.

Chief Medical Officers (2016) *Chief Medical Officers' Low Risk Drinking Guidelines* [online]. London, Cardiff, Belfast, Edinburgh: Department of Health (England), Welsh Government, Department of Health (Northern Ireland), Scottish Government, available at www.gov.uk/government/uploads/system/uploads/attachment_data/file/545937/UK_CMOs__report.pdf (accessed 24 May 2017).

Cicourel, A.V. (1964) *Method and Measurement in Sociology*. New York: Free Press.

Cilliers, P. (2001) 'Boundaries, hierarchies and networks in complex systems', *International Journal of Innovation Management*, 5(2): 135–47.

Clarke, R. (2002) *The Problem of Thefts of and from Cars in Parking Facilities*. Washington, DC: US Department of Justice, Office of Community Oriented Policing Services.

Clohesy, B. (2006) *The Damage Undone: Jane Rowe and the Mirabel Foundation*. South Melbourne, Vic.: Lothian Books.

Coast, J., Hensher, M., Mulligan, J.A., Sheppard, S. and Jones, J. (2000) 'Conceptual and practical difficulties with the economic evaluation of health services developments', *Journal of Health Services Research and Policy*, 5(1): 42–8.

Cochrane, A.L. (1972) *Effectiveness and Efficiency: Random Reflections on Health Services*. London: British Medical Journal/Nuffield Provincial Hospitals Trust.

Cohen, P.S. (1968) *Modern Social Theory*. London: Heinemann.

Cole, G. (1999) 'Advancing the development and application of theory-based evaluation in the practice of public health', *American Journal of Evaluation*, 20(3): 453–70.

Cole, I. (2012) 'Housing market renewal and demolition in England in the 2000s: the governance of "wicked" problems', *International Journal of Housing Policy*, 12(3): 347–66.

Commission on the Social Determinants of Health (2008) *Closing the Gap in a Generation: Health Equity through Action on the Social Determinants of Health*. Geneva: WHO.

Cook, T.D. (1990) 'The generalization of causal connections: multiple theories in search of clear practice', in L. Sechrest, E. Perrin and J. Bunker (eds), *Research Methodology: Strengthening Causal Interpretations of Nonexperimental Data*. Rockville, MD: US Department of Health and Human Services, pp. 9–31.

Cook, T.D. (1993) 'A quasi-sampling theory of the generalization of causal relationships', *New Directions for Evaluation*, 57: 39–82.

Cooley, C.H. (1992) *Human Nature and the Social Order*. Piscataway, NJ: Transaction Publishers.

Craig, P., Dieppe, P., MacIntyre, S., Michie, S., Nazareth, I. and Petticrew, M. (2008) 'Developing and evaluating complex interventions: the new Medical Research Council guidance', *BMJ*, 337: a1655.

Cronbach, L.J. (1975) 'Five decades of public controversy over mental testing', *American Psychologist*, 30(1): 1–14.

Cronbach, L.J. (1982) *Designing Evaluations of Educational and Social Programs*. San Francisco: Jossey-Bass.

Cronbach, L.J., Ambron, S.R., Dornbusch, S.M. et al. (1980) *Toward Reform of Program Evaluation*. San Francisco: Jossey-Bass.

Cruz, C.C.P., Motta, C.L.R., Santoro, F.M. and Elia, M. (2009) 'Applying reputation mechanisms in communities of practice: a case study', *Journal of Universal Computer Science, 15*(9): 1886–906.

Curnock, E., Ferguson, J., McKay, J. and Bowie, P. (2012) 'Healthcare improvement and rapid PDSA cycles of change: a realist synthesis of the literature' [online]. Glasgow: NHS Education for Scotland. Available at: www.nes.scot.nhs.uk/media/1389875/pdsa_realist_synthesis.pdf (accessed 25 May 2017).

Dalkin, S., Greenhalgh, J., Jones, D., Cunningham, B. and Lhussier, M. (2015) 'What's in a mechanism? Development of a key concept in realist evaluation', *Implementation Science, 10*(49): 1–7.

Davies, H.T.O., Nutley, S.M. and Smith, P.C. (2000) *What Works? Evidence-Based Policy Practice in Public Services*. Bristol: Policy Press.

Davies, K.S. (2011) 'Formulating the evidence based practice question: a review of the frameworks', *Evidence Based Library and Information Practice, 6*(2): 75–80.

Davis, C., Lexchin J., Jefferson, T., Gotzsche, P. and McKee, M. (2016) 'Adaptive pathways to drug authorisation: adapting to industry?', *BMJ, 354*(4437): 1–4.

Dawber, T.R. and Kannel, W.B. (1966) 'The Framingham Study: an epidemiological approach to coronary heart disease', *Circulation, 34*(4): 553–5.

Deci, E. and Ryan, R. (1985) *Intrinsic Motivation and Self-determination in Human Behaviour*. New York: Plenum.

Denham, J. (2001) *Building Cohesive Communities*. London: Home Office.

Dennis, J.G. (1973) *The Evangelistic Bureaucrat: A Study of a Planning Exercise in Newcastle upon Tyne*. London: Tavistock Publications.

Denyer, D. and Tranfield, D. (2009) 'Producing a systematic review', in D.A. Buchanan and A. Bryman (eds), *The Sage Handbook of Organizational Research Methods*. London: Sage, pp. 671–89.

Department of Communities and Local Government (2009) *Wider Performance Measures for the Housing Market Renewal Programme*. London: Department of Communities and Local Government.

Department of Health (2001) *A Research and Development Strategy for Public Health*. London: Department of Health.

Dibb, B. and Yardley, L. (2006) 'How does social comparison within a self-help group influence adjustment to chronic illness? A longitudinal study', *Social Science and Medicine, 63*(6): 1602–13.

Dickens, C. (1996) *Little Dorrit*. London: Penguin.

Dixon-Woods, M., Bonas, S., Booth, A. et al. (2006) 'How can systematic reviews incorporate qualitative research? A critical perspective', *Qualitative Research, 6*(1): 27–44.

Doll, R. and Hill, A.B. (1950) 'Smoking and carcinoma of the lung: preliminary report', *British Medical Journal, 2*(4682): 739–48.

Doll, R. and Hill, A.B. (1952) 'A study of the aetiology of carcinoma of the lung', *British Medical Journal, 2*(4797): 1271–86.

Drake, D.H. and Walters, R. (2015) '"Crossing the line": criminological expertise, policy advice and the "quarrelling society"', *Critical Social Policy, 35*(3): 414–33.

Drummond, M. (2010) 'Evidence-based decisions and economics: an agenda for research', in I. Shemilt, M. Mugford, L. Vale, K. Marsh and C. Donaldson (eds), *Evidence-Based Decisions* and Economics: Health Care, Social Welfare, Education and Criminal Justice. Oxford: Wiley-Blackwell.

Drummond, M. and Maguire, A. (2001) Economic Evaluation in Healthcare: Merging Theory with Practice. Oxford: Oxford University Press.

Drummond, M., Sculphier, M., Torrance, G., O'Brien, B. and Stoddart, G. (2005) Methods for the Economic Evaluation of Health Care Programmes. Oxford: Oxford University Press.

Duguid, S. and Pawson, R. (1998) 'Education, transformation and change', Evaluation Review, 22(4): 345–67.

Ebrahim, S., Montoya, L., El Din, M.K. et al. (2016) 'Randomized trials are frequently fragmented in multiple secondary publications', Journal of Clinical Epidemiology, 79: 130–9.

Eccles, M.P. and Mittman, B.S. (2006) 'Welcome to implementation science', Implementation Science, 1(1): 1–3.

Egger, M., Davey-Smith, G. and Altman, D. (2001) Systematic Reviews in Health Care: Meta-analysis in Context. London: BMJ Books.

Eichler, H.-G., Baird, L.G., Barker, R. et al. (2015) 'From adaptive licensing to adaptive pathways: delivering a flexible life-span approach to bring new drugs to patients', Clinical Pharmacology and Therapeutics, 97(3): 234–46.

Elder-Vass, D. (2004) 'Re-examining Bhaskar's three ontological domains: the lessons from emergence', in C. Lawson, J. Latsis and N. Martins (eds), Contributions to Social Ontology. New York: Routledge, pp. 160–76.

Ellwood, P., Grimshaw, P. and Pandza, K. (2016) 'Accelerating the innovation process: a systematic review and realist synthesis of the research literature' [online], International Journal of Management Reviews, available at: http://onlinelibrary.wiley.com/doi/10.1111/ijmr.12108/full (accessed 25 May 2017).

Elster, J. (1998) 'A plea for mechanisms', in P. Hedström and R. Swedberg (eds), Social Mechanisms: An Analytical Approach to Social Theory. Cambridge: Cambridge University Press.

Elster, J. (2007) Explaining Social Behaviour. Cambridge: Cambridge University Press.

Elster, J. (2015) Explaining Social Behaviour: More Nuts and Bolts for the Social Sciences. Cambridge: Cambridge University Press.

Emmel, N. (2013) Sampling and Choosing Cases in Qualitative Research: A Realist Approach. London: Sage.

Farrell, G. (2005) 'Progress and problems in the prevention of repeat victimisation', in N. Tilley (ed.), Handbook of Crime Prevention and Community Safety. Cullompton: Willan, pp. 143–70.

Farrell, G. and Pease, K. (2007) 'Preventing repeat residential burglary', in B. Welsh and D. Farrington (eds), Preventing Crime: What Works for Children, Offenders, Victims and Places. New York: Springer, pp. 161–76.

Festinger, L. (1954) 'A theory of social comparison processes', Human Relations, 7(2): 117–40.

Finfgeld-Connett, D. and Johnson, E.D. (2013) 'Literature search strategies for conducting knowledge-building and theory-generating qualitative systematic reviews: discussion paper', Journal of Advanced Nursing, 69(1): 194–204.

Flather, M., Delahunty, N. and Collinson, J. (2006) 'Generalising results from randomized trials in clinical practice: reliability and cautions', Clinical Trials, 3(6): 508–12.

Fleetwood, S. and Ackroyd, S. (2004) Critical Realist Applications in Organisation and Management Studies. London: Routledge.

Fox, D.M. (2017) 'Evidence and health policy: using and regulating systematic reviews', *American Journal of Public Health*, 107(1): 88–92.

Freedman, D. (2007) 'Statistical models for causation', in W. Outhwaite and S. Turner (eds), *The Sage Handbook of Social Science Methodology*. London: Sage, pp. 127–46.

Freeman, B., Chapman, S. and Storey, P. (2008) 'Banning smoking in cars carrying children: an analytical history of a public health advocacy campaign', *Australian and New Zealand Journal of Public Health*, 32(1): 60–5.

Fulop, N., Allen, P., Clarke, A. and Black, N. (2001) *Studying the Organisation and Delivery of Health Services: Research Methods*. London: Routledge.

Funnell, S. and Rogers, P. (2011) *Purposeful Program Theory: Effective Use of Theories of Change and Logic Models*. London: Wiley.

Garber, A. (1996) 'Theoretical foundations of cost-effectiveness analysis', in M. Gold, J. Siegel, L. Russell and M. Weinstein (eds), *Cost-Effectiveness in Health and Medicine*. New York: Oxford University Press, pp. 25–53.

George, A. and Bennett, A. (2005) *Case Studies and Theory Development in the Social Sciences*. Cambridge, MA: MIT Press.

Giddens, A. (1992) *The Transformation of Intimacy*. Cambridge: Polity Press.

Gilson, L. (2012) *Health Policy and Systems Research: A Methodology Reader*. Geneva: Alliance for Health Policy and Systems Research & World Health Organisation.

Gilson, L., Hanson, K., Sheikh, K., Agyepong, I.A., Ssengooba, F. and Bennett, S. (2011) 'Building the field of health policy and systems research: social science matters' [online], *PLoS Medicine*, 8(8), available at http://journals.plos.org/plosmedicine/article?id=10.1371/journal.pmed.1001079 (accessed 25 May 2017).

Godber, E., Robinson, R. and Steiner, A. (1997) 'Economic evaluation and the shifting balance towards primary care: definitions, evidence and methodological issues', *Health Economics*, 6(3): 275–94.

Goethals, G.R. (1986) 'Social comparison theory: psychology from the lost and found', *Personality and Social Psychology Bulletin*, 12(3): 261–78.

Goicolea, I., Vives-Cases, C., San Sebastian, M., Marchal, B., Kegels, G. and Hurtig, A.K. (2013) 'How do primary health care teams learn to integrate intimate partner violence (IPV) management? A realist evaluation protocol', *Implementation Science*, 8(36): 1–11.

Goicolea, I., Hurtig, A.-K., San Sebastian, M., Marchal, B. and Vives-Cases, C. (2015a) 'Using realist evaluation to assess primary healthcare teams' responses to intimate partner violence in Spain', *Gaceta Sanitaria*, 29(6): 431–6.

Goicolea, I., Hurtig, A.K., San Sebastian, M., Vives-Cases, C. and Marchal, B. (2015b) 'Developing a programme theory to explain how primary health care teams learn to respond to intimate partner violence: a realist case-study', *BMC Health Services Research*, 15(228): 1–13.

Goicolea, I., Vives-Cases, C., Hurtig, A.K. et al. (2015c) 'Mechanisms that trigger a good health-care response to intimate partner violence in Spain: combining realist evaluation and qualitative comparative analysis approaches' [online], *PLOS One*, 10(8), available at http://journals.plos.org/plosone/article?id=10.1371/journal.pone.0135167 (accessed 25 May 2017).

Goldthorpe, J. (2015) *Sociology as a Population Science*. Cambridge: Cambridge University Press.

Goodridge, D., Westhorp, G., Rotter, T., Dobson, R. and Bath, B. (2015) 'Lean and leadership practices: development of an initial realist program theory', *BMC Health Services Research*, 15(362): 1–15.

Greenhalgh, J. (2014) 'Synthesising published research: a realist approach', in P. Edwards, J. O'Mahoney and S. Vincent (eds), *Explaining Management and Organisation Using Critical Realism: A Practical Guide*. Oxford: Oxford University Press.

Greenhalgh, J., Dalkin S., Gooding, K. et al. (2017) 'Functionality and feedback: a realist synthesis of the collation, interpretation and utilisation of patient-reported outcome measures data to improve patient care', *Health Services and Delivery Research*, 5(2): 1–318.

Greenhalgh, T. (2001) *How to Read a Paper: The Basics of Evidence Based Medicine*. London: BMJ Books.

Greenhalgh, T. and Peacock, R. (2005) 'Effectiveness and efficiency of search methods in systematic reviews of complex evidence: audit of primary sources', *BMJ*, 331(7524): 1064–5.

Greenhalgh, T., Howick, J., Maskrey, N. et al. (2014) 'Evidence-based medicine: a movement in crisis?', *BMJ*, 348(3725): 1–7.

Greenhalgh, T., Humphrey, C., Hughes, J., Macfarlane, F., Butler, C. and Pawson, R. (2009) 'How do you modernize a health service? A realist evaluation of whole-scale transformation in London', *Milbank Quarterly*, 87(2): 391–416.

Greenhalgh, T., Raferty, J., Hanney, S. and Glover, M. (2016) 'Research impact: a narrative review', *BMC Medicine*, 14(78): 1–16.

Groff, R. (2004) *Critical Realism, Post-positivism and the Possibility of Knowledge*. London: Routledge.

Haddaway, N.R., Collins, A.M., Coughlin, D. and Kirk, S. (2015) 'The role of Google Scholar in evidence reviews and its applicability to grey literature searching' [online], *PLoS One*, available at http://journals.plos.org/plosone/article?id=10.1371/journal.pone.0138237 (accessed 25 May 2017).

Haig, B. and Evers, C. (2016) *Realist Inquiry in Social Science*. London: Sage.

Hammersley, M. (1989) *The Dilemma of Qualitative Method: Herbert Blumer and the Chicago Tradition*. London: Sage.

Hammersley, M. (1992) *What's Wrong with Ethnography?* London: Routledge.

Hamre, B.K. and Pianta, R.C. (2006) 'Student–teacher relationships', in G.G. Bear and K.M. Minke (eds), *Children's Needs III: Development, Prevention, and Intervention*. Washington, DC: National Association of School Psychologists, pp. 59–71.

Hardwick, R., Pearson, M., Byng, R. and Anderson, R. (2013) 'The effectiveness and cost-effectiveness of shared care: protocol for a realist review', *Systematic Reviews*, 2(12): 1–7.

Harré, R. (1972) *The Philosophies of Science*. Oxford: Oxford University Press.

Harré, R. and Madden, E.H. (1975) *Causal Powers: Theory of Natural Necessity*. Oxford: Blackwell.

Harris, J., Springett, J., Croot, L. et al. (2015) 'Can community-based peer support promote health literacy and reduce inequalities? A realist review', *Public Health Research*, 3(3): 1–192.

Hausner, E., Waffenschmidt, S., Kaiser, T. and Simon, M. (2012) 'Routine development of objectively derived search strategies', *Systematic Reviews*, 1(19): 1–10.

Hawe, P., Shiell, A. and Riley, T. (2004) 'Complex interventions: how "out of control" can a randomised controlled trial be?', *BMJ*, 328(7455): 1561–3.

Hawker, S., Payne, S., Kerr, C., Hardey, M. and Powell, J. (2002) 'Appraising the evidence: reviewing disparate data systematically', *Qualitative Health Research*, 12(9): 1284–99.

Hedström, P. (2005) *Dissecting the Social*. Oxford: Oxford University Press.

Hedström, P. and Swedberg, R. (1998) *Social Mechanisms: An Analytical Approach to Social Theory*. Cambridge: Cambridge University Press.

Henry, G.T., Julnes, G. and Mark, M.M. (1998a) *Realist Evaluation: An Emerging Theory in Support of Practice*. San Francisco: Jossey-Bass.

Henry, G.T., Mark, M.M. and Julnes, G. (1998b) 'Realist evaluation: an emerging theory in support of practice', *New Directions for Evaluation*, 78: 1–109.

Hernandez, A., Hurtig, A. and San Sebastian, M. (2014) 'More than a checklist: a realist evaluation of supervision of mid-level health workers in rural Guatemala', *BMC Health Services Research*, 14(112): 1–12.

Hickman, M., Drummond, N. and Grimshaw, J. (1994) 'A taxonomy of shared care for chronic disease', *Journal of Public Health Medicine*, 16(4): 447–54.

Higher Education Funding Council for England (HEFCE) (2014) *REF: Assessment Framework and Guidance on Submissions* [online]. Higher Education Funding Council for England, Scottish Funding Council, Higher Education Funding Council for Wales, Department for Employment and Learning, Northern Ireland, available at www.abdn.ac.uk/documents/assessment-framework-guidance-on-submissions.docx (accessed 25 May 2017).

Hjørland, B. (2002) 'Domain analysis in information science: eleven approaches – traditional as well as innovative', *Journal of Documentation*, 58(4): 422–62.

Hope, T. and Foster, J. (1992) 'Conflicting forces: changing the dynamics of crime and community in a "problem" estate', *British Journal of Criminology*, 32(4): 488–504.

Howick, J. (2011) *The Philosophy of Evidence-based Medicine*. London: Wiley.

Howick, J., Glasziou, P. and Aronson, J.K. (2013) 'Problems with using mechanisms to solve the problem of extrapolation', *Theoretical Medicine and Bioethics*, 34(4): 275–91.

Hume, D. ([1748] 2007) *An Enquiry Concerning Human Understanding*. Oxford: Oxford University Press.

Hyman, H.H. (1960) 'Reflections on reference groups', *Public Opinion Quarterly*, 24(3): 383–96.

Illich, I. (1977) *The Limits to Medicine*. Harmondsworth: Penguin.

Imbens, G.W. and Rubin, D.B. (2015) *Causal Inference for Statistics, Social, and Biomedical Sciences: An Introduction*. Cambridge: Cambridge University Press.

Ingold, J. and Monaghan, M. (2016) 'Evidence translation: an exploration of policy makers use of evidence', *Policy and Politics*, 44(2): 171–90.

Ioannidis, J.P. (2016) 'The mass production of redundant, misleading and conflicted systematic reviews and meta-analyses', *Millbank Quarterly*, 94(3): 485–514.

ISSG (2017) Information Specialists Subgroup Search Filters Resource website [online], available at https://sites.google.com/a/york.ac.uk/issg-search-filters-resource/home (accessed 25 May 2017).

Jackson, S.F. and Kolla, G. (2012) 'New realistic evaluation analysis method: linked coding of context, mechanism, and outcome relationships', *American Journal of Evaluation*, 33(3): 339–49.

Jagosh, J., Macaulay, A.C., Pluye, P. et al. (2012) 'Uncovering the benefits of participatory research: implications of a realist review for health research and practice', *Milbank Quarterly*, 90(2): 311–46.

Jagosh, J., Bush, P., Salsberg, J. et al. (2015) 'A realist evaluation of community-based participatory research: partnership synergy, trust building and related ripple effects', *BMC Public Health*, 15(725): 1–11.

Johnson, S., Tilley, N. and Bowers, K. (2015) 'Introducing EMMIE: an evidence rating scale for crime prevention policy and practice', *Journal of Experimental Criminology*, 11(3): 459–73.

Jones, J. (1986) 'Community development and health promotion', in J. Davies (ed.), *Health Promotion in Areas of Multiple Deprivation*. Report of a symposium held in the Royal College of Physicians. Edinburgh: Scottish Health Education Group.

Kahan, D.M., Braman, D., Cohen, G.L., Gastil, J. and Slovic, P. (2010) 'Who fears the HPV vaccine, who doesn't, and why? An experimental study of the mechanisms of cultural cognition', *Law and Human Behavior*, 34(6): 501–16.

Kane, S.S., Gerretsen, B., Scherpbier, R., Dal, P.M. and Dieleman, M. (2010) 'A realist synthesis of randomised control trials involving use of community health workers for delivering child health interventions in low and middle income countries', *BMC Health Services Research*, 10(286): 1–7.

Kant, I. ([1781] 2007) *The Critique of Pure Reason*. Basingstoke: Palgrave Macmillan.

Kelly, M.P. and Barker, M. (2016) 'Why is changing health related behaviour so difficult?', *Public Health*, 136: 109–16.

Kelly, M.P. and Moore, T.A. (2012) 'The judgement process in evidence based medicine and health technology assessment', *Social Theory and Health*, 10(1): 1–19.

Kelly, M.P., Kelly, R.S. and Russo, F. (2014) 'The integration of social, behavioural and biological mechanisms in models of pathogenesis', *Perspectives in Biology and Medicine*, 57(3): 308–28.

Kelly, M.P., Heath, I., Howick, J. and Greenhalgh, T. (2015) 'The importance of values in evidence-based medicine', *BMC Medical Ethics*, 16(69): 1–8.

Kelly, M.P., Morgan, A., Ellis, S., Younger, T., Huntley, J. and Swann, C. (2010) 'Evidence based public health: a review of the experience of the National Institute of Health and Clinical Excellence (NICE) of developing public health guidance in England', *Social Science and Medicine*, 71(6): 1056–62.

Kelly, M.P., Stewart, E., Morgan, A. et al. (2009) 'A conceptual framework for public health: NICE's emerging approach', *Public Health*, 123: e14–e20.

Kernick, D. (2002) 'The demise of linearity in managing health services: a call for post normal health care', *Journal of Health Servies Research and Policy*, 7(2): 121–4.

Killoran, A., Swann, C. and Kelly, M.P. (2006) *Public Health Evidence: Tackling Health Inequalities*. Oxford: Oxford University Press.

Kingdon, J. (1984) *Agendas, Alternatives, and Public Policies*. Boston, MA: Little, Brown.

Kislov, R., Wilson, P. and Boaden, R. (2017) 'The dark side of knowledge brokering', *Journal of Health Services Research and Policy*, 22(2): 107–12.

Kneale, D., Thomas, J. and Harris, K. (2015) 'Developing and optimising the use of logic models in systematic reviews: exploring practice and good practice in the use of programme theory in reviews', *PLoS One*, 10(11): 1–26.

Kulkarni, A.V., Aziz, B., Shams, I. and Busse, J.W. (2009) 'Comparisons of citations in Web of Science, Scopus, and Google Scholar for articles published in general medical journals', *JAMA*, 302(10): 1092–6.

Kwamie, A. (2016) 'The Tree Under Which You Sit: Realist Approaches to District-level Management and Leadership in Maternal and Newborn Health Policy Implementation in the Greater Accra Region, Ghana'. PhD, Wageningen University.

Kwamie, A., Van Dijk, H. and Agyepong, I.A. (2014) 'Advancing the application of systems thinking in health: realist evaluation of the Leadership Development Programme for district manager decision-making in Ghana', *Health Research Policy and Systems*, 12(29): 1–12.

Kwamie, A., Agyepong, I.A. and Van Dijk, H. (2015) 'What governs district manager decision making? A case study of complex leadership in Dangme West District, Ghana', *Health Systems and Reform*, 1(2): 167–77.

Lakatos, I. (1976) *Proofs and Refutations: The Logic of Mathematical Discovery*. Cambridge: Cambridge University Press.

Layard, R. and Glaister, S. (1994) *Cost-benefit Analysis*. Cambridge: Cambridge University Press.

Laycock, G. (1992) 'Operation identification or the power of publicity', *Security Journal*, 2(2): 67–72.

Leather, P., Nevin, B., Cole, I. and Eadson, W. (2012) *The Housing Market Renewal Programme in England: Development, Impact and Legacy*. Centre for Regional, Economic and Social Research, Sheffield Hallam University.

Leeuw, F.L. (2003) 'Reconstructing program theories: methods available and problems to be solved', *American Journal of Evaluation*, 24(1): 5–20.

Leeuw, F.L. and Donaldson, S.I. (2015) 'Theory in evaluation: reducing confusion and encouraging debate', *Evaluation*, 21(4): 467–80.

Leeuw, F.L. and Schmeets, H. (2016) *Empirical Legal Research*. Cheltenham: Edward Elgar.

Lefebvre, C., Manheimer, E. and Glanville, J. (2011) 'Searching for studies' [online], in J.P.T. Higgins and S. Green (eds), *Cochrane Handbook for Systematic Reviews of Interventions Version 5.1.0*, The Cochrane Collaboration, available at www.handbook.cochrane.org (accessed 25 May 2017).

Lefebvre, C., Glanville, J., Wieland, L.S., Coles, B. and Weightman, A.L. (2013) 'Methodological developments in searching for studies for systematic reviews: past, present and future?', *Systematic Reviews*, 2(78): 1–9.

Lessard, C. (2007) 'Complexity and reflexivity: two important issues for economic evaluation in health care', *Social Science and Medicine*, 64(8): 1754–65.

Lewis, D. (1986) *Philosophical Papers II*. Oxford: Oxford University Press.

Lincoln, Y.S. and Guba, E.G. (1985) *Naturalistic Inquiry*. Newbury Park, CA: Sage.

Linder, S.K., Kamath, G.R., Pratt, G.F., Saraykar, S.S. and Volk, R.J. (2015) 'Citation searches are more sensitive than keyword searches to identify studies using specific measurement instruments', *Journal of Clinical Epidemiology*, 68(4): 412–17.

Lipsey, M. (1993) 'Theory as method: small theories of treatments', *New Directions for Evaluation*, 57: 5–38.

Lipsey, M. and Pollard, J. (1989) 'Driving toward theory in program evaluation: more models to choose from', *Evaluation and Program Planning*, 12(4): 317–28.

McAdam, D., Tarrow, S. and Tilly, C. (2001) *Dynamics of Contention*. Cambridge: Cambridge University Press.

McCartney, M. (2012) *The Patient Paradox: Why Sexed Up Medicine Is Bad for Your Health*. London: Pinter & Martin.

McDaniel, R., Lanham, H. and Anderson, R. (2009) 'Implications of complex adaptive systems theory for the design of research on health care organizations', *Health Care Management Review*, 34(2): 191–9.

MacIver, R.M. (1942) *Social Causation*. New York: Ginn.

McLean, S., Gee, M., Booth, A. et al. (2014) 'Targeting the use of reminders and notifications for uptake by populations (TURNUP): a systematic review and evidence synthesis', *Health Services and Delivery Research*, 2(34): 1–184.

Mahoney, J. (2001) 'Beyond correlational analysis: recent innovations in theory and method', *Sociological Forum, 16*: 575–93.

Mahoney, J. (2003) 'Strategies of causal analysis in comparative historical analysis', in J. Mahoney and D. Rueschemeyer, *Comparative Historical Analysis in Social Sciences*. Cambridge: Cambridge University Press, pp. 337–72.

Maidment, I., McKeown, J., Mullan, J., Bailey, S., Booth, A. and Wong, G. (2016) 'Developing a framework for a novel multi-disciplinary, multi-agency intervention(s), to improve medication management in older people on complex medication regimens resident in the community: a realist synthesis' [online], available at: www.crd.york.ac.uk/PROSPERO/display_record. asp?ID=CRD42016043506 (accessed 25 May 2017).

Marchal, B., Dedzo, M. and Kegels, G. (2010a) 'Turning around an ailing district hospital: a realist evaluation of strategic changes at Ho Municipal Hospital (Ghana)', *BMC Public Health, 10*(787): 1–16.

Marchal, B., Dedzo, M. and Kegels, G. (2010b) 'A realist evaluation of the management of a well-performing regional hospital in Ghana', *BMC Health Services Research, 10*(24): 1–14.

Marchal, B., Van Belle, S., Van Olmen, J., Hoerée, T. and Kegels, G. (2012) 'Is realist evaluation keeping its promise? A literature review of methodological practice in health systems research', *Evaluation, 18*(2): 192–212.

Marchal, B., Van Belle, S., De Brouwere, V. and Witter, S. (2013a) 'Studying complex interventions: reflections from the FEMHealth project on evaluating fee exemption policies in West Africa and Morocco', *BMC Health Services Research, 13*(469): 1–9.

Marchal, B., Van der Veken, K., Essolbi, A., Dossou, J.-P., Richard, F. and Van Belle, S. (2013b) *Methodological Reflections on Using Realist Evaluation in a Study of Fee Exemption Policies in West Africa and Morocco*. Antwerp: FEMHealth.

Mark, M.M., Henry, G.T. and Julnes, G. (2000) *Evaluation – An Integrated Framework for Understanding, Guiding and Improving Policies and Programs*. San Francisco: Jossey-Bass.

Markman, A.B., Maddox, W.T. and Baldwin, G.C. (2005) 'The implications of advances in research on motivation for cognitive models', *Journal of Experimental and Theoretical Artificial Intelligence, 17*(4): 371–84.

Marmot, M. and Wilkinson, R. (1999) *Social Determinants of Health*. Oxford: Oxford University Press.

Marris, R. and Rein, M. (1967) *Dilemmas of Social Reform*. London: Routledge.

Marsh, C. (1982) *The Survey Method: The Contribution of Surveys to Sociological Explanation*. London: George Allen & Unwin.

Marteau, T.M., Hollands, G.J. and Kelly, M.P. (2015) 'Changing population behavior and reducing health disparities: exploring the potential of "choice architecture" interventions', in R.M. Kaplan, M. Spittel and D.H. David (eds), *Population Health: Behavioral and Social Science Insights*. Rockville, MD: Agency for Healthcare Research and Quality and Office of Behavioral and Social Sciences Research, National Institutes of Health, pp. 105–26.

Mason, P. and Barnes, M. (2007) 'Constructing theories of change: methods and sources', *Evaluation, 13*(2): 151–170.

Maxwell, J. (2012) *A Realist Approach For Qualitative Research*. Thousand Oaks, CA: Sage.

Maxwell, J. (2013) *Qualitative Research Design: An Interactive Approach*. London: Sage.

Mayhew, P. (2016) 'In defence of administrative criminology', *Crime Science*, 5(7): 1–10.

Mayne, J. (2001) 'Addressing attribution through contribution analysis: using performance measures sensibly' *The Canadian Journal of Program Evaluation*, 16(1): 1.

Menon, A. and Portes, J. (2016) 'You're wrong Michael Gove – experts are trusted far more than you' [online], *The Guardian*, 9 June, available at www.theguardian.com/commentisfree/2016/jun/09/michael-gove-experts-academics-vote (accessed 25 May 2017).

Merton, R.K. (1968) *Social Theory and Social Structure*. New York: Free Press.

Merton, R.K. and Kitt, A.S. (1950) 'Contributions to the theory of reference group behavior', in R.K. Merton and P.F. Lazersfeld (eds), *Continuities in Social Research: Studies in the Scope and Method of 'The American Soldier'*. New York: Free Press, pp. 40–105.

Millward, L.M., Morgan, A. and Kelly, M.P. (2003) *Prevention and Reduction of Accidental Injury in Children and Older People: Evidence Briefing*. London: Health Development Agency.

Mills, C.W. (1959) *The Sociological Imagination*. Oxford: Oxford University Press.

Mirabel Foundation (2016) *Annual Report*. Melbourne: Mirabel Foundation.

Monaghan, M. (2011) *Evidence versus Politics. Exploiting Research in UK Drug Policy Making?* Bristol: Policy Press.

Moore, B. (1966) *Social Origins of Dictatorship and Democracy*. Boston, MA: Beacon Press.

Moore, G.F., Audrey, S., Barker, M., Bond, L., Bonell, C., Hardeman, W., Moore, L., O'Cathain, A., Tinati, T., Wight, D. and Baird, J. (2015) 'Process evaluation of complex interventions: medical research council guidance.', *BMJ*, *350*, 1258.

Morgan, S. and Winship, C. (2015) *Counterfactuals and Causal Inference: Methods and Principles for Social Research*. New York: Cambridge University Press.

Morrell, C.J., Sutcliffe, P., Booth, A. et al. (2016) 'A systematic review, evidence synthesis and meta-analysis of quantitative and qualitative studies evaluating the clinical effectiveness, the cost-effectiveness, safety and acceptability of interventions to prevent postnatal depression', *Health Technology Assessment*, *20*(37): 1–414.

MRC (2000) *A Framework for the Development and Evaluation of RCTs for Complex Interventions to Improve Health*. London: Medical Research Council.

Mukherjee, S. (2011) *The Emperor of All Maladies: A Biography of Cancer*. London: Fourth Estate.

Mukumbang, F., Van Belle, S., Marchal, B. and Van Wyck, B. (2016a) 'A realist evaluation of the antiretroviral treatment adherence club programme in selected primary health care facilities in the metropolitan area of Western Cape Province, South Africa: a study protocol', *BMJ Open*, 6(4): 1–12.

Mukumbang, F., Van Belle, S., Marchal, B. and Van Wyck, B. (2016b) 'Towards developing an initial programme theory: programme designers' and managers' assumptions on the antiretroviral treatment adherence club programme in primary health care facilities in the Metropolitan area of Western Cape Province, South Africa', *PLOS One*, *11*(8): 1–31.

Mukumbang, F., Van Belle, S., Marchal, B. and Van Wyck, B. (2017) 'Exploring "generative mechanisms" of the antiretroviral adherence club intervention – a scoping review of research-based antiretroviral treatment adherence theories', *BMC Public Health*, *17*(385): 1–14.

Mukumbang, F., Van Belle, S., Marchal, B. and Van Wyck, B. (forthcoming) 'A systematic review (narrative synthesis) of group-based HIV/AIDS treatment and care models in Sub-Saharan Africa'.

Mulvihill, C. and Quigley, R. (2003) *The Management of Obesity and Overweight: An Analysis of Reviews of Diet, Physical Activity and Behavioural Approaches: Evidence Briefing*. London: Health Development Agency.

Mumford, S. (2007) 'Filled in space', in M. Kistler and B. Gnassounou (eds), *Dispositions and Causal Powers*. Aldershot: Ashgate, pp. 67–80.

National Audit Office (NAO) (2001) *Modern Policy Making: Ensuring Policies Deliver Value for Money*. London: Stationery Office.

Nebot Giralt, A., Nöstlinger, C., Lee, J. et al. (2017) 'Understanding the acceptability and adherence to paediatric antiretroviral treatment in the new formulation of pellets (LPV/r) – the protocol of a realist evaluation', *BMJ Open*, 7(3): 1–10.

NICE (2006a) 'Smoking: brief interventions and referrals' [online], available at www.nice.org.uk/guidance/ph1 (accessed 25 May 2017).

NICE (2006b) 'Four commonly used methods to increase physical activity: brief interventions in primary care, exercise referral schemes, pedometers and community based exercise programmes for walking and cycling' [online], available at www.nice.org.uk/guidance/PH54 (accessed 25 May 2017).

NICE (2007) 'Behaviour change: general approaches' [online], available at www.nice.org.uk/guidance/ph6 (accessed 25 May 2017).

NICE (2008) 'Community engagement: improving health and wellbeing and reducing health inequalities' [online], available at www.nice.org.uk/guidance/ng44 (accessed 25 May 2017).

NICE (2009) *Methods for the Development of NICE Public Health Guidance*. London: NICE.

NICE (2010a) 'Alcohol-use disorders: prevention' [online], available at www.nice.org.uk/guidance/ph24 (accessed 25 May 2017).

NICE (2010b) 'Cardiovascular disease prevention' [online], available at www.nice.org.uk/guidance/ph25 (accessed 25 May 2017).

NICE (2012) *Public Health Guidance Process and Method Guides*. London: NICE.

NICE (2016) *Developing NICE Guidelines: The Manual* [online], available at www.nice.org.uk/process/pmg20/chapter/introduction-and-overview (accessed 25 May 2017).

Nozick, R. (2001) *Invariances: The Structure of the Objective World*. Cambridge, MA: Harvard University Press.

Nutley, S.M., Walter, I. and Davies, H.T.O. (2003) 'From knowing to doing: a framework for understanding the evidence-into-practice agenda', *Evaluation*, 9(2): 125–48.

Nutley, S.M., Walter, I. and Davies, H.T.O. (2007) *Using Evidence: How Research Can Inform Public Services*. Bristol: Policy Press.

Nyssen, O.P., Taylor, S., Wong, G. et al. (2016) 'Does therapeutic writing help people with long-term conditions? Systematic review, realist synthesis and economic considerations', *Health Technology Assessment*, 20(27): 1–410.

O'Mara-Eves, A., Thomas, J., McNaught, J., Miwa, M. and Ananiadou, S. (2015) 'Using text mining for study identification in systematic reviews: a systematic review of current approaches', *Systematic Reviews*, 4(5): 1–22.

Ogilvie, D., Hamilton, V., Egan, M. and Petticrew, M. (2005) 'Systematic reviews of health effects of social interventions: 1. Finding the evidence: how far should you go?', *Journal of Epidemiology and Community Health*, 59(9): 804–8.

Otte-Trojel, T. and Wong, G. (2016) 'Going beyond systematic reviews: realist and meta-narrative reviews', in E. Ammenwerth and M. Rigby (eds), *Evidence Based Health Informatics: Promoting Safety and Efficiency through Scientific Methods and Ethical Policy*. Amsterdam, Berlin and Washington, DC: IOS Press, pp. 275–87.

Papaioannou, D., Sutton, A., Carroll, C., Booth, A. and Wong, R. (2010) 'Literature searching for social science systematic reviews: consideration of a range of search techniques', *Health Information and Libraries Journal*, 27(2): 114–22.

Papoutsi, C., Mattick, K., Pearson, M., Brennan, N., Briscoe, S. and Wong, G. (2017), 'Social and professional influences on antimicrobial prescribing for doctors-in-training: a realist review', *Journal of Antimicrobial Chemotherapy*. DOI: 10.1093/jac/dkx194.

Pawson, R. (1979) 'Empiricist explanatory strategies: the case of causal modelling', *Sociological Review*, 26(3): 613–45.

Pawson, R. (1980) 'Empiricist measurement strategies: a critique of the multiple indicator approach to measurement', *Quality and Quantity*, 14(5): 651–78.

Pawson, R. (1982) 'Desperate measures', *British Journal of Sociology*, 33(1): 35–63.

Pawson, R. (1989) *A Measure for Measures: A Manifesto for Empirical Sociology*. London: Routledge.

Pawson, R. (2000) 'Middle-range realism', *European Journal of Sociology*, 41(2): 283–325.

Pawson, R. (2002) 'Evidence based policy: in search of a method', *Evaluation*, 8(2): 157–81.

Pawson, R. (2003) 'Nothing as practical as good theory', *Evaluation*, 9(4): 471–90.

Pawson, R. (2006a) 'Digging for nuggets: how "bad" research can yield "good" evidence', *International Journal of Social Research Methodology*, 9(2): 127–42.

Pawson, R. (2006b) *Evidence-based Policy: A Realist Perspective*. London: Sage.

Pawson, R. (2008) 'Causality for beginners' [online], available at http://eprints.ncrm.ac.uk/245/1/Causality_for_Beginners_Dec_07.doc (accessed 26 May 2017).

Pawson, R. (2009a) 'Middle range theory and programme theory evaluation: from provenance to practice', in J. Vaessen and F. Leeuw (eds), *Mind the Gap: Perspectives on Policy Evaluation and the Social Sciences*. New Brunswick, NJ and London: Transaction Publishers, pp. 171–202.

Pawson, R. (2009b) 'On the shoulders of Merton: Boudon as the modern guardian of middle-range theory', in M. Cherkaoui and P. Hamilton (eds), *Raymond Boudon: A Life in Sociology*. Oxford: Bardwell Press, pp. 317–34.

Pawson, R. (2012) 'Re: Systematic and explicit methods for theory generation' [online], available at www.jiscmail.ac.uk/cgi-bin/webadmin?A2=RAMESES;e63f7910.1207 (accessed 26 May 2017).

Pawson, R. (2013) *The Science of Evaluation: A Realist Manifesto*. London: Sage.

Pawson, R. and Manzano-Santaella, A. (2012) 'A realist diagnostic workshop', *Evaluation*, 18(2): 176–91.

Pawson R. (2018) 'The realist foundations of evidence-based medicine: a review essay', *Evaluation*, 24(1): 42–50.

Pawson, R., Greenhalgh, T., Harvey, G. and Walshe, K. (2004) *Reaslist synthesis: an introduction Research Methods Programme ESRC* [online], available at https://pdfs.semanticscholar.org/4351/46e6e6617491ff1c4b32b76e0a534c86d6c7.pdf (accessed 11 May 2018).

Pawson, R. and Tilley, N. (1982) *Monstrous Thoughts: Weaknesses in the Strong Programme of the Sociology of Science*, University of Leeds Occasional Paper in Sociology No. 14.

Pawson, R. and Tilley, N. (1992) 'Re-evaluation: rethinking research on corrections and crime', in S. Duguid (ed.), *Yearbook of Correctional Education*. Burnaby: Institute of Humanities, Simon Fraser University, pp. 19–49.

Pawson, R. and Tilley, N. (1994) 'What works in evaluation research?', *British Journal of Criminology*, 34(3): 291–306.

Pawson, R. and Tilley, N. (1997) *Realistic Evaluation*. London: Sage.

Pawson, R. and Tilley, N. (1998a) 'Caring communities, paradigm polemics, design debates', *Evaluation: International Journal of Theory, Research and Practice*, 4(1): 73–90.

Pawson, R. and Tilley, N. (1998b) 'Cookbook methods and disastrous recipes: a rejoinder to Farrington', *Evaluation: International Journal of Theory, Research and Practice*, 4(2): 211–13.

Pawson, R. and Tilley, N. (2001) 'Realistic evaluation bloodlines', *American Journal of Evaluation*, 22(3): 317–24.

Pawson, R. and Tilley, N. (2004) 'Realist evaluation' [online], available at www.communitymatters. com.au/RE_chapter.pdf (accessed 26 May 2017).

Pawson, R. and Tilley, N. (2009) 'Realist evaluation', in H. Uwe, A. Polutta and H. Ziegler (eds), *Evidence-based Practice: Modernising the Knowledge Base of Social Work?* Opladen and Farmington Hills, MI: Barbara Budrich Publishers, pp. 151–80.

Pawson, R. and Wong, G. (2013) 'Public opinion and policy-making', in I. Greener and B. Greve (eds), *Evidence and Evaluation in Social Policy*. Oxford: Wiley Blackwell, pp. 81–96.

Pawson, R., Greenhalgh, J. and Brennan, C. (2016) 'Demand management for planned care: a realist synthesis', *Health Services and Delivery Research*, 4(2): 1–252.

Pawson, R., Owen, L. and Wong, G. (2010a) 'Legislating for health: locating the evidence', *Journal of Public Health Policy*, 31(2): 164–77.

Pawson, R., Owen, L. and Wong, G. (2010b) 'The Today progamme's contribution to evidence-based policy', *Evaluation*, 16(2): 211–13.

Pawson, R., Wong, G. and Owen, L. (2011a) 'Myths, facts and conditional truths: what is the evidence on the risks associated with smoking in cars carrying children?', *Canadian Medical Association Journal*, 183(10): E680–E684.

Pawson, R., Wong, G. and Owen, L. (2011b) 'Known knowns, known unknowns, unknown unknowns: the predicament of evidence-based policy', *American Journal of Evaluation*, 32(4): 518–46.

Pawson, R., Greenhalgh, T., Harvey, G. and Walshe, K. (2004) *Realist Synthesis: An Introduction*. Manchester: ESRC Research Methods Programme, University of Manchester.

Pawson, R., Greenhalgh, T., Harvey, G. and Walshe, K. (2005) 'Realist review – a new method of systematic review designed for complex policy interventions', *Journal of Health Services Research and Policy*, 10(Suppl. 1): 21–34.

Payne, K. and Thompson, A. (2015) 'Economic evaluations of complex interventions', in D. Richards and I. Rahm Hallberg (eds), *Complex Interventions in Health: An Overview of Research Methods*. Abingdon: Routledge, pp. 248–57.

Payne, K., McAllister, M. and Davies, L. (2013) 'Valuing the economic benefits of complex interventions: when maximising health is not sufficient', *Health Economics*, 22(3): 258–71.

Pearson, M., Moxham, T. and Ashton, K. (2011) 'Effectiveness of search strategies for qualitative research about barriers and facilitators of program delivery', *Evaluation and the Health Professions*, 34(3): 297–308.

Pearson, M., Hunt, H., Cooper, C., Sheppard, S., Pawson, R. and Anderson, R. (2015) 'Providing effective and preferred care closer to home: a realist review of intermediate care', *Health and Social Care in the Community*, 23(6): 577–93.

Pease, K. (1998) *Repeat Victimisation: Taking Stock*, Crime Prevention Detection and Prevention Series Paper 90. London: Home Office.

Peto, R., Collins, R. and Gray, R. (1995) 'Large-scale randomized evidence: large, simple trials and overviews of trials', *Journal of Clinical Epidemiology*, 48(1): 23–40.

Philip, K. and Spratt, J. (2007) *A Synthesis of Published Research on Mentoring and Befriending*. Manchester: Mentoring and Befriending Foundation.

Psillos, S. (1999) *Scientific Realism: How Science Tracks Truth*. Routledge: London

Popper, K. (1945) *The Open Society and Its Enemies*. London: Routledge.

Popper, K. (1957) *The Poverty of Historicism*. London: Routledge.

Popper, K. (1963) *Conjectures and Refutations: The Growth of Scientific Knowledge*. London: Routledge.

Popper, K. (1972) *Objective Knowledge: An Evolutionary Approach*. Oxford: Oxford University Press.

Popper, K. (2002) *The Logic of Scientific Discovery*. London: Routledge.

Popper, K.R. (1979) Truth, rationality and the growth of scientific knowledge. Vittorio Klostermann.

Popper, M. and Lipschitz, R. (1998) 'Organizational learning mechanisms – a structural and cultural approach to organizational learning', *Journal of Applied Behavioral Science*, 34(2): 161–79.

Prashanth, N., Marchal, B. and Hoerée, T. (2012) 'How does capacity building of health managers work? A realist evaluation study protocol', *BMJ Open*, 2(2): 1–12.

Prashanth, N., Marchal, B., Devadasan, N., Kegels, G. and Criel, B. (2014a) 'Advancing the application of systems thinking in health: a realist evaluation of a capacity building programme for district managers in Tumkur, India', *Health Research Policy and Systems*, 12(42): 1–20.

Prashanth, N., Marchal, B., Kegels, G. and Criel, B. (2014b) 'Evaluation of capacity building programme of district health managers in India: a contextualised theoretical framework', *Frontiers in Public Health* [online], available at http://dx.doi.org/10.2139/ssrn.2451132 (accessed 26 May 2017).

Psillos, R. (2005) *Scientific realism: how science tracks truth*. London: Routledge.

Punton, M. (2016) 'How can capacity development promote evidence-informed policy making?' [online], available at www.itad.com/wp-content/uploads/2016/04/BCURE-Literature-Review-FINAL-010416.pdf (accessed 26 May 2017).

Punton, M., Vogel, I. and Lloyd, R. (2016) 'Reflections from a realist evaluation in progress: scaling ladders and stitching theory' [online], available at https://opendocs.ids.ac.uk/opendocs/bitstream/handle/123456789/11254/CDIPracticePaper_18.pdf?sequence=1 (accessed 26 May 2017).

Pyne, J., Fortney, J., Tripathi, S., Maciejewski, M., Edlund, M. and Williams, D. (2010) 'Cost-effectiveness analysis of a rural telemedicine collaborative care intervention for depression', *Archives of General Psychiatry*, 67(8): 812–21.

Ragin, C.C. (1992) 'Casing and the process of social inquiry', in C.C. Ragin and H.S. Becker (eds), *What Is a Case? Exploring the Foundations of Social Inquiry*. Cambridge: Cambridge University Press, pp. 217–26.

Ragin, C.C. (1994) *Constructing Social Research*. Thousand Oaks, CA: Pine Forge Press.

Ragin, C.C. (1998) 'The logic of qualitative comparative analysis', *International Review of Social History*, 43(S6): 105–24.

Ragin, C.C. (1999) 'Using qualitative comparative analysis to study causal complexity', *Health Services Research*, 34(5): 1225–39.

Ragin, C.C. (2000) *Fuzzy Set Social Science*. Chicago: University of Chicago Press.

Ragin, C.C. and Becker, H.S. (1992) *What Is a Case? Exploring the Foundations of Social Inquiry*. Cambridge: Cambridge University Press.

Raphael, D., Bryant, T. and Rioux, M. (2010) *Staying Alive: Critical Perspectives on Health Illness and Health Care*. Toronto: Canadian Scholars' Press.

Reed, M. and Harvey, D.L. (1992) 'The new science and the old: complexity and realism in the social sciences', *Journal for the Theory of Social Behaviour*, 22(4): 356–79.

Robert, E., Ridde, V., Marchal, B. and Fournier, P. (2012) 'Protocol: a realist review of user fee exemption policies for health services in Africa', *BMJ Open*, 2(1): 1–8.

Rogers, E. (1995) *The Diffusion of Innovations*. New York: Free Press.

Rosas, S. (2005) 'Concept mapping as a technique for program theory development: an illustration using family support programs', *American Journal of Evaluation*, 26(3): 389–401.

Rost, K., Pyne, J., Dickinson, L. and Losasso, A. (2005) 'Cost-effectiveness of enhancing primary care depression management on an ongoing basis', *Annals of Family Medicine*, 3(1): 7–14.

Rothwell, P. (2005) 'Treating individuals 1: External validity of randomised controlled trials: "to whom do the results of this trial apply?"', *The Lancet*, 365(9453): 82–93.

Royal College of Physicians (1962) *Smoking and Health: Summary of a Report of the Royal College of Physicians of London on Smoking in Relation to Cancer of the Lung and Other Diseases*. London: Pitman.

Rovelli, C. (2016) *Reality is Not What it Seems: A Journey into Quantum Gravity*. Harmondsworth: Penguin.

Russo, F. and Williamson, J. (2007) 'Interpreting causality in the health sciences', *International Studies in the Philosophy of Science*, 21(2): 157–70.

Ryan, R. and Deci, E. (2000) 'Self-determination theory and the facilitation of intrinsic motivation, social development and well-being', *American Psychologist*, 55(1): 68–78.

Rycroft-Malone, J., Burton, C., Wilkinson, J. et al. (2015) 'Collective action for knowledge mobilisation: a realist evaluation of the Collaborations for Leadership in Applied Health Research and Care', *Health Services and Delivery Research*, 3(44): 1–200.

Sackett, D.L., Rosenberg, W.M.C., Muir Gray, J.A., Haynes, R.B. and Richardson, W.S. (1996) 'Evidence based medicine: what it is and what it isn't', *BMJ*, 312: 71–2.

Sargeant, J., Curran, V., Jarvis, S.S. et al. (2004) 'Interactive on-line continuing medical education: physicians' perceptions', *Journal of Continuing Education in the Health Professions*, 24(4): 227–36.

Saul, J., Willis, C., Bitz, J. and Best, A. (2013) 'A time-responsive tool for informing policy making: rapid realist review', *Implement Science*, 8(103): 1–15.

Sayer, A. (1984) *Method in Social Science: A Realist Approach*. London: Hutchinson.

Sayer, A. (2000) *Realism and Social Science*. London: Sage.

Sayer, A. (1992) *Method in Social Science: A Realist Approach*, 2nd edn. London: Routledge.

Schulthess, D., Baird, L.G., Trushelm, M. et al. (2016) 'Medicines adaptive pathways to patients (MAPP): a story of international collaboration leading to implementation', *Therapeutic Innovation and Regulatory Science*, 50(3): 347–54.

Schunk, D.H. and Ertmer, P.A. (2000) 'Self-regulation and academic learning: self-efficacy enhancing interventions', in M. Boekaerts, P.R. Pintrich and M. Zeidner (eds), *Handbook of Self-regulation*. London and New York: Academic Press, pp. 631–49.

Scott, I. and Spouse, J. (2013) *Practice Based Learning in Nursing, Health and Social Care: Mentorship, Facilitation and Supervision*. New York: Wiley-Blackwell.

Sculpher, M. (2001) 'Economic evaluation', in N. Fulop, P. Allen, A. Clarke and N. Black (eds), *Studying the Organisation and Delivery of Health Services: Research Methods*. London and New York: Routledge, pp. 107–23.

Sculpher, M., Claxton, K., Drummond, M. and McCabe, C. (2006) 'Whither trial-based economic evaluation for health care decision making?', *Health Economics*, 15(7): 677–87.

Sculpher, M., Pang, F., Manca, A. et al. (2004) 'Generalisability in economic evaluation studies in healthcare: a review and case studies', *Health Technology Assessment*, 8(49): 1–192.

Seebohm, F. (1968) *Report of the Committee on Local Authority and Allied Personal Social Services*. London: HMSO.

Shadish, W.R., Cook, T.D. and Campbell, D.T. (2002) *Experimental and Quasi-experimental Designs for Generalized Causal Inference*. Boston and New York: Houghton Mifflin.

Shadish, W.R., Cook, T.D. and Leviton, L.C. (1991) *Foundations of Program Evaluation: Theories of Practice*. Newbury Park, CA: Sage.

Shafir, E. and Mullainathan, S. (2013) *Scarcity: Why Having Too Little Means So Much*. New York: Times Books.

Shaw, I. (2016) *Social Work Science*. New York: Columbia University Press.

Shiell, A., Hawe, P. and Gold, L. (2008) 'Complex interventions or complex systems? Implications for health economic evaluation', *BMJ*, 336(7656): 1281–3.

Shils, E. (1960) 'Imaginary sociology', *Encounter*, 14(6): 77–9.

Smith, S.M., Allwright, S. and O'Dowd, T. (2007) 'Effectiveness of shared care across the interface between primary and specialty care in chronic disease management', *Cochrane Database of Systematic Reviews*, 3: 1–158.

Stern, E. (1997) 'No title', in R. Pawson and N. Tilley (eds), *Realistic Evaluation*. London: Sage, back cover.

Stevens, A. (2007) 'Survival of the ideas that fit: an evolutionary analogy for the use of evidence in policy', *Social Policy and Society*, 6(1): 25–35.

Summerfield, C. and Babb, P. (eds) (2003) *Social Trends No. 33*. London: The Stationery Office.

Sytkowski, P.A. and D'Agostino, R.B. (1996) 'Sex and time trends in cardiovascular disease incidence and mortality: the Framingham heart study, 1950–1989', *American Journal of Epidemiology*, 143(4): 338–50.

Tieberghien, J. and Monaghan, M. (forthcoming) 'Public scholarship and the evidence movement: understanding and learning from Belgian policy development', *European Journal of Criminology*.

Tilley, N. (1981) 'The logic of laboratory life', *Sociology*, 15(1): 59–67.

Tilley, N. (1982) 'Popper, historicism and emergence', *Philosophy of the Social Sciences*, 12(1): 59–67.

Tilley, N. (1992) *Safer Cities and Community Safety Strategies*, Crime Prevention Unit Paper No. 38. London: Home Office.

Tilley, N. (1993a) *After Kirkholt – Theory, Method and Results of Replication Evaluations*, Crime Prevention Unit Paper No. 47. London: Home Office.

Tilley, N. (1993b) *Understanding Car Parks, Crime and CCTV: Evaluation Lessons from Safer Cities*, Crime Prevention Unit Paper No. 42. London: Home Office.

Tilley, N. (1996) 'Demonstration, exemplification, duplication and replication in evaluation research', *Evaluation, 2*(1): 35–50.

Tilley, N. (1999) 'Evaluation and evidence-(mis)led policy', *Evaluation Journal of Australasia, 11*(2): 48–63.

Tilley, N. (2000) 'Experimentation and criminal justice policies in the UK', *Crime and Delinquency, 46*(2): 194–213.

Tilley, N. (2001) 'Evaluation and evidence-led crime reduction policy and practice', in R. Matthews and J. Pitts (eds), *Crime, Disorder and Community Safety*. London: Routledge, pp. 90–8.

Tilley, N. (2002) *Evaluation for Crime Prevention*. Cullompton: Willan.

Tilley, N. (2004) 'Applying theory-driven evaluation to the British Crime Reduction Programme: the theories of the programme and of its evaluations', *Criminal Justice, 4*(3): 255–76.

Tilley, N. (2006) 'Knowing and doing: guidance and good practice in crime prevention', in R. Clarke and J. Knutsson (eds), *Putting Theory to Work: Implementing Situational Prevention and Problem-oriented Policing*. Monsey, NY: Criminal Justice Press, pp. 217–52.

Tilley, N. (2009a) 'Sherman vs Sherman: realism vs rhetoric', *Criminology and Criminal Justice, 9*(2): 135–44.

Tilley, N. (2009b) *Crime Prevention*. Cullompton: Willan.

Tilley, N. (2014) 'There is nothing so practical as a good theory: teacher-learner relationships in applied research for policing', in E. Cockbain and J. Knutsson (eds), *Applied Police Research: Challenges and Opportunities*. London: Routledge, pp. 141–52.

Tilley, N. (2016) 'EMMIE and engineering: what works as evidence to improve decisions?', *Evaluation, 22*(3): 304–22.

Tilley, N. and Selby, J. (1976) 'An apt sociology for polytechnics', *Higher Education Review, 8*(2): 38–56.

Tilly, C. (2001) 'Mechanisms in political processes', *Annual Review of Political Science, 4*(1): 21–41.

Tranfield, D., Denyer, D. and Smart, P. (2003) 'Towards a methodology for developing evidence-informed management knowledge by means of systematic review', *British Journal of Management, 14*(3): 207–22.

Trochim, W. (1989) 'Outcome pattern matching and program theory', *Evaluation and Program Planning, 12*(4): 355–66.

Turner, A., Mulla, A., Booth, A. et al. (2016) 'An evidence synthesis of the international knowledge base for new care models to inform and mobilise knowledge for Multispecialty Community Providers (MCPs)', *Systematic Reviews, 5*(167): 1–7.

US Department of Health Education and Welfare Public Health Service (1964) *Smoking and Health: Report of the Advisory Committee to the Surgeon General of the Public Health Service*, Public Health Service Publication 1103. Washington, DC: US Department of Health Education and Welfare Public Health Service.

Van Belle, S. (2014) 'Accountability in Sexual and Reproductive Health: How Relations Between INGOs and State Actors Shape Public Accountability. A Study of Two Local Health Systems in Ghana'. PhD, London School of Hygeine and Tropical Medicine.

Van Belle, S. and Mayhew, S.H. (2016) 'Public accountability needs to be enforced – a case study of the governance arrangements and accountability practices in a rural health district in Ghana', *BMC Health Services Research, 16*(568): 1–14.

Van Belle, S., Van de Pas, R. and Marchal, B. (2017) 'Towards an agenda for implementation science in global health: there is nothing more practical than good (social science) theories', *BMJ Global Health*, 2(2): 1–4.

Van der Zee, K., Oldersma, F., Buunk, B.P. and Bos, D. (1998) 'Social comparison preferences among cancer patients as related to neuroticism and social comparison orientation', *Journal of Personality and Social Psychology*, 75(3): 801–10.

Van der Zee, K., Buunk, B., Sanderman, R., Botke, G. and Van den Bergh, F. (2000) 'Social comparison and coping with cancer treatment', *Personality and Individual Differences*, 28(1): 17–34.

Van Straten, A., Hill, J., Richards, D. and Cuipers, P. (2015) 'Stepped care treatment delivery for depression: a systematic review and meta-analysis', *Psychological Medicine*, 45(2): 231–46.

Vareilles, G., Kane, S., Marchal, B. and Pommier, J. (2017) 'Understanding the performance of community health volunteers involved in the delivery of health programmes in underserved areas: a realist synthesis', *Implementation Science*, 12(22): 1–12.

Vareilles, G., Marchal, B., Kane, S., Petric, T., Pictet, G. and Pommier, J. (2015a) 'Understanding the motivation and performance of community health volunteers involved in the delivery of health programmes in Kampala, Uganda: a realist evaluation', *BMJ Open*, 5: e006752.

Vareilles, G., Pommier, J., Kane, S., Pictet, G. and Marchal, B. (2015b) 'Understanding the motivation and performance of community health volunteers involved in the delivery of health programs: a realist evaluation protocol', *BMJ Open*, 5(1): 1–14.

Von Korff, M., Katon, W., Bush, T. et al. (1998) 'Treatment costs, cost offset, and cost-effectiveness of collaborative management for depression', *Psychosomatic Medicine*, 60(2): 143–9.

Waldner, D. (2012) 'Process tracing and causal mechanisms', in H. Kincaid (ed.), *The Oxford Handbook of Philosophy of Social Science*. New York: Oxford University Press, pp. 65–84.

Walter, I., Nutley, S. and Davies, H. (2003) *Research Impact: A Cross Sector Review – Literature Review*. St Andrews: Research Unit for Research Utilisation, University of St Andrews.

Ward, V., House, A. and Hamer, S. (2009) 'Knowledge brokering: the missing link in the knowledge to action chain', *Evidence and Policy*, 5(3): 267–79.

Ward, V., Smith, S.O., House, A. and Hamer, S. (2012) 'Exploring knowledge exchange: a useful framework for practice and policy', *Social Science and Medicine*, 74(3): 297–304.

Watt, A. and Rodmell, S. (1988) 'Community involvement in health promotion: progress or panacea?', *Health Promotion International*, 2(4): 359–68.

Weatherly, H., Drummond, M., Claxton, K. et al. (2009) 'Methods for assessing the cost-effectiveness of public health interventions: key challenges and recommendations', *Health Policy*, 93(2): 85–92.

Webb, D. (2010) 'Rethinking the role of markets in urban renewal: the Housing Market Renewal Initiative in England', *Housing, Theory and Society*, 27(4): 313–31.

Weiss, C.H. (1979) 'The many meanings of research utilization', *Public Administration Review*, 39(5): 426–31.

Weiss, C.H. (1980) 'Knowledge creep and decision accretion', *Knowledge, Creation, Diffusion, Utilisation*, 1: 381–404.

Weiss, C.H. (1995) 'The Four "I's" of school reform: how interests, ideology, information and institution affect teachers and principals', *Harvard Educational Review*, 65(4): 571–93.

Weiss, C.H. (1997) 'Theory-based evaluation: past, present and future', *New Directions for Evaluation*, 76: 41–55.

Weiss, C.H. and Bucuvalas, M.J. (1980) *Social Science Research and Decision-Making*. New York: Columbia University Press.

Westhorp, G.S. (2008) *Development of Realist Evaluation Models and Methods for Use in Small-Scale Community Based Settings*. Nottingham Trent University, UK.

Westhorp, G. (2012) 'Using complexity-consistent theory for evaluating complex systems', *Evaluation*, 18(4): 405–20.

WHO (1986) *Ottawa Charter for Health Promotion*. Ottawa, Ontario: WHO.

Wieringa, S. and Greenhalgh, T. (2015) '10 years of mindlines: a systematic review and commentary', *Implementation Science*, 10(45): 1–11.

Williams, M. (2000) *Science and Social Science: An Introduction*. London: Routledge.

Williams, M. (2003) 'The problem of representation: realism and operationalism in survey research' [online], *Sociological Research Online*, 8(1), available at www.socresonline.org.uk/8/1/williams.html (accessed 26 May 2017).

Williams, M. (2009) 'Social objects, causality and contingent realism', *Journal for the Theory of Social Behaviour*, 39(1): 1–18.

Williams, M. (2010) 'Can we measure homelessness? A critical evaluation of "capture–recapture"', *Methodological Innovations Online*, 5(2): 49–59.

Williams, M. (2011) 'Contingent realism – abandoning necessity', *Social Epistemology*, 25(1): 37–56.

Williams, M. and Cheal, B. (2001) 'Is there any such thing as homelessness? Measurement, explanation and process in "homelessness" research', *European Journal of Social Research: Innovation*, 14(3): 239–53.

Williams, M. and Husk, K. (2013) 'Can we, should we measure ethnicity?', *International Journal of Social Research Methodology*, 16(4): 285–300.

Williams, M., Maconachie, M., Ware, L., Chandler, J. and Dodgeon, B. (2008) 'Using longitudinal data to examine living alone in England and Wales 1971–2001', in R. Edwards (ed.), *Researching Families, Community and Generational Change*. London: Routledge, pp. 164–80.

Willis, C.D, Saul, J., Bevan, H. et al. (2014) 'Sustaining organizational culture change in health systems', *Journal of Health Organization and Management*, 30(1): 2–30.

Wills, T.A. (1981) 'Downward comparison principles in social psychology', *Psychological Bulletin*, 90(2): 245–71.

Wills, T.A. and Mendoza, D. (2004) 'Social comparison and subjective well-being', in C. Spielberger (ed.), *Encyclopedia of Applied Psychology, Volume 3*. London: Academic Press, pp. 405–9.

Wohlin, C. (2014) *Guidelines for Snowballing in Systematic Literature Studies and a Replication in Software Engineering*. Proceedings of the 18th International Conference on Evaluation and Assessment in Software Engineering.

Wolff, N. (2000) 'Using randomized controlled trials to evaluate socially complex services: problems, challenges and recommendations', *Journal of Mental Health Policy and Economics*, 3(2): 97–109.

Wong, G., Greenhalgh, T. and Pawson, R. (2010) 'Internet-based medical education: a realist review of what works, for whom and in what circumstances', *BMC Medical Education*, 10(12): 1–10.

Wong, G., Pawson, R. and Owen, L. (2011) 'Policy guidance on threats to legislative interventions in public health: a realist synthesis', *BMC Public Health*, *11*(222): 1–11.

Wong, G., Greenhalgh, T., Westhorp, G. and Pawson, R. (2014a) 'Development of methodological guidance, publication standards and training materials for realist and meta-narrative reviews: the RAMESES (Realist and Meta-narrative Evidence Syntheses – Evolving Standards) project', *Health Service Delivery Research*, *2*(30): 1–278.

Wong, G., Greenhalgh, T., Westhorp, G. and Pawson, R. (2014b) 'Quality standards for realist syntheses and meta-narrative reviews' [online], available at http://betterevaluation.org/sites/default/files/Quality_standards_for_RS_and_MNR_v3final.pdf (accessed 26 May 2017).

Wong, G., Brennan, N., Mattick, K., Pearson, M., Briscoe, S. and Papoutsi, C. (2015) 'Interventions to improve antimicrobial prescribing of doctors in training: the IMPACT (IMProving Antimicrobial presCribing of doctors in Training) realist review', *BMJ Open*, *5*(10): 1–9.

Wong, G., Greenhalgh, T., Westhorp, G., Buckingham, J. and Pawson, R. (2013) 'RAMESES publication standards: realist syntheses', *BMC Medicine*, *11*(21): 1–14.

Wong, G., Westhorp, G., Manzano, A., Greenhalgh, J., Jagosh, J. and Greenhalgh, T. (2016) 'RAMESES II reporting standards for realist evaluations', *BMC Medicine*, *14*(96): 1–18.

Wright Mills, C. (1959) *The Sociological Imagination*. New York: Oxford University Press.

Wright, K., Golder, S. and Rodriguez-Lopez, R. (2014) 'Citation searching: a systematic review case study of multiple risk behaviour interventions', *BMC Medical Research Methodology*, *14*(73): 1–8.

Yllner, N. (2008) *Just a Little White Sleeping Pill: The Story of the Neurosedyn Catastrophe*. Stockholm: Recito.

Young, K., Ashby, D., Boaz, A. and Grayson, L. (2002) 'Social science and the evidence-based policy movement', *Social Policy and Society*, *1*(3): 215–24.

INDEX

Note: Tables and Figures are indicated by page numbers in bold print.